Cops and Constables

Cops and Constables:
American and British Fictional Policemen

Edited by
Earl F. Bargainnier
George N. Dove

Popular Press

Bowling Green State University Popular Press
Bowling Green, Ohio 43403

Copyright © 1986 Bowling Greeen State University Popular Press
Bowling Green, Ohio 43403

Library of Congress Catalogue Card No.: 86-71642

ISBN: 0-87972-333-5 Clothbound
      0-87972-334-3 Paperback

Cover design by Gary Dumm

CONTENTS

Introduction

No conventional character in mystery fiction has experienced a more varied career than the police detective. He was on the scene in the Rue Morgue before Dupin began to show an interest in the case, but Poe and his successors habitually assigned him a role subordinate to that of the gifted eccentric who solved the mystery—often even as a figure of contempt. Early in the history of the genre he was on occasion able to rise above this modest level in the person of Dickens' Inspector Bucket or Collins' Sergeant Cuff, but it was not until the 1930s that he was permitted the status of Simenon's Jules Maigret or Tey's Alan Grant.

The police detective as fictional protagonist emerged much later in America than in Britain. Anna Katharine Green made Ebenezer Gryce, a New York policeman, the detective in *The Leavenworth Case* (1878), but it was almost a half century before the advent of Earl Derr Biggers' Charlie Chan, another policeman in a major role. Chan experienced a tremendous popularity during the 1920s and 1930s (albeit more in the world of film than that of books), but the American mystery writer has never seemed to develop a taste for the great police detective of the stature of Marsh's Alleyn and James's Dalgleish.

It may be that the habitual American irreverence for authority figures has discouraged the introduction of great policemen into mystery fiction. Charlie Chan, with his insistent humility, was after all an exotic operating in far-off Honolulu. Actually, the only character resembling a great policeman in the United States during the 1920s and 1930s was Dick Tracy, a fantasy figure who translated more readily into a travesty like Fearless Fosdick than to a celebrity like Maigret. The only other protagonists with police associations to emerge during this period were William MacHarg's O'Malley (one of the smart "dumb cops") and Police Commissioner Thatcher Colt in the novels of Anthony Abbot.

The decade following the end of World War II brought forth a different kind of police story in America, represented by the Mitch Taylor-Jub Freeman series of Lawrence Treat and the Frank Ford-Fred Fellows novels of Hillary Waugh. In these stories the detection was carried on by policemen, without the participation of gifted amateurs or private investigators, and some important differences resulted: in these accounts the police usually worked as a team instead of turning the major job over to a gifted individual, and the methods employed were those normally used by policemen, like the questioning of witnesses, the use of informants, and an especially heavy reliance on the police laboratory. The popularity of this kind of story, called the police procedural, was stimulated during the late 1940s and early 1950s by the reception accorded the radio-television series *Dragnet*, with the result that writers of procedural series like Ed McBain (Evan Hunter) and Dell Shannon (Elizabeth Linington) have enjoyed considerable continuing popularity.

A close relative of the police procedural is the kind of story written by Thomas Chastain, whose Deputy Chief Inspector Max Kauffman customarily occupies the spotlight to a greater degree than the procedural cops do. Chastain is closer to the British tradition of the great police detective, who flourished in the period between the two world wars and paralleled the brilliant amateur, Ngaio Marsh's Superintendent Roderick Alleyn being the prime example. However, since the first British police procedural, Maurice Procter's *The Chief Inspector's Statement,* appeared in 1951—only six years after Lawrence Treat's *V as in Victim*, the first American procedural—both types of police novel, ranging from the comic to the grim, have been equally a part of British crime fiction.

The formula of the mystery story with a police detective is basically the same as that for any other detective story: there is a mystery (or a group of mysteries) solved by a detective (or a team of detectives). The condition is that the detective is a professional rather than a gifted amateur, and he or she is a civil servant rather than a private detective.

This is not to say that a policeman in a mystery story can operate as if he were not a policeman. In the first place, the police detective is the only kind of fictitious detective of whom the reading public has any pre-conception carried over from real life, and those pre-conceptions will set limits with regard to the behavior of policemen in stories. Part of that pre-conception is the knowledge that police can never afford to operate in a leisurely fashion and hence are under pressure to solve a case as quickly as possible, if they are to solve it at all. Moreover, most readers must know that much of police work relies upon luck, and the outcome is to a degree dependent on how the breaks fall. One other condition of supreme importance is the public perception of the policeman as a rather ordinary individual, competent but not brilliant, more likely to achieve success through methodical plodding than dramatic breakthroughs. Much more than the amateur or the private investigator, he is more interested in preventing crime than in detecting it. Finally, his position gives him a kind of clout that is never available to the other detectives of fiction.

If we seek a niche for the police story within the traditional rubrics of mystery fiction, we can place it in the classic category in terms of plot, and generally within the hard-boiled school with respect to its ambiance and general tone, although there are exceptions, especially in British works, for example those of Lovesey, Innes, and Watson.

The structure of a police story usually follows the classic step-by-step development, except that many police stories have multiple parallel plots, especially the procedural, in which the police may be engaged upon several cases at once. When the story features a single gifted protagonist, like Crofts' Inspector French, the structure follows the classic plot-line of the Poe-Conan Doyle tradition, because the methods of such great policemen are closer to those of Dupin and Holmes than to those of the lesser mortals of the detective squad. The procedural has tended to develop the same plot-structure, probably because its earliest practitioners were already experienced writers of mysteries in the classic mold.

At the level of myth, the police story frequently deviates from the classic line, particularly with respect to the relationship between the policeman and society. In the older tradition, the detective acts as the "genius from outside" who enters the scene only long enough to purge the guilty community, then withdraws forever. When the police detective is one of those superior detective-superintendents sent down from Scotland Yard to help the local constabulary with a difficult case, the image of the "genius from outside" holds true, but not when he is himself a resident of the precinct and hence a member of the guilty community, and he and his family are participants in the outcome.

The police story can be accurately placed in the hard-boiled category of mystery with respect to its atmosphere and detectival method. This does not mean that fictional policemen deal exclusively with junkies and impoverished prostitutes, any more than do the private investigators of the hard-boiled school, who actually spend more of their time in affluent apartments than in the "mean streets" of Chandler's manifesto. It does mean that the policeman, like the private eye, is inclined to take a more physical, pragmatic approach than the genius of the Nero Wolfe category.

There are some differences. The police story will not fit the characteristic ramified plot of the private investigator school, wherein the investigation of one mystery uncovers several others, until the private detective finds himself off on all kinds of tangents, for the plausible reason that no policeman would have the time, or the curiosity, to follow so many leads. The policeman, moreover, does not enjoy the privilege of accepting only those cases that appeal to him. Most particularly, he is denied the luxury of those private codes of ethics that permit the private eye to violate the standards of society in the light of his own interpretations and loyalties. Though the policeman operates by a code that frequently deviates from that of the community, it is the corporate code of the police sub-culture, which is class-oriented, intended for the protection of his special community. It is based in large measure on an assumption that the law is sometimes wrong and that the courts often impede justice instead of promoting it. The dynamic of the police code is pressure: pressure from the police establishment, the public, and the policeman's own family; and it is expressed in the tendency of the police to take matters into their own hands, often settling cases without an arrest, and handing out rewards and punishments in secret.

Partly as a result of the reading public's pre-conceptions, the policeman must make a somewhat different approach to the business of detection from that of the gifted amateur or the private investigator. Almost invariably his personal makeup in the stories is different from theirs: he tends to be a plodder (if he is not one of the British "super" policemen), canny rather than brilliant, automatically suspicious of people and things, rich in knowledge of the rough side of humankind.

More specifically, though, his whole operation as a detective has certain qualities that identify him as a policeman. In terms of police methodology, we can say that there are two "schools" of fictional police detection. The older one relies, for its results, on intelligence and broad acquaintance, on common sense and especially on what is called "cop sense." The other, which has emerged more recently, relies on technology, forensic science, the police laboratory, and sophisticated systems for the storing, analysis, and retrieval of information.

Besides the dependence on "cop sense" and technology, however, there are two other elements that tend to characterize the police detective in fiction. A heavy reliance on informants, which comes close to being a violation of the "rules" of the older tradition of detective fiction, is acceptable in police fiction, because it is through the use of "stool pigeons" or "narks" that most crimes are solved in real life. We have earlier mentioned the other element, the tendency of the police to work in teams, so that the responsibility and credit for investigative work are a shared business. The actual sharing is more apparent in the police procedural, though those gifted police detectives like Alleyn and

Dalgleish inevitably have their partners and right-hand men, and the rest of the detective squad is within the margin of the picture.

In spite of his official position, quite often the actions of a fictional policeman are extra-legal or outright criminal. At one level, the police detective may use methods forbidden by law or police regulations to expedite the business of enforcement. These may range from using unauthorized means of interrogation to planting a few "decks" of heroin on a suspect to insure his conviction, all the way up to the "execution" of a dangerous criminal who may otherwise go free. At another level they involve graft, bribery, and the rakeoff and payoff schemes well known in the non-fictional police world.

The public ordinarily plays a more insistent role in the police story than in other tales of detection, almost always fearful of the police and almost invariably hostile to them. The usual police response is to develop an attitude that considers the public not so much a great faceless enemy as an oversized and very ignorant child to be coped with as firmly and expeditiously as possible.

One of the most difficult problems of the writer of police detection is avoidance of the humdrums. Brilliant amateur detectives can be endowed with all kinds of interesting eccentricities, and private detectives (those in fiction, at least) lead lives of constant glamor and excitement, but everybody knows that police work is deadly dull and a ghastly bore. One solution is to use the special character of police work to advantage, namely police methodology. Ed McBain is especially gifted in presenting absorbing accounts of the techniques of the police laboratory. So is Bill Knox, who can build creditable suspense through highly detailed descriptions of the employment of police technology.

There are other devices, familiar to writers of all kinds of popular fiction, for making police stories interesting. One is the development of an absorbing theme, such as race-relations, the place of women in society, or even the occult and supernatural. Then there is a whole bag of well-tested tricks, such as the alternating point of view and the resort to cliffhangers, concealed clues, hints, and suggestions. Many writers of police stories can use humor effectively to keep the readers' attention, though American police humor in its untreated form may be somewhat too gritty for the average reader. The British are much more apt to write comic police novels than are Americans. Perhaps because there is less violence in their society, they can more easily indulge in the amusement of comic crime. Some British authors, such as Michael Innes and Colin Watson, have made a specialty of this type of fiction, and others have used it occasionally: Cyril Hare, Elspeth Huxley, and

Peter Dickinson to name just three. (Unique "crossovers" are the comic novels of Martha Grimes, an American, featuring the British cases of Superintendent Richard Jury of Scotland Yard.)

The policeman as fictional protagonist shows some marked differences from other detectives, especially in his home life. Unlike most of the amateurs and the private detectives, the policeman is customarily married, and his marriage (or hers) is a reasonably successful one, though usually marred by a few problems. The policeman's family becomes part of the dominant myth, in the sense that they too belong to the "guilty community" and are themselves potential victims or criminals. The existence of spouse and children necessarily affects the policeman's view of his society, especially when the children become drug addicts or get themselves involved in criminal activities.

The policeman's constant exposure to corruption is another factor likely to affect his performance as protagonist, especially in American works. As a result of his low pay the police detective is always vulnerable to graft, a condition exacerbated by the automatic assumption of the criminal world that payoffs to the police are part of their normal expenses. Most of the police protagonists of mystery fiction have immunized themselves to such pressures, though many of them will accept a free meal in a restaurant or a "good price" on a re-decorating job on occasion.

Most policemen, as a matter of fact, feel more at home with the criminal element than with the public they are expected to protect. The policeman normally shares a whole set of values with the criminal world, speaks its language, and often feels easy using its methods.

The theme of the policeman's alienation from society, what a character in Sjowall and Wahloo's *Murder at the Savoy* calls the policeman's "occupational disease," has appeared more frequently in American (and continental European) police fiction than in British. As with the susceptibility to corruption, this sense of estrangement from society is more common among the second-stringers than among the major protagonists in the stories.

Policemen, as popular wisdom has it, are much the same the world over, and the similarities are especially marked between those in Britain and America, as might be expected in societies with so many shared conceptions of justice and order.

Possibly the most striking likeness lies in their mutual diversity. In both professional and personal quality they range all the way from the Adam Dalgleishes to the county clods in Britain, and from the Virgil Tibbses to the flatfoots in America. In both countries, however, the public conception of the policeman tends to be based upon the lower rather than the middle or higher reaches of the spectrum.

In the context of the whole system, British and American policemen are much alike in the way they cherish and promote the rivalries between branches and departments. In Britain the competition expresses itself in the resentment felt by the locals toward somebody sent in by Scotland Yard to take over *their* case, and in America by the very suggestion of an outside cop's foot being set inside one's precinct. They are alike in the way they are bound by the realities of a free society, which means that no solution to any crime is satisfactory unless it will stand up before a jury. The similarity extends to their sense of professionalism, which is increasing in both countries to the extent that the old-fashioned uneducated, heavy-handed policeman is disappearing from both systems. Occupational pride is as strong as ever, manifesting itself in Britain and America in a scorn of amateurs and of "civilians" generally. So is their inclination toward the use of extra-legal methods: both groups will break down doors when the occasion demands, though the British detective is more likely to send 'round a repairman next day.

The similarities naturally extend also to the personal level. British and American police tend toward political conservatism, which is evident in their attitudes toward capital punishment (almost universally favored on both sides of the Atlantic). They share most of the same biases, usually paying lip-service to the principle of equality of the sexes and the races, but in practice manifesting most of the traditional prejudices against women and members of ethnic minorities.

Like these similarities, the differences between British and American police probably reflect the basic differences between the expectations of the two reading publics. Fictional British policemen are much less susceptible to corruption than are those in the United States. British detectives tend to "go wrong" on an isolated individual basis, while American police graft is usually systemic and even syndicated. In the context of the profession, British and American conceptions of the role of the policeman vary chiefly in respect to their attitudes toward the uses and limits of police violence, exemplified in the fact that a British policeman seldom carries a firearm, whereas the American is expected to have his handy at all times. A further reflection of this attitude is apparent in their handling of suspects and other "subjects": the British tradition of humanitarian treatment usually holds as long as the culprit maintains a proper respect; Americans are a little quicker to teach respect, with a fist if necessary, at the outset. On the personal level, the British detective is more likely to demonstrate a higher cultural level, with a heavier reliance on elitist, abstract knowledge, the American to call upon practical, utilitarian expertise.

The British detective usually takes more seriously his role as citizen and example to his fellow-citizens, to the extent that the stern lecture on the responsibilities of citizenship, addressed to the culprit, is a familiar operation of the police. The American is inclined rather to repudiation: "We don't make the laws; we just enforce them." Both groups deplore the decline of morality and social standards, though the British detective is more inclined to worry about the character of the whole country, the American to be concerned only with his own community.

All of these qualities naturally affect their approach to the business of detection. Consequently, the British policeman is more likely to perceive patterns by backing away from the situation and taking the broad view, while the American throws himself into the middle of it. Likewise, the British detective is inclined to verbalize his thoughts and understandings, the American to talk only about the necessity for getting on with the job.

A final difference, which would seem to reflect literary convention, is in their willingness to make colleagues of "civilians." The figure of the police detective who teams up with an intelligent amateur is fairly common in the British story, but non-existent in the American. The American cop tends to be more guarded in his contacts outside the detective squad, and in those rare instances where he does collaborate with an outsider, it is more likely to be a private detective than an amateur.

This brief introduction to the fictional policeman cannot cover all aspects of his nature, but it does indicate some of the principal elements which appear again and again, the diversity within the convention, and significant similarities and differences between the American and British varieties. The thirteen essays that follow provide extended and specific illustrations of ways in which authors present policemen and their investigations of crime. The editors wish to thank their colleagues for their informed, thoughtful, and provocative essays, which add considerably to an understanding of the creation of fictional cops and constables.

George N. Dove   Earl F. Bargainnier

Cops

Edited by
George N. Dove

Anthony Abbot's Thatcher Colt

Barrie Hayne

The prototypes of Thatcher Colt, Police Commissioner, fall into three classes: literary, historical, and mytho-religious. Not only the son of Philo Vance and Theodore Roosevelt, but also very nearly the central figure of *The Greatest Story Ever Told,* he fits easily into the category of the God-Like Detective, finding there a place less important than those occupied by Holmes or Vance, but no less infallible.

In 1930, Willard Huntington Wright, who wrote as "S.S. Van Dine", and who once said that everyone had six good books in him, and no more, published the fifth of his Philo Vance novels; in the same year those two cousins Frederic Dannay and Manfred Lee published the second of their many collaborations as Ellery Queen. Van Dine was still the most popular of detective story writers of the day, and Queen, his principal, and most successful, imitator, was beginning on a career which would last for four decades. In that same year of 1930, Fulton Oursler, popular journalist, soon to be editor of *Liberty,* published under the name of "Anthony Abbot" the first of his eight Thatcher Colt novels,[1] and became, in historical importance, second only to Queen as the heir to Van Dine.

By the end of the decade, Van Dine was dead, but his detective's popularity, true to his own six-book prediction, had died long before the twelfth book was written. Vance's leading characteristics are repeated over and over in each of the novels, and are essentially those of the detached dilettante: he is a conflation of Dupin's Bi-part soul, Mycroft Holmes' sedentary nature, and Sherlock's tendency to dispense justice himself. But he differs from all of them in that he not only plays God, but almost may be said to be God, albeit a rather remote one. "He looked upon life like a dispassionate and impersonal spectator at a play, secretly amused and debonairly cynical at the meaningless futility of it all" (*The Canary Murder Case, 11*).[2]

From the beginning, Ellery Queen's similarities to Vance are apparent, but the movement is already underway towards a greater realism of character, and a warmer personality. It is in the formulas of plot and theme that Ellery Queen hews so close to S.S. Van Dine: the formulaic titles, the absolutely mechanical nature of the plot, and, in Queen, the even greater departure from realism in the pause just before the denouement in which a "challenge to the reader" puts that reader on the same footing as the detective and invites him to solve the mystery.

When Fulton Oursler, then, in the year after Queen's first appearance, published *About the Murder of Geraldine Foster,* he too was subscribing to the formula. Van Dine's novels are all titled, except the second last, within the strait-jacket of *The (six-letter) Murder Case.* Ellery Queen's early novels are titled just as restrictively: *The (national adjective) (noun) Mystery.* Oursler's first six Colt novels are titled *About the Murder of...* It is customarily reported, and there seems to be no reason to doubt this, that the preposition with which each title begins represents Oursler's determination to have his novels first on any alphabetical list of detective fiction.[3]

His pseudonym of "Anthony Abbot", as well, must have been chosen for the same reason, though here again is a subscription to the formula. Philo Vance finds his amanuensis or Boswell in "S.S. Van Dine," the lawyer who knew Vance at Harvard and who quits his legal partnership to record the young genius' cases with the unabashed admiration such a gesture implies. Ellery Queen the detective has two such historians, though the first is little more than a messenger to the publishers: J.J. Mc C., a stockbroker who in the preface to the first novel, *The Roman Hat Mystery,* discovers Ellery and his father living in an Italian hamlet, only too eager to have their adventures recorded for posterity.

Ellery Queen, or rather Dannay and Lee, greatly complicate the relation they found between author (Willard Huntington Wright), persona (S.S. Van Dine, whose name appears on the spine), and character ("Van" who is little more than an interlocutor and one-man admiration society for Vance; and of course a true double, as the similarity of his name to his principal's would suggest). For Dannay and Lee, Ellery Queen is the author (Ellery Queen the detective story writer, who is recording the tale, even in the third person), and the character (Ellery Queen the detective); the admiration and the obtuse verification are projected off on to the largely absent J.J. The advantage of Queen's method, since the next turn of the screw is that he does not tell his tale in the first person, is that the authorial consciousness can shift during the novel, and the rules of fair play so dear to detective story readers can be observed without the facts being received through the mind of an obtuse Watson.

If Ellery Queen, however, takes a few steps forward from Van Dine, Fulton Oursler takes about as many back. He gives himself as author the name of "Anthony Abbot" (whose name appears on the spine), and also makes Abbot the persona, a younger friend of Thatcher Colt's, who as a journalist knew him before the Great War, who served with him during it, and who becomes his private secretary when Colt is appointed Police Commissioner for the city of New York. "Anthony Abbot," therefore, represents a return to "S.S. Van Dine," with none of the —albeit largely unconscious in Queen—hall of mirrors effect and implicit examination of the entry of the author into his work that makes "Fielding," say, a character in *Joseph Andrews* or *Tom Jones*.[4]

And as Oursler followed the authorial formula of S.S. Van Dine, so he closely patterned Thatcher Colt after Philo Vance. The introductory description of Colt, indeed, though less precious, might be of Vance: "A man born to wealth, family and position, he made crime his hobby while he was still in college. He knows the modern criminology in all its schools, from Lombroso to Adler" (*Geraldine Foster*, xi). In his very first appearance we are told that far from wishing, as his detractors would believe, to be Mayor of New York, what Colt really wanted "was to be a musician and poet" (*Geraldine Foster*, 18). And in his very last appearance he is described as "a down-to-earth detective," a description which follows by only one page the information that the sole 'C' he had at college was in Mathematics (*Shudders*, 4-5). Colt is, like Vance, the Bi-Part Soul, poet and mathematician, though more intuitive than rational. He solves "the crime of the century" (*Clergyman's Mistress*, 9), by what he calls "common sense and straight police work" (*Clergyman's Mistress*, 252), yet he approaches the bizarre crime in that case as though it were a work of art, to be interpreted only by an artist; his own "artistic confidence" is shaken when he finds a lapse on the part of the criminal: "It is an impropriety, an incongruity, a solecism in an otherwise virtuoso exhibition" (62). More often than not, it is an intuition that solves the crime rather than a strict piece of scientific reasoning; and the title of Book Three of *About the Murder of a Startled Lady*, quoting Colt, strikes the right note—"We Know Who Did It, But We Can't Prove It."

Like Vance, Colt is an impeccable dresser, and a personage of great presence: "a striking figure, with his huge and powerful frame and soldier's face. He was the best dressed man in public life, and regarded by the more frivolous newspapers as a *flaneur* or, at best, a dilettante in crime, yet not since the days of Theodore Roosevelt had the Department known a chief of such strength, courage, and decision.

His black hair was crisp and closely cut, his brown eyes sombre and resolved and in his firm features lived action and authority" (*Geraldine Foster*, 4). It is perhaps enough to add that he was played, in the only two film versions of the novels,[5] by that epitome of formally dressed, sophisticated elegance, Adolphe Menjou. Yet, like Ellery, Colt has given up Regies for a pipe, and there is in Menjou a down-to-earth, raspy-voiced quality carried over from the more or less humane, not quite uncanny wordliness of the roles that made his name, in *A Woman of Paris*, or *The Marriage Circle*. He is less heartless than the most successful visual equivalents of Philo Vance—William Powell, whose cool detachment stood him in good stead in a string of famous screwball comedies, and Paul Lukas, who also played heartless comic sophisticates, as well as colder villains (*The Lady Vanishes*).

Colt is aware of the abysses that lie beneath the elegant art deco of 1930s New York, as of course Vance was, but Colt is emotionally upset by the awareness. So when a woman under his protection is murdered: "His hair was disarranged; his face glistened with sweat; his eyes were opened wide and full of fury" (*Man Afraid*, 245). Philo Vance's hair is rarely disarranged, and sweat has infrequently appeared on his brow; on the only notable such occasion, when he falls off a wall and meets Gracie Allen, though "disheveled," he has little in common with ordinary suffering humanity, looking like "some roving mendicant" (*The Gracie Allen Murder Case*, 29), and so still seen through an artistic-literary glass.

Vance's erudition is legendary. Colt's version of that side of Vance, too, is more human, down-to-earth. His knowledge enables him to identify a mysterious substance as dulse, surely a rather obscure seaweed, found mostly in Canada; so he introduces a crucial marine element into a seemingly landlocked case (*Clergyman's Mistress*, 63). He talks on a wide variety of subjects, easily holding his own with the still more down-to-earth District Attorney in a reminiscent rhapsody over the burlesque theater of days gone by (which leaves the younger Tony Abbot speechless in his ignorance). In another conversation he ranges from the "latest experiments in getting power from tides" to the insurance risks on the Dionne quintuplets (*Startled Lady*, 252). And the mixture of down-to-earth and sophisticated knowledge is reflected in the food he eats, which sometimes falls well below Vance's epicurean tastes (toasted chicken sandwiches and beer sent into the office— *Startled Lady*, 146), but can rise at other times to the same level— as when under the eye of Oscar of the Waldorf he sits down to a "never-to-be-forgotten luncheon of Maryland oysters on the half shell; bisque d'homard; lobster a la Foyot; then pressed duck done quite as delicately as one eats it at Laperouse; a light desert (*sic*) of pears stewed in champagne; and, as a fitting after-clap, a liqueur from Avignon, known by the unprepossessing title of "The Sweat of the Holy Virgin," but very soothing and tasty just the same" (*Startled Lady*, 252). The tone of the speaker is of one who enjoys good food but who can take it or let it alone; it is Tony's tone, but just as surely Colt's. And it is perhaps remarkable that Colt rises from Oscar's table to follow a lead in the case. It is, in fact, at this point that he announces that he knows who committed the murder but cannot prove it! The intuitive powers may be similar, but Colt's taste for beer, a beverage which may never have passed Vance's lips, marks him as a more American hero. His brownstone in midtown Manhattan contains a connoisseur's cellar of fine wines, but no hero to be mentioned in the same breath as Theodore Roosevelt could be less than distinctively American.

In one other, crucial, way, Colt differs from Vance, and incidentally from Queen as well. In answer to Dashiell Hammett's question, "Mr. Queen, will you be good enough to explain your famous character's sex life, if any?"[6] Philo Vance would have to stand more or less mute; he is as much averse (if not adverse) to the wiles of women as Sherlock Holmes himself. He does meet his Irene Adler, and characteristically solaces himself for her loss with a trip to Egypt. "With the multiplicity of intellectual interests that occupied him," Van notes, "he doubted (and I think rightly so) his capacity to make any woman happy in the conventional sense" (*The Garden Murder Case*, 330). But the young sportswoman who takes his fancy on this case is a rather brashly flippant and ambiguous flapper, with a "swaggering" manner and "muscular boyish hips" (62). Irene Adler may have dressed as a young man, but Zalia Graem, in her woman's clothes, looks like a boy to begin with. It is perhaps predictable that to Philo Vance she would always be *the* woman.

Ellery Queen's answer to Hammett's question, with perhaps a hint from Willard Huntington Wright,[7] was, "In all sincerity, aren't there enough conjugal criminologists as it is?" Indeed, Queen's sex-life is of little importance, and perhaps much impotence—he falls in and out of love with his leading ladies with a regularity suggestive of at least infantilism,[8] and we can take J.J. McC's statement in the first book that he is living with a wife and child, or his later relations with Nikki, with the same grain of salt we apply to the child inadvisedly bestowed upon Nick and Nora Charles—not, be it noted, by Hammett, but by several of the film series.[9]

Colt, however, has something of an eye for women, and once discoursed at length on the very fashions which seem to have endeared Zalia to Vance. Noting, in 1935, "the tendency to emphasize breasts in the current female fashions," he deplores it as a reflection "of a strumpet influence from Hollywood but nevertheless an outstanding improvement over the decadence of the boyish silhouette. Now that women were pretending to have breasts, he declared, there was hope they might some day begin to grow them again" (*Startled Lady,* 252).

All these three detectives are descendants of Sherlock Holmes in their celibacy, of course, but in Colt's case the rather Byronic qualities are enhanced by the presence of a lost love. A less flippant Wimsey who did not allow himself the luxury of a nervous breakdown, Colt cherishes through several novels the memory of "a red-headed girl who had ditched him for a duke while he was fighting in France" (*Geraldine Foster,* 18). In the fifth Colt novel, the girl, Florence Dunbar, mistreated and beaten by her Spanish nobleman, returns to New York and is for three hundred pages an offstage telephone voice. Such she remains in the sixth of the series, where the case begins a few days before Colt is finally due to be married to her, and ends with his solving the crime just in time to keep his appointment at the church. And in the diegetically last of the series, *The Creeps* (*The Shudders* takes us back to an earlier time), they are a married couple. But in her presence as in her absence, she tends to confirm the wisdom of the interdict against the intrusion of love into the detective story. If Dorothy Sayers could write "A Love Story with Detective Interruptions,"[10] here the case is the other way around, and the interruptions almost as tiresome. Their only interest, indeed, is to invest Colt with a humanity somewhat more convincing than those of the more epicene Philo Vance or the early Ellery Queen—and for all Dannay and Lee's disclaimer,[11] these two names, "Philo" and "Queen" do suggest the epicene, just as "Thatcher Colt" brings together a masculine avocation with a tool of American, frontier individualism. And Florence Dunbar herself reflects the greater masculinity: no boyishness, but only the unattainability of perfection—

In that instant I recalled a photograph that hung on the wall of Thatcher Colt's library; the only picture in that huge quiet room, and, aside from the pictures of his mother and father, which he kept on his dressing table, the only photograph in the entire house that he called home. Often I had looked at that portrait and wondered what manner of girl had owned the beautiful face that half smiled, half chided the world she gazed at. Florence Dunbar—who had once been engaged to marry Thatcher Colt! She had a remote, legendary beauty; you felt somehow that she spoke strange languages, and understood least of all what we hedonists call "civilization." Yet there was a wistful glimmer in her large, dark eyes, and a soft womanliness in the rich masses of black hair in a day of bobs. Only the imperious tilt to her head, the aristocratic curve to the proud sharp nose set her apart, as if she were quite unattainable, and knew it to her sorrow.

(*Startled Lady,* 8)

Vance and Queen may hark back to the aestheticism of the '90s refracted, to a lesser or greater degree, through the brutalities of the War, so that there may be touches of a more macho physicality like Bulldog Drummond's in even Vance or Wimsey, not to mention Queen. But Colt, with his powerful frame and soldier's face, seems to be a generation removed from Wilde or Saki, his aestheticism an acquisition rather than an inheritance.

This lesser prissiness of Colt reflects itself in his circle of associates. Vance, Queen, Colt, are all rather Quixotic figures, though Colt, already a more hard-headed realist, needs his Sancho Panzas rather less than they. Vance has his District Attorney Markham and Sergeant Heath to carry on the official obtuseness of Dupin's Prefect or Holmes' Lestrade, and Ellery has his Sergeant Velie. Vance's Van is a characterless figure whose *raison d'etre* is his devotion to Vance. But Tony Abbot is closer than any of these to John H. (or was it James?) Watson, M.D. Indeed, in the very first reported case he falls in love with one of the leading suspects and throughout the series he is shown in happy conjugal relations with her. Unlike Holmes in *The Sign of Four,* Colt finds no fault in the match, and in fact closes the case with a celebratory supper for the happy pair. When the game is afoot, Tony must be hauled out of the marital bed, but he is a police official, on proper call, not a physician in private practice; even so, he takes much greater exception than Watson to these impositions upon his married life, and, unlike the long-suffering Mary Morstan, so does she: "My wife was probably the most indignant woman in New York—I was pretty mad myself—as I dressed in three minutes and took a taxi to West Seventieth Street" (*Man Afraid,* 207-208).

But the character in the Colt novels second only in importance to Colt himself is the District Attorney, Merle K. Dougherty, overweight, perspiring, uninhibited, eloquent in a homespun way, and a distinctly political figure. Vance's D.A., John F.X. Markham, is inevitably, given Vance's amateur status, a somewhat adversarial figure, but so to an extent is Dougherty, for the presumed amity between Commissioner and D.A. sometimes breaks down in the face of independence versus the political machine. Yet Colt and Dougherty are friends and equals as Vance and Markham could never quite be, though they almost never agree on the prosecution and solution of the case. Dougherty becomes more prominent as the series proceeds, entering the first novel in the sixth chapter, the second in Chapter three, but there on the first page in the fifth and sixth novels. It is in the second novel that his role is most clearly defined:

> Where Colt viewed life as a gourmet, Dougherty was always the gourmand. In his official capacity, he was a hard-working vigorous, if often blundering man, incorruptibly honest in his dealings. But in his private bachelor life, he was one of the most edacious eaters, and one of the most conscientious drinkers I have ever known. His frank fondness for chorines, his sheer delight in dancing and brazen noise, was a simple enjoyment comparable to that of a puppy romping with a colored ball. Dougherty, with his red curls, his thick jowls, his bulging eyes, and his loud laugh, was a vulgar politician, but without a mean bone in his body, or real malice toward any human being, and with real ability of a kind. On the principle of the attraction of opposites, Colt and he had persevered in a long and trying friendship.
>
> (*Clergyman's Mistress*, 184-185)

In *About the Murder of a Startled Lady*, Dougherty is most unequivocally seen as a politician, as he seeks to protect a powerful Tammany figure from suspicion, and as he warns Colt against using the services of the eccentric "crime sculptor" who is out of favor with the powers downtown. As Colt says, however, " 'We can't let political squabbles stand in the way of results. We are good Democrats but we want those bones identified' " (46). Never is the line so clearly drawn between Dougherty's relative probity, and Colt's absolute incorruptibility. But a further distinction is drawn with Vance, who would certainly be a Republican if his remoteness allowed him to belong to a political party at all. In the very first novel, Colt chats with the policeman on the beat (248), takes on a family of great wealth, ignores, as he pursues the more important clue, the presence of some home-brew in the kitchen of a woman of the people: the whole ambience is that of a police force working together democratically and efficiently, and without fear or favor.

It is the portrait of a police department at work, in fact, which moves us now beyond literary considerations and models and brings us to Colt's even more striking historical ancestry. A police department "is seldom stronger than its chief," runs the publisher's statement in the first preface to the first volume, in words quoted in later volumes and attributed to Abbot himself. "But it is also true that New York has been fortunate in its succession of Commissioners, from Woods and Roosevelt down to the latest reign of Whalen and Mulrooney.... Greater than any of these was Thatcher Colt, greater because of his peculiar fitness for the job" (*Geraldine Foster*, xi).

Roosevelt had been Police Commissioner (or, more precisely, President of the Police Commission) for the City of New York in 1895-97, on his way to being Assistant Secretary for the Navy, hero of San Juan Hill, Governor of New York, briefly Vice-President, and then President of the United States. One of his successors as Commissioner had been Arthur Woods, who held the office in 1914-18, a Bostonian and a Harvard man who had had graduate study at Harvard and Berlin, and had been for ten years a master at Groton. Grover A. Whalen and Edward Pierce Mulrooney were Commissioners even as Abbot was writing: in 1928-30 and 1930-33 respectively. Whalen was a merchant and career administrator who served on countless boards in the city; graduate of military academy and New York law school, he crowned his career as President of the New York World's Fair of 1939, and was no doubt entitled to call his autobiography, published in the mid-1950s, *Mr. New York.* Mulrooney began his career as a patrolman, in 1896, and took thirty-five years to work his way to the top. It becomes apparent, as one surveys these careers, that though Woods may have had the Ivy League and upperclass background, and though Whalen may have had the prominence within the city and the reluctance to enter the world of politics, it is Theodore Roosevelt, "greater than any of these," who is the ultimate historical model for Thatcher Colt.

Colt's view of the job of police commissioner is most clearly expounded at the beginning of *About the Murder of a Man Afraid of Women,* as he announces his intention of resigning his police career and going into "more important work"—"crime prevention" rather than detection after the fact. " 'We should fight crime just as cities organize against an epidemic, as nations mobilize for war. The situation is unthinkable. We shudder at the French Revolution. Poppycock! Careless automobile driving in the United States alone kills twice as many people in one year as died in the whole shambles of the terror... Just try to do something about restricting the manufacture, sale or shipment of firearms. The public has got to be aroused, otherwise—' " (5).

The man who fought the entry of politics into the administration of his police-force sounds a lot like a politician in this passage, and the running imagery of warfare that he uses sounds a lot like TR's, especially as Roosevelt described his tenure as Police Commissioner, both immediately in his letter of resignation to the Mayor, in 1897, and retrospectively in his *Autobiography,* fifteen years later.[12] But the comparison between Colt and Roosevelt goes much further, and is detailed in the demurrer that his friend Dougherty makes to Colt's determination to resign:

You put speed into the department; you gave it armor plate and modern weapons; you told the politicians to go to hell; you kept the Mayor back of you—and that was something—and you brought science into the police work of this burg for the first time in a big way. You're the one that recognized how sociology has a part in police work; that psychiatry has, too, and that key detectives, at least, need a foundation in law, if they are going to bring in evidence on which my juries will convict—and you're the first police commissioner we ever had who could tell not only what was wrong with our existing system of bail bondsmen, but how to rectify it, or could handle shyster lawyers and suggest reforms in court procedure, parole system and prisons. I think it's a shame, Thatch, for you to desert now. And thats just what it is—plain desertion."

(Man Afraid, 6)

Roosevelt too gave his force more modern weapons (one of them was a double-action Colt!), and he noted in his autobiography[13] the improvement in marksmanship following his establishment of a school of pistol practice. It was of course one of his characteristics to tell politicians to go to hell, and the prevailing theme in his statements about his tenure is that of having instituted a system of promotion which ignored political loyalty; he even cites the case of an officer who deserved promotion but had it delayed because a friend was importuning for it on his behalf.[14] His battles against the boss system of his own Republican party resulted in Boss Thomas Platt's acquiescence in his transfer from New York to official Washington, and later his ultimate advancement. He kept the Mayor back of him, a Reform mayor who interrupted a long line of Tammany figures of the kind that Colt also fought with. Above all, Roosevelt, like Colt, fought for reforms in the essential corruptness of the system that he inherited. Real life is less tractable than fictional life, however, and Roosevelt expended a great deal of energy on his winning fight over Sunday closing (Colt's final quarry was drug trafficking), and his second year on the Police Board was paralyzed by internecine warfare, largely engineered by a retaliatory Platt.[15] Colt's adversaries are disembodied, and consequently less formidable.

"In addition to greater physical fitness, we have also stiffened the mental caliber of our graduates. Today, the rating of each police rookie in New York City must equal the I.Q. of an officer accepted for the United States Army...." —so writes Commissioner Colt in the last book of the series (*Shudders*, 5). Roosevelt, in his fullest statement about his tenure shortly after leaving it, noted that "we raised the requirements, mental, moral and physical" of the force. When Roosevelt brought the police force under the Civil Service Act and so made candidates for entry into it subject to a written examination system, he raised the "mental caliber" of the force, and in rewarding, characteristically, physical courage and heroism (a theme which runs throughout his statements), he raised its physical fitness as well as its moral qualities. The "very type" he wished to see on the force were "men of strong physique and resolute temper, sober, self-respecting, self-reliant, with a strong wish to improve themselves".[16]

Of course, the great exponent of the Strenuous Life was less interested in psychiatry, but he was certainly interested in sociological questions. He wrote much about the relation between economic hardship and crime, and saw, especially in the case of prostitution, the necessity of relieving the one to eliminate the other. And Roosevelt's legendary nocturnal walks through the city, keeping the patrolman up to the mark, find an echo in Colt's relations with the man on the beat, just as there is a strong parallel between Roosevelt's insistence on equality of opportunity in his department, and Colt's sense of the democratic nature of his.

Finally, though Roosevelt was very little like Colt in appearance, being a man of shorter stature and by no means handsome in Colt's conventional way, the two commissioners are linked by such general characteristics as the soldier's face, and even their flamboyant air, for both have something of the dandy. Indeed, the name of "Thatcher Colt" rather aptly conjures up the contradictory nature of the New York dude who came to his maturity in the Badlands, the cultivated Easterner who wrote *The Winning of the West,* the embodiment of the heroic America of his day.

But if Philo Vance, in particular, is Colt's literary prototype, and Theodore Roosevelt his historical one, it is not too much to say, thirdly, that there is a certain continuity of interest between Oursler's creation of Colt and his creation of the central figure in *The Greatest Story Ever Told.* Oursler's determination to tell the story of "a real man, and the only perfect one,"[17] which took root during the writing of the Thatcher Colt series, suggests not, of course, that Colt's creation was suggested by Oursler's view of Jesus, but that his already very successful creation of a paragon ("greater than any of these was Thatcher Colt") was related to his interest in writing the story, very much in the form of a novel, of the greatest of all men.

Oursler conceived the idea of rewriting the Gospels in modernized account on a trip to Palestine in 1935; "after twenty-five years of contented agnosticism" he took up his pen and published the famous work, an enormous bestseller, in 1949. The hero, "a human being like ourselves," is presented by Oursler as a great teacher and explicator, but above all a rebel: "But in His daily life Jesus was also looking around

Him; He was learning a great deal through His own observations. Already He was beginning to challenge in His own thoughts the tyrannical power exerted by the religious authorities."[18] Roosevelt and Colt took on the constituted order; so did Jesus. It is no blasphemy to see Oursler re-enacting Colt's battles with Tammany (or Roosevelt's with Platt) in Jesus's relentless criticsm of the Pharisees, or in His determination that true Judaic principles should be followed rather than those administered by the likes of Annas and Caiaphas. The old system must be renewed, and this corrupt ruling class swept aside. Roosevelt and Colt were innate democrats; so was Jesus.

My subject here cannot be infinitely or even unduly amplified. As Hawthorne said of the symbolic ramifications of his marble faun, "The idea grows coarse as we handle it, and hardens in our grasp." But clearly enough, the hand that drew Thatcher Colt is the same hand that sketched a Christ for the mid-twentieth century. To imagine Philo Vance contributing to a fictionalized portrait of the Son of God would be grotesquely blasphemous. It is a tribute to the larger-than-life, down-to-earth, yet transcendently noble, qualities of Thatcher Colt, who patently feels compassion for both victims and criminals, that in his case the absurdity of the comparison is scarcely an absurdity at all. As no less a witness than Theodore Roosevelt himself once wrote, "Our success in striving to help our fellow-man, and therefore to help ourselves, depends largely upon our success as we strive, with whatever shortcomings, with whatever failures, to lead our lives in accordance with the great ethical principles laid down in the life of Christ, and in the New Testament writings which seek to expound and apply his teachings."[19]

With these considerations of Colt's ancestry, and his affinities, in mind, we may now concentrate upon the novels themselves. The first six of the eight in which he appears are all accounts of cases which, we are informed in the portentous tones of a Van, have had to wait until now to be told—"The only reason Thatcher Colt has permitted me to publish these memoirs is for the greater glory of the department which he administered so fairly and efficiently under two Mayors, of opposite political faiths" (*Startled Lady*, ix). But time has swept away the necessity for secrecy: "with the recent departure from this country of two persons who would be most affected, and who, under changed names, will finish their lives in a different land..." (*Clergyman's Mistress*, ii); "But now, in the news recently arrived from Australia—news of still another suicide, the last uncaptured survivor of an abominable clique..." (*Man Afraid*, x).

The intended effect of such heavy breathing, with its attendant superlatives, also a Van Dine trademark, is of course to authenticate the narrative that follows, as well as to encourage one to read on. The unintended effect is perhaps to let the reader down a little, for what narrative could live up to this preview? Van Dine avoids the letdown because Vance is at once both heroic and mock-heroic; Abbot allows Colt no comic touches, not even those of self-mockery, so that the sense of reality becomes all important, and the descent from the preface sometimes disappoints.

There are, however, two other major means Abbot uses to give the Colt novels an ultimately higher kind of reality than Van Dine's. Ever since Poe, "locale" has been one of the prime elements in detective fiction: late-Victorian London lives in our imaginations at least partly through its evocation in the Sherlock Holmes stories, as even so hostile a critic of the genre as Edmund Wilson noted; people who have never entered British village life have a fair right to say they know it through the pages of Agatha Christie; even today, much of the popularity of a Robert B. Parker or a Ruth Rendell belongs to a wish to see a recognizable Boston or a by now familiar Kingsmarkham. Van Dine evoked a well-signposted Art Deco New York, a world dominated by aging brownstones and apartment balconies, the world below the Park. Abbot moved his focus further north, though still seventeen blocks below the cluttered apartment shared by Ellery and his father. The difference between Vance's apartment on East 38th Street and Colt's lived-in bachelor house on West Seventieth is the difference between aestheticism and a more functional design: Vance characteristically has an olde English butler and major-domo by the name of Currie, a second cousin not too far removed from Lord Peter's impossible Bunter; Colt a "cat-foot Negro butler" who has something of the sway of Jupiter over the hero of "The Gold-Bug." If Colt is more of a working detective, "down-to-earth," than Vance, this is expressed in the still greater specificity of that earth. Vance's work is a world of artifacts; for all its solidity, one visualizes it as a set of Whistler etchings rather than a gallery of Alvin Langdon Coburn photographs. And the comparison is not without its associative point: the RCA building (*Man Afraid*) or the Waldorf Astoria (*Startled Lady*) are brought before our eyes, ears and noses with a reality and a feel for their symbolic weight which Van Dine's calibrated descriptions do not achieve; although infinitely more pedestrian, and intellectually less detailed, Abbot's description of the great hotel on Park Avenue looks back, without suggesting the absurdity of the comparison, on Henry James' opulent evocation of it (in its earlier incarnation on 34th Street) in *The American Scene*.[20]

To see the difference between Van Dine's precise and measured New York and Abbot's more *felt*, and so more real, metropolis, we should place two of their characteristic descriptions side by side. The house where the first murder in *The Bishop Murder Case* is committed is introduced with a typical Philoism—" 'Come, let us find out something more about it at what the Austrian police officials eruditely call the *situs criminis*' "—, and then continues:

We left the house at once and drove uptown in Markham's car. Entering Central Park at Fifth Avenue, we emerged through the 72nd-Street gate, and a few minutes later were turning off of West End Avenue into 75th Street. The Dillard house—number 391—was on our right, far down the block toward the river. Between it and the Drive—occupying the entire corner was a large fifteen-story apartment house. The professor's home seemed to nestle, as if for protection, in the shadow of this huge structure.

The Dillard house was of gray, weather-darkened limestone, and belonged to the days when homes were built for permanency and comfort. The lot on which it stood had a thirty-five foot frontage, and the house itself was fully twenty-five feet across. The other ten feet of the lot, which formed an areaway separating the house from the apartment structure, was shut off from the street by a ten-foot stone wall with a large iron door in the center.

The house was of modified Colonial architecture. A short flight of shallow steps led from the street to a narrow brick-lined porch adorned with four white Corinthian pillars. On the second floor a series of casement windows, paned with rectangular leaded glass, extended across the entire width of the house. (These, I learned later, were the windows of the library.) There was something restful and distinctly old-fashioned about the place: it appeared like anything but the scene of a gruesome murder.

What must strike the reader of this passage is the remarkable accumulation of detail, of what James called "the solidity of specification," or what Walter Scott had called still earlier *vraisemblance,* both of them formulas for anchoring the incredible in the inescapably real and familiar. And in that familiarity is shelter from the horrible as well, as Van Dine's final remark makes clear. Such a description, more often than not, comes with its visual equivalent, a carefully specific floor plan or chart. When, however, we turn to a typical Abbot description, there is an affinity rather than a separation between crime and scene of crime; the tone is one of foreboding:

Neil headed back to First Avenue and we rolled southward at a pace permitted only to a Police Commissioner when he is in a great hurry. Very quickly we were in that contradictory region where an abattoir lifts its own peculiar incense in the face of the Pan-Hellenic skyscraper; a region where squalid red and brown brick tenements exist cheek by jowl with costly new co-operative apartments; a mingling of mean stationery stores and haughty beauty parlors. Towering above this strange commingling is the immense steel-gray lacery of the Queensborough Bridge. Strong and graceful, it lifts its span above all the pomp and poverty. Beneath the gallant and mighty structure of this bridge was the settlement to which we had hastened—Sangster Terrace—which is so much like its companion settlement of Sutton Place, that it would be hard to tell them apart. As we stepped from the car, I found we were in the very shadow of the bridge. Hastily I looked around me, wondering if indeed we were warm on the scent; if the scene of the murder could possibly be found in this retired quarter of New York. Both sides of the street were lined with old-fashioned brick and stone houses, probably of the first President Cleveland administration. They had painted doors in the new manner-red portals, and green and blue; the house numbers were brass and nailed to the panels, and they ran from one to twenty-five. At this season, the residents were probably off to Europe, Maine, or Newport—not a light was visible behind the several hundred windows glaring blankly out upon the highway.

(*Clergyman's Mistress,* 49-50)

The solidity of specification remains, but it has been generalized, poeticized into a sense of man's penetration of the landscape ("Cheek by jowl," "gallant and mighty structure," "windows glaring blankly"). Whereas Van's descriptions are in the spirit of the old hymn—"And every prospect pleases/ And only man is vile"—Abbot's shows that man's vileness is part of the prospect. Van's New York is an intellectualized city, however recognizable; Abbot's is an emotionally experienced one:

The flow of Broadway was on his face, as light flooded through the side window. Danger seemed wholly out of key with the lit-up world all around us just then—a playtime world of theaters and dance halls and restaurants; darkness turned into noon by millions of mazda bulbs and frenzied electric boards over the fronts of buildings; of night clubs getting ready for their busy time, they hoped; pleasure's high road on old Broadway. Danger seemed only a stage prop for one of those showhouse melodramas.

(*Man Afraid,* 344-35)

Moreover, Abbot's New York is grounded in another, wider kind of *vraisemblance.* Where Vance's and Van's allusions are all to the world of art and the intellect, of Menander and LaPlace, of Cezanne and Gracie Allen (for even she prompts Vance to quote a line from Longfellow), Abbot's and Colt's allusions are again more down-to-earth, and so conjure up, much more specifically, their time and place. A drive through Greenwich Village calls Dreiser to mind, the enlistment of a fingerprint expert recalls the Lindbergh kidnapping, a trip to the Circus brings a reference to Barnum and Will Rogers, the entrance of a Tammany politician brings a recollection of the Seabury investigation.

But above all, the Colt novels derive their ultimate reality from their careful attention to police methods and routine; and it is this element, too, that gives Colt his place in the history of detective fiction. Thatcher Colt brings together the qualities of the private detective with those of the police official. In those eight novels, at least in the first six, we see a remarkable hybrid of S.S. Van Dine and Freeman Wills Crofts—oil and water indeed, but no more incongruous than the mix of P.G. Wodehouse and John Buchan that went to the creation of Bulldog Drummond.

It is, of course, one of the truisms of the detective genre that from the beginning the police were inept, from Poe's Prefect to the advent of the police procedural and even beyond. The early, Victorian, exceptions, like Bucket, Cuff, and Ebenezer Gryce, are all professionals who need some assistance from their class superiors; in a classed system, there are doors still not open to them which they cannot merely kick down. Two early twentieth-century exceptions are A.E.W. Mason's Inspector Hanaud, and Robert Barr's Eugene Valmont; but Hanaud, as I have argued elsewhere,[21] is an amateur detective in police uniform, and the "triumphs" or Eugene Valmont are mostly failures, vehicles for an English writer to poke fun at French police methods. Crofts' Inspector French is an astute police officer, but there is little imagination in him; no one would call him a Bi-Part Soul, and Julian Symons dubs him the best of the Humdrum school.[22] So that Thatcher Colt is the first notable example of a policeman with flair who is still inescapably a policeman, engaged in the daily routine of tracking criminals. Fulton Oursler, in his early journalistic career, had walked the police and detection beat. He made on three occasions the graduating address at the F.B.I. Academy, and, as Anthony Abbot, clearly had it as one of his main purposes to redeem the police force from nearly a hundred years of detective-fiction calumny.

"It is all too true that the American public does not sufficiently appreciate its police," he says in that very first preface, and goes on:

There is a romantic fallacy that the Force is hopeless when faced with a clever crime; indeed many persons hold the departments of the country in contempt and derision. From short stories and novels they seem to have gained the impression that puzzling crimes are solved only by brilliant amateurs. These whimsical creatures of the storyteller's imagination, a printed army of amiable dilettantes of the current fiction, are gentlemen of inexhaustible knowledge and accomplishment. They are experts in chemistry and astronomy, psycho-analysis and fire-arms; they know rugs, music, chess and wines; they are languid fellows with a great fund of humor, and a mischievous liking for cryptic utterances until they are ready to put a delicate finger on the malefactor. Their avocation is to catch elusive murderers, when the police detectives are ready to confess their utter ineptitude for their own business.

Of course there are no such detectives in real life. Yet the crimes of reality are infinitely stranger than the fanciful misdeeds which these imaginary detectives are asked to unravel. The police face crime and mystery as a part of their daily routine, and they solve their cases by knowing their business and attending to it—by vast and competent organization, patience and determined hard work, together with some ingenuity and an occasional streak of good luck. We should not be deluded into believing that such men are incompetent or corrupt.[23]

(Geraldine Foster, x-xi)

Patience and determined hard work, together with ingenuity. The police force presided over by Colt has both Poe's *acumen* and the calculating power, the intuitive and the rational. And one of the many classic statements of the Bi-Part Soul by Sherlock Holmes finds its echo in Colt himself: " 'Tony,' he said solemnly, 'the trouble with the police in this investigation is that we see but we do not observe.' 'Seems to me I read that somewhere when I was a kid, chief.' 'So did I, and it is still true.' " (*Clergyman's Mistress,* 160).

The police are shown in their ballistics department—"the last word" in that science in that day (*Man Afraid,* 251). A leaf discovered in the same boat as the bodies sends Colt to the City Forester and his cross-index of every tree in New York; after a good deal of information about Chinese sumachs, the scene of the crime is discovered through "nothing but observation and guess work'" (43). While the novels abound in careful detailings of the routine of police discovery, the most marvellous example, so often cited by critics, is the method by which the Startled Lady, who when she is discovered in a box in the river is no more than "a scrap-heap of human bones" (31), "the two hundred pieces of Madeline," is reconstructed by the "crime sculptor." And the method of the sculptor follows the pattern of the intuitive and the scientific— he works on the skull "with hands of great tactile sensitiveness, his manner that of a hierophant intent upon heavenly mysteries," even as he tells Colt that, "speaking as an anatomist," "the length of the nose from the bridge to the base is fixed by the size of the roots of the teeth." (55)

With the realism of police routine in Abbot's novels comes a graphic presentation of murder not often seen in the detective fiction of the Golden Age. Geraldine Foster is hacked to death with an axe, and the "tortured body" is found, nude, with a pillow case tied over its head. The scene of the murder is not surprisingly doused with blood, and one of the more bizarre features of the scene is a flock of dead pigeons which have drunk their fill of that blood. A circus acrobat falls from the high wire, and Tony duly, even dully, records the "nightmare" of the sound of her repeated impact with the ground (*Circus Queen,* 53). Even sex is treated with rather more than 1930s freedom: when Tony has his doubts about the wisdom of Colt marrying Florence Dunbar, "Betty laughed at me. She said I was jealous, that my nose was out of joint, and then she sat on my knee and asked me if I would deny Thatcher Colt joys such as I had known with her. I spanked her and took her to bed." (*Man Afraid,* 207). Lest room be left for doubt, when Colt telephones shortly afterwards to call Tony out on the case, it is "one of life's embarrassing moments."

One final element of Abbot's realism in the Colt novels is the foundation of more than one of them in an actual crime. Again, such a procedure is hardly original: Marie Roget was really Mary Rogers, and both Sergeant Cuff and the crime he was investigating had their real-life genesis in the Constance Kent case. And S.S. Van Dine's first novel was based on the Joseph Elwell case. Some alert or ingenious minds have found the origin of *About the Murder of Geraldine Foster* in Lizzie Borden's celebrated rampage, and, rather more closely, *About the Murder of the Clergyman's Mistress* is patterned after that tangled love murder on the Hall-Mills case, which had already produced Frances Noyes Hart's *The Bellamy Trial* four years before.

One method which many writers have used to underline the verisimilar qualities of their detective heroes has been to show them growing older with each passing book: the series becomes a running biography of the detective. We can chart the life of Sherlock Holmes from his college days with the *Gloria Scott* to his end as a Sussex beekeeper, or Poirot's from Styles to his own final curtain; and we now follow Reg Wexford through his heart regimens, and Mike Burden through the loss of his wife and his subsequent remarriage. Some detectives do not grow appreciably older: Vance, Father Brown, even Lew Archer, seem to solve their cases within a vast simultaneity. Vance may translate a book of Xenophon here, trip off to Egypt there, or Archer's broken marriage may invoke an earlier existence, but these people seem not to exist within a continuum of passing time—would we be able to place the cases in sequence if we were not told? Thatcher Colt belongs to this second group, save only that Florence Dunbar is the register of time passing. Colt's marriage to Florence, in fact, is what separates the first six novels from the last two. In those first six, reminders of her aside, we are in that temporal never-never land. With the marriage, and his retirement as Commissioner, Abbot has nowhere to take Colt, and so the last novel takes him backwards, into a reminiscence.

How, finally, are we to assess these eight novels of Anthony Abbot's? The standard treatments of the genre over the years have not dealt very kindly with them: Haycraft mentions Abbot only in a listing of contemporary writers; A.E. Murch passes over him rather rapidly; Julian Symons mentions him not at all; only that eccentrically chatty, though much underrated, buff of the form, Sutherland Scott, has more than a few good words to say of him. More recent, encyclopedic works, aiming at wider coverage, include him in their canvass, and Charles Shibuk's essay in *Twentieth-Century Crime and Mystery Writers* is a sympathetic treatment. Barzun and Taylor, who admit to reading him for the first time in 1968, find that the books have "faded less than the once more highly esteemed Van Dine," and that "Thatcher Colt is credible in everything save his impeccable attire." They single out *About the Murder of the Clergyman's Mistress* as the one to read, and Scott and Shibuk, the only writers to attempt a rating, agree that it must be ranked high. Scott rates it best; Shibuk prefers the last, *The Shudders*.[24] My present survey must now end with a similar, summary evaluation.

The first six novels are written in fair conformity to the Van Dine, or Golden Age, formula: a murder is committed, clues are detected, and the detective gathers the dramatis personae in "discordant convocation" (*Night Club Lady*, 238) for the explication, and the unmasking of the criminal. None of them contains more than two murders, another mark of Abbot's greater realism over Van Dine's; in *The Greene Murder Case* almost all the suspects are eliminated one by one, until the most obtuse reader is left with the criminal before him.

Each of the Colt novels turns upon a formal problem; a change is rung in turn on each of the standard elements of the form—scene of the crime, identity of the victim, motive, the method of murder. *About the Murder of Geraldine Foster* mystifies the reader with a seemingly motiveless crime: the solution reveals that the murderer did not even know the victim, but killed her only to convict the man who stands in the way of the murderer's inheriting several million dollars. The formal problem in *About the Murder of the Clergyman's Mistress,* which also obscures the motive, is a variation on what Francis M. Nevins has called, in its use upon use by Ellery Queen, "the Birlstone Gambit,"[25] most memorably used by Doyle in *The Valley of Fear:* the roles of murderer and victim are reversed, so that the body found by the police is that of the intending killer. In the third novel, *About the Murder of the Night Club Lady*, the focus is upon the murder method: a woman, whose death is predicted at a certain hour, duly dies at that hour, in a variation of the locked room enigma, to all appearances of natural, if sudden, causes. The murderer has changed identities, and has revenged the night club lady's seduction of a near relative years before; in yet another of the central formulas of the genre, the past enters the present to stalk its victim. In all these first three cases, the solution is not given to the public, for no useful purpose (*pace* the contemporary investigative reporter) would be served by its being known. In two of them, the murderer commits suicide, and in the other the murderer, having acted in self-defence, is allowed to go free, and even provided with a new identity.

The next two novels alter this formula of having the crime solved semi-privately by the Commissioner and the solution withheld from the public, and these two novels are also less concerned with a single formal problem. *About the Murder of the Circus Queen* finds Colt looking into a series of mishaps at the circus which culminate in the murder of an acrobat. Also part of the circus is a troupe of Ubangi tribesmen; when their witch doctor is also killed by the murderer of the acrobat, they provide the climax to Colt's explication by projecting a poison dart—again a retributive gambit borrowed from a Holmes novel, *The Sign of Four*—into the murderer's neck. For the fourth time the criminal has not been brought to the bar of justice, though his guilt is disclosed to the world. In *About the Murder of a Startled Lady*, the killer will go to trial, but will be let off leniently, for the killing has been accidental. The final novel of these first six, *About the Murder of a Man Afraid of Women,* returns to the formula: the central problem is a formal one, and the solution is not publicly revealed. As in *The Night Club Lady*, the murderer is a figure from out of the victim's past, and as in *The Clergyman's Mistress* and *A Startled Lady*, he has killed by accident, and in self-defense as well; with the acquiescence of the D.A., Colt lets him go at the end. Of these six novels, the most successful is the one which most convincingly and effectively exploits the formula, and which, even at an emotional level, justifies both the final suppression of the true facts and Colt's playing God in allowing the killer, in one way or the other, to escape the operation of the law. That one is *About the Murder of the Clergyman's Mistress,* which of all the Colt novels is the one most steeped in both subjective atmosphere and objective locale, the one most closely based on an actual case, and the one most convincing, though not the most spectacular, in its presentation of solid, hard-working police routine.

The last two novels fall largely outside the formulas and the explication of formal problems which mark the first six. *The Creeps* certainly gives us a standard formula, but not a formula looked at anew so much as a cliche rehashed: the closed circle of a house party (in Buzzard's Bay) during a memorable snowstorm. It is the only Colt novel given a specific date, Thanksgiving 1938, and it culminates once more in a gathering of the suspects that even Tony finds "melodramatic," and once more the villain, having been unmasked, kills himself, running from the room to leap over a convenient cliff. And *The Shudders* is perhaps the most factitious of all the eight novels, and the one most incommoded by its formula; again we have the closed circle, as Colt is lured to a rural estate in Connecticut to engage in a long duel of wits with a criminal bent on killing him by the use of an obscure poison. Since the tale is told retrospectively, any suspense is removed by our certainty that he will survive this bogus encounter with one whom he sent in years gone by to the electric chair, who survived the experience through the help of some venal prison officials, and who has set out to murder, one by one, not only these accomplices, but also those who brought him to justice, including and especially Thatcher Colt.

The titles of these last two novels, too, suggest a difference in kind, as well as in quality, changing the dossier-objectivity of the first six to a fortuitous chill factor, fortuitous not least because neither title bears much relation to the content. Despite their titles, both these novels remain deadly serious, though the emphasis is upon suspense rather than detection, especially in *The Shudders*; and this is emphasized by Colt's being less in his official role—a retired house guest in *The Creeps,* and away from his official desk for most of *The Shudders.*

It is finally appropriate, however, that *The Shudders* should be told retrospectively, for there is a valedictory air about this last Colt novel. Colt stakes his life as he never has before (though in *The Creeps,* too, he is more reckless than usual, eliciting the villain's guilt at the cost of a machete wound in the shoulder). "I'd merely made up my mind," he says, "to close this case by morning—dead, or living" (*Shudders,* 306). And there is a moving, if perhaps also commercial,[26] passage in which Tony reviews Colt's career and the cases he has solved. Solved, as both detective and scribe tell us several times in the novels, but here again in the very last paragraph of the last novel, by "Patience, industry, and perseverance." These are certainly the salient qualities of this detective created by "one of the first apologists for the police in detective fiction," as Oursler called himself, also looking back.[27] But

Colt might have been truer to himself and his ancestry in Dupin, Holmes, and Vance, had he added intuition and imagination to those qualities.

Notes

[1]All references are to the first editions, except for *About the Murder of the Clergyman's Mistress*, for which I have found it necessary to use the English first edition: *The Crime of the Century* (London: Collins, 1931).

About the Murder of Geraldine Foster (New York: Covici Friede, 1930).

About the Murder of the Clergyman's Mistress (see above).

About the Murder of the Night Club Lady (New York: Covici Friede, 1931).

About the Murder of the Circus Queen (New York: Covici Friede, 1932).

About the Murder of a Startled Lady (New York: Farrar & Rinehart, 1935).

About the Murder of a Man Afraid of Women (New York: Farrar & Rinehart, 1937).

The Creeps (New York: Farrar & Rinehart, 1939).

The Shudders (New York: Farrar & Rinehart, 1943).

[2]All references to the S.S. Van Dine novels are to the first editions (New York: Charles Scribner's Sons).

[3]See Sutherland Scott, *Blood in Their Ink* (London: Stanley Paul, 1953), p. 61.

[4]See Wayne C. Booth, *The Rhetoric of Fiction* (Chicago: University of Chicago Press, 1961), pp. 215-218.

[5]*The Night Club Lady* (Columbia, 1932), and *The Circus Queen Murder* (Columbia, 1933).

[6]See "The Sex Life of a Gentleman Detective," *In the Queens' Parlor* (New York: Simon & Schuster, 1957), pp. 47-49.

[7]Though many of the rule-makers have interdicted love and marriage in detective fiction, Van Dine put it most succinctly: "*Sherlock Holmes* in mellow mood, holding a lady's hand and murmuring amorous platitudes, would be unthinkable." (Introduction to *The Great Detective Stories* (New York Charles Scribner's Sons, 1928, p. 10).

[8]The most striking example being the nature-girl Rima of *Double, Double*.

[9]"Nick Charles, Jr." ages from babyhood to ten or so (played by Dean Stockwell) over the last four *Thin Man* films: *Another Thin Man, Shadow of the Thin Man, The Thin Man Goes Home, Song of the Thin Man* (1939-47).

[10]The subtitle of *Busman's Honeymoon* (1937).

[11]"The Origin of Ellery Queen," *In the Queens' Parlor*, pp. 65-67.

[12]*Works*, National Edition, 20 volumes (New York: Charles Scribner's Sons, 1926), XIV, 236-238; *An Autobiography* (New York: Macmillan, 1913), Chapter VI.

[13]p. 178.

[14]*Works*, XIV, 208.

[15]See, especially, Edmund Morris, *The Rise of Theodore Roosevelt* (New York: Coward, McCann, & Geoghegan, 1979), Chapter 20.

[16]*Autobiography*, p. 192.

[17]*The Greatest Story Ever Told* (Kingswood, Surrey, 1949), p. vii.

[18]p. 79.

[19]*Outlook*, May 27, 1911.

[20](London, 1907), pp. 105-106.

[21]"A.E.W. Mason," *Twelve Englishmen of Mystery* ed. Earl F. Bargainnier (Bowling Green: Popular Press, 1984), p. 60.

[22]*Bloody Murder* (London: Faber & Faber, 1972), p. 114.

[23]The idea is put somewhat more whimsically by another professional policeman, in G.K. Chesterton's "The Mirror of the Magistrate" (*The Father Brown Omnibus*, New York: Dodd, Mead, 1951, p. 429): " 'Ours is the only trade...in which the professional is always supposed to be wrong. After all, people don't write stories in which hairdressers can't cut hair and have to be helped by a customer; or in which a cabman can't drive a cab until his fare explains to him the philosophy of cab-driving.' "

[24]*Blood in Their Ink*, p. 61; *Twentieth-Century Crime and Mystery Writers*, ed. John M. Reilly (New York: St. Martin's Press, 1980), p. 15.

[25]*Royal Bloodline: Ellery Queen, Author and Detective* (Bowling Green: The Popular Press, 1974), p. 27.

[26]Pp. 45-46.

[27]*Behold This Dreamer!* (Boston: Little Brown, 1964), pp. 257-258.

Joseph Harrington's Francis X. Kerrigan

Martha Alderson and Neysa Chouteau

Even though Joseph Harrington wrote only three mystery novels,[1] his work deserves a place in any study of cops and constables because his hero of those three novels, Francis X. ("Frank") Kerrigan of the New York Police Department, is the quintessential cop.

Joseph Harrington was a newspaper reporter for many years before he became a free-lance writer. As a reporter, he knew many detectives, and those real-life detectives served as models for his fictional hero. The dust jacket of *Doorbell* includes a description by Harrington of the detectives who served as his role models:

As individuals they varied a lot but they all had certain traits in common—an incredible tenacity, infinite patience, and an unlimited capacity of hard and often dull work. To them there was no such thing as a good clue, or a bad one. A clue was a clue was a clue; something to be pursued to the very end, hopeless or not.

Harrington is such a firm believer in the values of tenacity, patience, and hard work that he manages to create substantive suspenseful novels through focusing upon these elements almost exclusively, making very little use of the other conventions that writers of police procedurals have developed to create interest. This feat becomes even more impressive when we consider that a writer of police procedurals already is operating under certain limitations that the writer of classic or hard-boiled mysteries does not face. As Hillary Waugh points out, "Not only does realism require that the hero of the procedural be human rather than superhuman, so do the restrictions of his job and his obligations to society."[2] As is stated in the introduction to *Cops and Constables*, "One of the most difficult problems of the writer of police detection is the avoidance of the humdrum."

To counterbalance the limitations imposed by realism, writers of police procedurals have developed their own conventions, which were not inherited from the older forms of detective fiction.[3] One such convention is that of the police officer with family problems, a theme which some writers of police procedurals use very effectively to add interest to the story. For example, Lillian O'Donnell takes her series hero, Norah Mulcahaney of the N.Y.P.D., through a romance, a strong but often troubled marriage, and, after eight books, widowhood when her fellow officer and husband Joe Capretto is killed in the line of duty. In this progression, O'Donnell also develops clear portraits of Norah's father, stepmother, mother-in-law, and several sisters-in-law.

Harrington does not use the family problem convention at all. For all we are told of Kerrigan's past, he might have materialized on the subway on a grimy afternoon. From the name Francis X. (surely Xavier) Kerrigan, we infer that he is Irish Catholic, but we are told nothing of his religious beliefs or practices, his socio-economic background, his parents, or his siblings. Eventually, we learn much about Francis X. Kerrigan, but little of what Sergeant Friday of *Dragnet* so regularly asks for, "just the facts, ma'am." We learn that he lives in a one-and-a-half room apartment, is thirty-two years old (*Address,* 12), is not a college graduate, and looks like nothing else but a cop (*Spot,* 7); but we never see the inside of the apartment or learn where or how the previous thirty-one years were lived.

Interservice hostility, the tendency to "cherish and promote the rivalries between branches" as it is described in the introduction to the present volume, is a convention used by a number of writers of police procedurals, including McBain, O'Donnell, Procter, and Shannon, among others. This friction occurs between squads, between departments, and between the police and other public servants.[4] Harrington almost turns this convention upside down in that he points it up as a potential problem, then makes it a nonproblem, thanks to Kerrigan's humanity and skill. In *Address,* Kerrigan and his rookie partner Jane Boardman, working out of Special Service, are on loan to the First Detective Division. Their job is to locate a man that Detectives Yelanski and MacAllister of the First Division have failed to find in spite of diligent legwork. After Kerrigan and Boardman have discussed the case with them and left to take up the cold trail, MacAllister expresses the hope that they will fail, because if they succeed, "It'll certainly make monkeys of us..." (62). Yelanski reassures MacAllister that "Frank is pretty careful when it comes to making monkeys of people" (61). Yelanski's statement is proved correct when Kerrigan goes out of his way to see that MacAllister and Yelanski are called in to share the credit after he and Boardman solve the case.

While pursuing an apparently irrelevant, useless clue in *Spot,* Kerrigan goes beyond the New York state border and into the state of Connecticut. Harrington points out that police officers can be jealous of their turf, that "there were certain amenities to be observed in cases which crossed state lines, even county lines" (172) and that if those amenities were not observed, hard feelings would result. Kerrigan, of course, observes the amenities as he must have in dealing with the Connecticut state police earlier, since he gets superb cooperation from them as he fishes for leads in several rural and suburban locations in that state (138-152).

When Kerrigan encounters hostility from a building inspector in *Doorbell,* this hostility pleases him because it shows that the young inspector is honest. He suspects that Kerrigan is going to ask him to ignore violations of the building code (110-111). When Kerrigan cannot avoid interservice hostility by going through channels in a cordial, courteous manner, he is perfectly willing to fight it out, as when he encounters classic resistance from a postal employee at a postal substation. Kerrigan goes to the main post office where he speaks to "a high authority, then to a higher authority, then to the highest authority" (*Doorbell,* 122). He then returns to the employee who is now eager to help, claiming that he hadn't realized who Kerrigan was on the earlier visit. Kerrigan knows that the postal employee knew very well who he was, but he accepts the face-saving device cordially, because Kerrigan never picks bones. Here, as elsewhere, Harrington uses the convention of interservice hostility sparingly, and primarily as a vehicle for pointing up how carefully and smoothly Kerrigan operates.

The long hours that police officers work on a hot case and the problems that such overwork can cause are another convention of the police procedural. Harrington uses the convention of the overworked force in somewhat the same manner as he uses the convention of interservice hostility, not as a problem that adds tension, but as a device to point up how Kerrigan operates. After Kerrigan and Boardman are assigned to the missing witness case in *Address,* they begin work immediately. Toward the end of the normal work day, Kerrigan points out that five-thirty or six is the best time to catch people at home. They proceed to interview people for three more hours. Kerrigan suggests that they try "the rest of the neighbors." When Jane responds that they have already been on the job for eleven hours, she sees a trace of disappointment in Kerrigan's face. When he suggests that she go on home while he finishes the interviews, her pride will not let her give up, and so they work on until nearly ten o'clock (107-108). The next day, they work until past eleven o'clock in the evening. Kerrigan suggests that they meet later than usual in the morning. Boardman asks how much later. He suggests a time only a half-hour later than usual. At first Boardman thinks he is joking, but, of course, he isn't. (165).

In *Doorbell,* Kerrigan is on vacation when Boardman is assigned an eleven-year-old kidnapping case. They meet for dinner that night and Boardman tells him about the case. What little interest Kerrigan had displayed in vacationing in Canada or Portugal vanishes as they spend the rest of the evening going over the case records. Kerrigan asks if he may go with Boardman the next day to interview the family. Meanwhile, Jane Boardman has realized that Frank Kerrigan is one of those cops "who said it was a pleasure to get away from crime and didn't mean it at all, even though they really believed it as they said it. They said it, and a few minutes later it was clear that they didn't want to talk about anything else, weren't interested in anything else" (35).

Thus Jane and Frank work long hours, but not because of pressures from outside. Jane works such hours in order to keep up with her role model, Frank. Frank works long hours because he wants to, because he would rather follow a case than do anything else. Again, Harrington employs a police procedural convention in a somewhat unconventional manner. The system does not overwork Kerrigan; Kerrigan overworks himself.

Francis X. Kerrigan would never be the sort of cop who feels closer to the criminal than to the citizen nor one who thinks of cops and citizens as "us against them," but Harrington does use the convention of the hostile public with some regularity. Kerrigan suffers an exceptionally severe blow from public pressure, a blow from which his career can never entirely recover. At the beginning of *Address,* Kerrigan is walking a beat on Staten Island. Only a few months before, he had been an acting lieutenant, "as sure as anybody could be sure of anything that he'd make full lieutenant in three months, captain in five years, with a good chance of making deputy inspector before he was forty" (12). Then he arrested a young man for drunken driving. The young man, vengeful and with powerful connections, alleged brutality and succeeded in having Kerrigan demoted as far as possible: back to sergeant, in uniform, pounding a beat.

The brutality tag haunts Kerrigan throughout all three books. In *Address,* Kerrigan is correctly perceived as too good a cop to be kept on a quiet beat and so is soon pulled back to Special Service. When he and Jane Boardman nab a mugger in Central Park, however, Jane is forced to take all the credit so that it won't come out that Frank has sent another man to the hospital. When the case is brought to a successful conclusion, the success is so great that a letter from the District Attorney's Office reaches the Commissioner himself. He recognizes the name Francis X. Kerrigan and angrily protests that "this gun-happy, fist-happy troublemaker" has been brought back from Staten Island (188). Frank is promptly sent back to his Staten Island beat, although the District Attorney plans to offer him a spot as Acting Detective Lieutenant.

Kerrigan does win the job of Acting Detective Lieutenant on the staff of the District Attorney and holds this position during the cases he works on in *Spot* and *Doorbell.* In *Doorbell,* the story of the unfair charge is repeated when Jane Boardman almost mentions that another officer is going places in the department. She stops for fear of hurting Frank because for Kerrigan, "all hope of future promotion was gone" (32). When the case is brought to a successful conclusion, Jane wins another promotion, as does her immediate superior, but Kerrigan must stay in the background again. In *Spot,* while Kerrigan is working in the District Attorney's Office, he is assigned to a "hopeless" case because an influential citizen has put pressure on the department.

Kerrigan also encounters hostility from some of the individuals he contacts in the course of tracking down leads. The school principal and Dr. McPartridge of *Address* both begin interviews with Kerrigan and Boardman on a hostile note. Jane notes that Dr. McPartridge has "the air of a man who knew his rights and wasn't prepared to sell them out" (167). A few witnesses begin by being unhelpful and/or hostile and stay that way, notably Dr. McPartridge's nurse, Miss Tavish. Many others, however, begin by being wary or hostile witnesses, then become helpful as Kerrigan employs his bag of tricks. Harrington uses the convention of the hostile public both to add tension—Kerrigan has been wronged, and we yearn to see this injustice corrected—and as another device for showing us what a great cop Kerrigan is.

Another police procedural convention that Harrington makes full use of in two of the three books is that of the young cop. In the first book, *Address,* Kerrigan is assigned to work with an attractive young probationary policewoman, Jane Boardman. The result of this pairing is touted on the dust jacket:

For Jane—and for the reader—the assignment is a graduate course in detection work, and Kerrigan is an accomplished teacher.

Kerrigan works alone in the second book, *Spot,* with Jane mentioned only at the beginning and the end. In the third book, *Doorbell,* Frank again assumes the role of teacher, educating Jane about the quirks of eye witnesses, the tendency of people to use their own initials when they choose an alias, and ways to spot patterns of operation (102-103).

Jane Boardman not only functions as the rookie against whom Harrington can balance the skilled Kerrigan, but she also provides romance. By the end of *Address,* MacAllister says of Jane, "You know, Sam, I think she fell for that Kerrigan guy" (190). In *Spot,* though Jane appears only twice, in the first instance, Kerrigan often wonders about the warmth between them (7) and in the second instance, they are on a date (190). In *Doorbell,* they have been dating something over six months, as we know from the report that Frank has "taken to kissing her good night" for "these six months past" (48). The romance between Frank and Jane is exceptionally chaste, even for a book published in 1969. The chasteness does not spring from the times, but from the character of Kerrigan. He is not comfortable with women (*Address,* 29) and he is a clumsy kisser (*Spot,* 48), an attribute that might be expected of a high school boy, but not a street-wise cop. Kerrigan has spent twelve years on the force seeing the seamiest side of life. For all that, Frank's heart is pure. As a character, he could easily be a western hero whose only real passion is for his horse.

Harrington not only uses Boardman as a student to be taught the tricks of the trade and as a romantic interest but also as a contrast to Kerrigan. In *Spot,* as Frank is slowly plodding through a 1200-page file, he thinks ruefully of Jane, who can easily read two novels in a day. He goes on to think of other differences between them. Jane's career has been quite successful. At twenty-three and after only a year in the department, she has reached a grade that Frank took five years to make. She is a college graduate, with the poise and wholesome good looks of an all-American girl, looking "nothing like a police officer" (7). Kerrigan is ten years older than Jane, is not a college graduate, and looks so much like a cop that he is pleased when a bouncer fails to recognize him as such. He is not handsome. "Twelve years on the force, twelve years of seeing a great deal that was sordid and brutal, had left a veneer of hardness on a face that had been rough to begin with" (*Spot,* 7). As Frank sees it, Jane is smart and quick, but he is only ploddingly thorough. Of course, Jane realizes time and again how smart Frank is, and each one's attitude toward the other adds the contrast of their points of view to the obvious contrasts of age, education, and style.

Boardman is not only the classic rookie and love interest, but she also serves as the only continuing character of significance. Hillary Waugh points out that through the use of continuing character, "the squad room can become the equivalent of a daytime serial setting, meaning that readers can get to know the people, their personalities, and their problems so well that they look forward to the next book as a chance to rejoin old friends."[5] Harrington seldom uses this opportunity. Assistant District Attorney Robert Rosetti appears briefly in *Spot* and *Doorbell*. Inspector Arnold appears briefly in *Address* and even more briefly in Doorbell, where he is described but not named. Even Jane Boardman has only a walk-on role in *Blind Spot*.

Harrington barely uses continuing characters, does not use the convention of the young cop with family problems at all, inverts the conventions of interservice hostility and the overworked force (and to a lesser extent, that of the hostile public), and makes extensive use only of the convention of the young cop. If Harrington so seldom uses the normal devices that make police procedurals interesting, then how does he engage the reader so completely?

There are three elements that stand out in making Harrington's novels good reading. One is the reality with which minor characters are portrayed. In the course of his investigations, Kerrigan interviews many characters, and a surprising number of them rise above the level of stock figures. Mrs. Sachs, Jack Loring, and Miss Tavish of *Address*, Barbara Ogilvie and Mr. Goheen of *Spot*, and Miss Deakin and Mrs. Gibney of *Doorbell* are among the minor characters who are so fully fleshed out that we remember them as individuals rather than as part of a large crowd of witnesses. Further, some characters prove unexpectedly complex, either because of Kerrigan's (and therefore the reader's) expectations or their own natures. The profane, combative Barbara Ogilvie, whom Kerrigan had expected from the interrogation notes "to be a sharp-nosed stinging woman of middle age" is young and "a soft round little brunette, with great dark eyes and a musical voice" (*Spot*, 103). Furthermore, she is exceptionally perceptive. Jack Loring of *Address* drinks too much and may be a chaser, but even while drunk he produces a remarkable description, "A tightly knit tapestry of a picture" displaying "a gift of recollection and observation" (106). Wholesome Albert Schmidt of *Spot* is completely unexpected as the proprietor of a nightclub. In *Doorbell*, Jane Boardman's perceptions of Ernie Detweiler change as she learns more about his motivations, but the most extensive and interesting shift in perceptions occurs as Kerrigan learns more about Eva Midnight in *Spot*. From the first description of her as an earthy, coarse (but very sexy) stripper to whom "a lay is a lay is a lay" (36), each revelation moves Eva slightly further away from the first description until Kerrigan has to acknowledge "that the lot of them, himself included, had a blind spot when they looked at Eva Midnight" (185).

A second important element in Harrington's novels is pacing. Each book begins with a hopeless case, one that other good officers have failed to solve. The first steps of Kerrigan and/or Boardman are to retrace the steps of others, proving once again how hopeless the case is. Then an idea or an event gives Kerrigan a sudden insight that sends him off in new directions. A few more hitches, the pace quickens, success!

The reality of the secondary characters and the pacing of the story are important elements in the success of Harrington's novels, but the most important element by far is Harrington's hero, Frank Kerrigan. Waugh and others have emphasized that the protagonist in a police procedural is not a superhero, but in one respect, Kerrigan comes closer to the superhero than to the traditional police procedural cop. In delineating Kerrigan, Harrington makes little use of devices other than the "procedural" of the police procedural. He doesn't inject sex: Kerrigan is a clumsy kisser. He doesn't inject derring-do—Kerrigan never draws a gun. Francis X. Kerrigan embodies boring virtues: tenacity, patience, and hard work. Still, Kerrigan is almost a superhero because he is a citizen's dream of the Perfect Cop. He is dedicated; in fact, it is his dedication to duty, his decision to double-check a few stake-outs, that leads to his run-in with the drunken citizen who gets him busted to Staten Island (*Address*, 9-24). He gives every case his complete attention, no matter what the nature of the case. In *Address,* he solves a case of four missing pigeons stolen from a twelve-year-old boy (25-27). A colleague recalls similar dedication in an earlier case involving a forty-dollar burglary, "So help me, you'd think he was investigating a gold robbery at Fort Knox." (61)

Kerrigan's dedication includes working long hours, no matter how important the case. Not only do Kerrigan and Boardman work thirteen hours on the first day in *Address,* and work on the case during Kerrigan's vacation in *Doorbell,* but the missing pigeon investigation is conducted on Kerrigan's lunch hour and after his tour of duty ends because it is technically not a matter for a uniformed officer.

Kerrigan cares about people. In *Address,* he shares the credit with the two detectives who had worked (unsuccessfully) on the case earlier, and he carries out an extensive charade of being an acquaintance of the man they finally track down so that the man's daughter will not be alarmed. In *Spot,* he cannot bring himself to ask Gerald Mackey how he feels about the fact that Neil Jefferson owned keys to Laurie

Callender's apartment (93). In *Doorbell,* he intervenes with the Building Department on behalf of Mrs. Gibney. In *Address,* he berates himself because he failed to congratulate Jane for a good piece of work and "tried to rehearse a little speech about how she was teaching an old dog new tricks" (127). When he and Boardman interview a Jewish woman whose daughter had been an apostate, Kerrigan shares the woman's suffering as he is "uncomfortably aware that he had raked the scab off an old wound and left a running red sore" (*Address,* 148).

Kerrigan is a first-rate psychologist. He repeatedly uses just the right technique to bring witnesses around. He elicits information from two witnesses in *Spot* by using quite different methods. He notes of Mrs. Dodd that "She reacted to courtesy as Goheen had reacted to rudeness" (155). Kerrigan is also intuitive. When he is interviewing Eva Midnight, he asks a question which throws her off guard. The question "wasn't a shot in the dark. In the twilight, perhaps, but not in the dark" (111).

Kerrigan has a sense of his own worth but is essentially a modest man. In *Spot,* when Mackey reports that Rosetti has called him the most brilliant detective they have, Kerrigan is embarrassed:

He wasn't brilliant, never had been, never would be. His closest friends didn't say that about him. They said a lot of other kind things about him. They said he was stubborn, perhaps foolishly so, that he put in a hard day's work even when it wasn't necessary, that he never let go until the last stone was turned, and then he usually went back and turned the damned things over again. But no one, not even Jane, ever called him brilliant (86).

Of course, Kerrigan *is* brilliant. In each case, it takes more than dogged persistence to win the day. He asks the question that no one else thought to ask; he sees connections that no one else sees.

A cop like Kerrigan is bound to have friends, to inspire loyalty, as Boardman learns:

There were men in the department who had a queer loyalty to Francis X. Kerrigan; some of them she knew he covered for; some of them just had a blind loyalty to him (*Doorbell,* 153).

It is not surprising that he inspires such loyalty. Dedicated, thoughtful, caring, empathetic, modest, a very human superhuman, he arouses the reader's loyalty, too. He involves us, makes us a member of the team, proud to be working with Francis X. Kerrigan.

Joseph Harrington's three novels are unusual for police procedurals in that he spurned the use of a large cast of continuing characters, elaborate subplots, crime lab razzle-dazzle, sex, personal danger, and gunplay, embracing instead the pedestrian virtue of dogged persistence. Considering this narrow scope of action, one might wonder how Harrington created even three novels for Francis X. Kerrigan. Yet Harrington put Kerrigan into quite different situations—tracking a missing friendly witness, proving that a beautiful girl was wrongly convicted of murder, and capturing a repulsive sex offender who had murdered with impunity for years. Perhaps Harrington could have created any number of plot variations that would have been as engaging as *Blind Spot, The Last Doorbell,* and *The Last Known Address.* It is disappointing that there are only three Kerrigan novels, but these three provide fully satisfying studies of the tireless pursuit of justice by a superior cop.

Notes

[1]The editions of Joseph Harrington's novels, all featuring Francis X. Kerrigan, are listed below, preceded by the original date of publication. All quotations will be cited in the text using the abbreviation given after an entry:

1965: *The Last Known Address* (Philadelphia: Lippincott, 1965). (*Address*)

1966: *Blind Spot* (Philadelphia: Lippincott, 1966). (*Spot*)

1969: *The Last Doorbell* (Philadelphia: Lippincott, 1969). (*Doorbell*)

[2]Hillary Waugh, "The Human Rather Than the Superhuman Sleuth," in *The Murder Mystique: Crime Writers on Their Art,* ed. Lucy Freeman. (New York: Frederick Ungar Publishing Co., Inc., 1982), p. 42.

[3]George N. Dove, "Realism, Routine, Stubbornness and System: The Police Procedural," in *The Armchair Detective,* (April 1977), 133.

[4]George N. Dove, *The Police Procedural* (Bowling Green, OH: The Popular Press, 1982), p. 98.

[5]Hillary Waugh, p. 43.

John Ball's Virgil Tibbs and Jack Tallon
George N. Dove

Not many mystery series have started with anything like the acclaim of John Ball's *In the Heat of the Night,* which received both the Mystery Writers of America Edgar as the best first novel of 1965 and the Gold Dagger of the British Crime Writers' Association for the best non-British mystery. The film adaptation, starring Sidney Poitier as police detective Virgil Tibbs, won five Motion Picture Academy awards in 1967.[1]

In the Heat of the Night is not exceptional as a crime novel, and the mystery element, except for some classy Sherlock Holmes-style deduction by Tibbs, is not really remarkable either. The success of this story, and the reason for its continuing distinctiveness, is the combination of the portrayal of the wholesome character of Virgil Tibbs and the markedly skillful handling of the irony of the racial theme, which combine into a story not easily forgotten.

The controlling paradox is developed early in the book. Virgil Tibbs, a detective on the Pasadena police force, is picked up in the waiting room of a railroad station in a small deep-South town on suspicion of murder, for the reason that, as a black man at large in the middle of the night with money in his pocket, he is an obvious suspect. When the white police learn his identity and try to send him on his way, they are deterred by the insistence of a local influential white citizen who knows of Tibbs' reputation and insists that the police use him in the murder investigation. Thus Chief Gillespie and the rest of the police force of Wells, South Carolina, are forced to collaborate with the obvious racial inferior whose skill and intelligence are so far above theirs that he successfully solves the problem that is plainly beyond their reach.

Virgil Tibbs' nobility becomes manifest in his dealings with the white police, whose prejudices he understands and whose self-esteem he seeks to preserve. He is quick to compliment Officer Sam Wood on the way he handles a car, with the result that Wood finds himself liking the black man (75)[2], and when Chief Gillespie misses a clue Tibbs has noticed, Tibbs is careful to attribute the oversight to a difference in the angles from which they viewed the suspect. When the Chief remarks on his unusual given name and asks what people call him in Pasadena, Virgil's diplomatic reply is possibly the best-known line in police fiction,

"They call me Mr. Tibbs" (31). His detectival abilities, which place him much more decisively in the class of such great detectives as Nero Wolfe and Ellery Queen and decidedly above the ranks of the fictional policeman, come across with special force when he is able to eliminate a suspect because the man is left-handed, is wearing hard leather heels, and needs a shave (29-30). The unfolding of the mystery in the final chapter of the book is so completely his show that the badly outclassed white cops can only marvel.

The white social order that provides so opportune a backdrop to Virgil Tibbs' success is almost a textbook-style treatment of the stratification of a Southern town. There is, in a minor position for narrative purposes but a very important one for determining community predispositions, the White Power Structure, composed of three influential men who want the murder solved but make it clear to the Chief that they will not tolerate a "bunch of nigger lovers" from the North telling them how to act in Wells (70-3). There is the familiar Good Ole Boy, Mayor Frank Schubert, who shares the local bias against Blacks but who yields to the voice of authority when local influence forces him to use Virgil Tibbs in the case. More important to the story as background is the White Middle Class, represented by Sam Wood and the other regular police, who, talking about a black fighter, automatically assume that he can take inordinate punishment because "they don't feel it when they get hit the way you or I would" (5), and who avoid sitting by a black man or shaking hands with him. Considerably further down the scale are the local poor whites, typified especially by the Purdys, whom Chief Gillespie and Officer Wood frankly designate as Poor White Trash. The Purdys are more aggressively hostile toward Blacks than any others in the story, greeting Tibbs, when he comes to interview them, with "Niggers go to the back door" (113) and refusing to discuss the pregnancy of the sexy daughter Delores "with no nigger in the room" (97). Chief Gillespie constitutes a class of his own, the transplanted Southwestern White, who will not let anybody tell him a colored man can do anything he can't do (23) but whose attitude toward the common population of Wells is that "no southern white trash was going to tell a Texan what to do" (85). The picture is completed by the Enlightened Whites, the Endicotts, who have moved in from the North. It is George Endicott who uses his influence to get Virgil Tibbs assigned to the murder case under investigation.

The strength of *In the Heat of the Night* is grounded rather in Ball's selection and development of a first-class narrative situation than in any special skill with the technique of suspense writing or any of the flourishes that show up in some of his later mysteries. In one of the earliest reviews of the novel, Anthony Boucher recognized its main strength: "Virgil Tibbs is quite a remarkable individual, who may well wind up in the great Detecitve Category." He also pointed to a weakness in the handling of the language ("a tendency to let all characters speak the same prose," as Boucher put it) that was to draw fire from other critics in later Tibbs stories.[3]

In the Heat of the Night was followed the next year by *The Cool Cottontail,* in which Tibbs, now back in Pasadena, investigates a murder in a nudist park. A more considerable novel, in terms of development of the social-racial theme, is *Johnny Get Your Gun* (1969), the story of an eight-year-old boy who steals his father's handgun to shoot a schoolmate, then flees in panic and is tracked down by Virgil Tibbs. A paperback revision, with the title *Death for a Playmate,* was published in 1972. *Five Pieces of Jade* (1972) follows Tibbs through the investigation of the murder of a Chinese jade merchant, and *The Eyes of Buddha* (1976) takes him to Hong Kong and Nepal in search of a missing young woman. A somewhat different story is *Then Came Violence* (1980), in which Tibbs undertakes the investigation of a sordid hanging murder and also the job of serving as bodyguard to the wife of the president of an African republic, who is endangered by political terrorists.

Virgil Tibbs has also appeared in three short stories in *Ellery Queen's Mystery Magazine* between 1976 and 1978.[4]

We need to make special mention of *Death for a Playmate,* which is not just a paperback reprint but a substantial revision of *Johnny Get Your Gun.* It deviates from the original, with regard to the facts of the case and to the treatment of the character of Virgil Tibbs.[5] The paperback's account of his confrontation with the black mob, for instance, places more emphasis on Tibbs' physical prowess than does the hardback (92-3), and he is permitted the observation that Stokely Carmichael "had set the Negro cause back by a generation" (56), which is not in the first edition.

Virgil Tibbs does not like the word "black" as applied to race, preferring to think of himself as a Negro. The racial theme is brought home in all the novels from *The Cool Cottontail* onward, with the prejudice of the Deep South replaced by the racism of California, as manifested by a white woman who enters the Pasadena station house in that story asking to see a "detective" and walks out when Tibbs identifies himself as one (38). We return to the theme of Southern racial hostility in *Johnny Get Your Gun* when Tibbs confronts the McGuires, the parents of the fugitive boy, who recently migrated to Pasadena from

Tennessee. The McGuires are lower-middle class whites, a cut above the Purdys of *In the Heat of the Night* but below Officer Sam Wood and his colleagues. Mike McGuire, the father, is a sullen, taciturn man who resents all authority and is offended by the necessity of talking to a black policeman. The racial theme is modified as the series progresses; in *The Eyes of Buddha* Tibbs looks at his dark hands and finds strength (in *The Cottontail* he had looked at those same hands and hated them), and searching for the missing woman in Katmandu he is pleased that the Nepalese do not pay attention to his color and ancestry (26, 146-7).

The nobility of Virgil Tibbs gets increasing attention as the series proceeds. Always considerate of the feelings of the people he works with, he even sympathizes with the hostile McGuires in *Johnny Get Your Gun* because he recognizes the fearful strain they are under (12). To the distraught mother of the murdered youth in *Then Came Violence* who weeps, "His sins have been forgiven by the Lamb of God" Tibbs replies, "I hope He will do as much for me" (43).

The personal aspect of Virgil Tibbs that separates him from the ordinary run of policemen, however, is his remarkable cultural level, which was only suggested in *In the Heat of the Night* but makes itself felt full force in *The Cool Cottontail,* when alone in his apartment he relaxes by listening to Ravel and Falla, and in *Five Pieces of Jade,* where he makes an offhand reference to an episode in the second act of *Tosca* (19).

In view of his cultural attainments, it is small wonder that Virgil Tibbs as detective is much closer to the Great Policeman tradition of Freeman Wills Crofts' Inspector French than to the Ordinary Cop convention of the police procedural stories. Tibbs' mental powers are nothing if not overwhelming, reaching such heights as in *Five Pieces of Jade,* when he deduces the purpose of a top-secret industry after a ride in a company car and a walk across the office carpet (12-13). It reaches the mind-boggling level in *The Eyes of Buddha* when he knows a young woman is still alive because her closest friend speaks of her in the *present* tense (99), and it transcends the bounds of plausibility when he deduces that a suspect knows the death of a youth was the result of murder and not a suicide because the man uses "hanged" instead of "hung" in reference to the method of his death (*Then Came Violence,* 201). Besides these mental powers, Tibbs has to his credit a black belt in the martial art of karate and a brown belt in aikido.

One remarkable exception to all the deductive gymnastics is the account of some really fine police work in *Johnny Get Your Gun* involving the efficient handling of a potential mob. As the angry black crowd gathers to protest the supposed murder of one of their own by Johnny McGuire, the Pasadena police carefully work their way around the edges of the throng, purposely ignoring incidents of rock-throwing at themselves and their cruisers. The sergeant in charge sets up a public address system for use if necesssary, then places policemen at strategic points where they can testify that the announcements were audible. They refrain from any action until a speaker urges violence, whereupon the sergeant declares the assembly unlawful and orders it to disperse. Finally, as the crowd calms down, the police around the edges begin turning individuals and moving them out of the area (ch. 11).

Suspense in the Virgil Tibbs stories is largely dependent upon the conventional mystery-story technique of presenting the reader with a complex problem and permitting him to watch the detective solve it. A successful departure from this formula is the one Ball uses in *Johnny Get Your Gun:* as the eight-year-old flees with the loaded gun, the point of view switches from him to his frightened potential victims and to Virgil Tibbs, who is trying to find him before he panics and uses the gun again. The resolution of the story is one of the most spectacular endings in all mystery fiction. Tibbs, having learned that Johnny McGuire has one great passion in his young life, for the Los Angeles Angels and their owner Gene Autry, correctly guesses that the boy will be drawn eventually to the Angels' stadium. The sequence in which the frightened Johnny, still lethally armed, takes refuge in the service car high on the scoreboard and is finally enticed out of hiding when Autry rides onto the field in full cowboy regalia while the stadium organ plays "Ghost Riders in the Sky" and "Tumbling Tumbleweeds," is undistilled Hollywood schmaltz that in any hands but John Ball's would be sheer travesty.

The Ball touch in the Tibbs series is based upon a habit of careful research, with a resulting high degree of accuracy and the application of an impressive amount of specialized knowledge, and upon the creation of an ambiance that tends at some times toward the esoteric and at others toward affectation to the point of priggishness.

Almost every Ball mystery is prefaced by a full page of acknowledgements of sources of the information used in the story, ranging from forensic medicine to jade collecting to nudism. In an essay in *The Writer's Handbook* in 1976 John Ball cautions young writers against writing about things they do not really know, and he adds the highly useful caution, "Guessing at facts that can be established is an invitation to disaster."[6] That he takes his own advice is attested by the fact that an inaccuracy in a Ball story is an exceptional rarity. Besides his dedication to detail, John Ball has brought to the Tibbs stories an understanding of Oriental culture that is reflected in the treatment of such subjects as karate, jade collecting, and Buddhism.

The overriding quality of the Tibbs stories that continues to evoke comment from critics and reviewers is the tone of almost incredible refinement, usually centered upon what Frank Ochiogrosso has called an "impeccable sense of decorum and discretion."[7] We remarked a little earlier upon Virgil Tibbs' effortless reference to a scene in *Tosca,* but we discover that he is not alone in such civilized knowledge when Chief McGowan of the Pasadena P.D. refers just as easily to "the famous catalogue aria in *Don Giovanni*" (*Eyes of Buddha,* 175). Virgil Tibbs' model in the detective business is Sherlock Holmes, and his acquaintance with the Canonical Writings is so extensive that we are not surprised when he remarks during an investigation that he is reminded of the dog in the nighttime, but when a uniformed sergeant responds, "The dog did nothing in the nighttime," we begin to wonder if all policemen are not indeed versed in the lore of the classic mystery, more particularly when Tibbs remarks a little later about the helicopter nobody noticed and the sergeant suggests, "Father Brown's postman," demonstrating an additional acquaintance with the stories of G.K. Chesterton.[8] The police of the Tibbs novels are generally courteous to the extent that they are almost unrecognizable when compared with the roughnecks in most police fiction, like the sergeant in *Then Came Violence,* who assembles the witnesses at the scene of a holdup and apologizes for detaining them (5). Their courtesy is contagious, apparently having infected the population of the Los Angeles area: as Johnny McGuire makes his way out to the stadium where the Angels are playing, he meets successively with a courteous clerk who makes him a special price on a cowboy outfit, a Disneyland gate guard who stamps his hand for re-admission and points the way to the stadium, a passing motorist who gives him a lift and asks if he has money for a ticket to the game, and finally a gracious stadium usher who gives him directions and calls him "son" (149-57).

One manifestation of this refined atmosphere is the language of the Tibbs stories, about which Anthony Boucher had offered a restrained caution in his review of *In the Heat of the Night,* and which becomes at times inordinately stilted. Occasionally it is merely self-conscious, as in the reference in one of the short stories to a "gymnasium instructor" who in anybody else's story would be a gym teacher.[9] More frequently, it takes on a starched quality, especially in Tibbs' conversation, as when he tells the father of the missing woman in *The Eyes of Buddha* "I may require information that you would greatly prefer to keep to yourself, such as minutiae of a very intimate nature concerning your daughter" (17). At times it is out of the inkwell of Edward L. Stratemeyer: When an astounded character asks, "Mr. Tibbs, how do you do these things?" our author's comment is, "It was a moment of trial for the talented Negro detective" (*Eyes of Buddha,* 126).

When we move from the Virgil Tibbs stories to the Jack Tallon series, starting with *Police Chief* in 1977, we enter a world where the language loses most of its stiffness, deductive gymnastics are replaced by rule-book police work, and humanity is rather sharply divided between the Professionals and the Non-Professionals.

Early in *Police Chief* Tallon, a detective on the Los Angeles police force, takes the job of chief in "Whitewater," Washington (a moderately disguised Cheney), a town with a population of 8500 and a police force of ten. An obvious born leader, Tallon undertakes to shape up a force that has almost been allowed to go to seed; he institutes a training program and, above all else, seeks to endow his new charge with a spirit of professionalism. Tallon makes it clear during his first day on the job that he will not fix a ticket, including his own (30); in his first meeting with his people he tells them he will be brief because he does not want to leave the city unguarded even for a minute (33); he later discovers that somebody in the department has given a city councilman an informal account of what went on in that meeting, and he proceeds to lay down the law on the subject of confidentiality with regard to police business (35). His physical prowess is impressive; he is not a karate black belt like Virgil Tibbs, but when a belligerent suspect dodges his fist Tallon gives him an elbow smash, knocks his legs from under him, and flips him on his back (152). Even stronger, though, is his sense of commitment. Just about to catch a rapist, Tallon is thrown by another man who thinks him to be the culprit; when the man comes to the hospital to apologize, Tallon assures him he did what too many people fail to do just because they don't want to get involved. "I hate their Goddamn guts," he says (177).

Tallon, who is 34 in *Police Chief* and is described by a Whitewater councilman as a "handsome devil," is a good and loving husband who has very little time to spend at home and whose method of relaxation when he tires of administrative work is to take a police cruiser out on routine patrol.

Tallon lacks Virgil Tibbs' polish; he makes no references to operas, and he has apparently never read Arthur Conan Doyle or G.K. Chesterton. He is like Tibbs in his ability to get along with Federal officers, and he works as well with the F.B.I. in *Police Chief* as Tibbs did with the Bureau of Narcotics and Dangerous Drugs in *Five Pieces of Jade,* although like Tibbs (and like most other fictional local cops who are thrown into association with Feds) he considers Whitewater *his* territory, not to be yielded to Federal agents. Finally, Tallon has a much stronger sense of professionalism, is much more the cop and less the Great Detective than Tibbs.

Trouble for Tallon (1981) is a further development of Tallon the consistent professional. Praised for an heroic rescue from a burning vehicle he reponds only, "It goes with the territory" (83), and when the celebration party at the end of the story is interrupted by the inevitable phone call, "Let's go, gentlemen. We've got work to do" (179). The "Trouble" of the title is a suspicion of murder directed against a religious cult that has set up a community on the outskirts of Whitewater. Interviewing the Swami and his associates, Tallon is strictly objective, treating them as citizens. For him, efficient action consists in going by the book. When the rookie Gary Mason calls in that he has wrecked a police cruiser in pursuit of the arsonist, Tallon (who personally monitors all police radio traffic) goes immediately on the air and activates a mental check-list: (1.) Anything broken or feel numb? (2.a.) If so, remain still; an ambulance is on the way. (2.b.) If not, get out of the cruiser and stand by. (3.) Cut the ignition and turn off the radio (62.).

Trouble for Tallon is a parable of professionalism. The effective people in the story are the professionals: trained, registered, certified, and disciplined. The key is discipline, which separates the men from the boys (and in the case of the nurse, Mary Clancy, who fills in occasionally as policewoman, the women from the girls). When Tallon hears that the arsonist claims to be a karate black belt, he doubts that it is so, because "he could never stand for the discipline" (154). Training is the salvation of young Gary Mason and of Mary Clancy. Mason refuses to let his chief drive the police cruiser with his badly burned hands and insists on driving himself: "And I know how; you taught me" (155). When Tallon tells Mary to stay away from the shooting, she replies, "Like hell. I've been shooting on the sheriff's range. I'm up to expert" (155).

Not only the police but the other professionals in the story share the quality of effectiveness. Mrs. Weintraub, the librarian, is confidential and efficient, quickly supplies the police with the background material they need on the Swami and the religious community and keeps quiet about the business. The non-professionals, in contrast, are sloppy and ineffective. Mortimer Brown, the wealthy developer and shady operator, smokes constantly, curses, threatens, evades, can't stand being thwarted. The arsonist, who is big and mean and dangerous but lacks discipline, is no match for the police pros, one of whom throws him single-handed.

We must take note that not a single one of the police in the story behaves in a non-professional manner. Absent from the Whitewater scene is any evidence of goofing off, inter-departmental rivalry, police corruption, or the standard interface of favors and revenge. The language of Tallon's police lacks the stilted quality of Virgil Tibbs', but it is free of sentence fragments, subject-verb disagreement, confusion of case-forms or of adjectives and adverbs. Profanity is remarkably absent.

The third book, *Chief Tallon and the S.O.R.* (1984), casts the Whitewater police in a familiar role, caught between two ideological extremes. The Society for Open Relationships (S.O.R.), which practices non-marital family life and nude swimming, holds its national convention in Whitewater, and the town is invaded by the Army for Scriptural Morality, determined to break up the S.O.R. The police handle the situation with superb skill, thanks in part to the intervention of the local professional clergy, who use their own type of informed consecration to counteract the bigotry of the Army for Scriptural Morality. Tallon and his people practice a high level of objectivity, maintaining complete neutrality between the extreme groups.

Not so their author, who to a greater degree than in the earlier books colors his language to show which side he is on. We sense the bias immediately when Tallon visits the home of an S.O.R. "triad" (two men, one woman, unmarried) early in the story. The first man is "very well dressed," the woman "attractive"; the second man has a "neatly trimmed moustache" (3). Not so the advance agent of the A.S.M., who enters a few pages later: he has a "sense of his own importance" and he swings his briefcase "just enough to attract the right kind of attention" (13-15). The contrast deepens as the story progresses, the S.O.R. people "tall, amiable-appearing," "obviously capable," the leaders of the A.S.M. blatant hypocrites who try to seduce unattached women and who cynically drop their pretense of scriptural indignation when they are out of the public eye.

The world of Jack Tallon, especially in this third novel, is a world of sharp cleavage between Good People and Bad People, with little in between. Both groups are easy to recognize by their physical appearance: Good People tend to be tall, fit-looking, neat; Bad People are usually pompous, slovenly, out of shape. The pattern is so constant that when an unidentified woman, described only as being "between fifty and seventy pounds overweight" enters Tallon's office, we know at once that here is a Bad Person (143). Sure enough, she turns out immediately to be a female activist who tries to intimidate Tallon into offering her a job. She is devastatingly put down, we should notice, by the arrival of Mary Clancy, who is a person of "extraordinary attractiveness."

The Elite in this scheme are the professionals, who go by the book and do things right. To a degree almost unparalleled in police fiction, the Tallon stories offer a clear dichotomy of competence versus incompetence, and the main advantage of the competent is the professional spirit. Good, productive things are those which are systematized and authorized. Intelligent living consists in familiarity with procedures and the ability to apply them quickly and efficiently. The purpose of training is discipline, particularly internal discipline for self-control and the avoidance of costly mistakes.

Because the basic puzzles in the Tallon stories are not so complex as were those in the Tibbs series, suspense is maintained through a greater variety of techniques. In *Trouble for Tallon* Ball repeats the alternating point of view that was so effective in *Johnny Get Your Gun,* and it seems even more natural here because he uses, as strands of the narrative, the assignments of the police who are working on the various aspects of the case. Much of the suspense is dependent upon the bombshell, the big development that is only partly explained, like the one near the end of *Chief Tallon and the S.O.R.,* where Tallon first reveals a solution that is already half expected and then a big one that takes the reader completely by surprise (181).

Certain themes recur, as they frequently do in mystery series. Commenting on his own work, John Ball explains that he is not a "message" author but that he builds books on ideas, like the racial theme in *In the Heat of the Night.*[10] He used the idea of "differentness" in *The Cool Cottontail,* in which Virgil Tibbs feels a closeness with the Nunns, whose nudism tends to isolate them as his color does him; in *Five Pieces of Jade,* with regard to the mixed-race woman Yumeko; and in the second and third Tallon stories, where the religious community and the S.O.R. are subjected to hostility because of their differentness from the mainstream of society. The theme of changing morality is another constant, voiced several times by Virgil Tibbs, who reminds various people in the stories that the Puritan era is long past, and by

Jack Tallon, who several times suggests that the police are not concerned with the intimate lives of responsible adults.

Critical evaluations of John Ball's police stories tend to vary in terms of the expectations of the reviewers. The novels are regularly praised for their "solid professionalism" and their accurate information.[11] Negative criticism is usually directed at the artificial atmosphere and the weak detection, and, in the Tibbs stories, at the stilted style.[12] A reasonably balanced assessment may be found in a review by Francis M. Nevins, Jr., who summarizes weaknesses of plot and motivation and then goes on to say that those readers who like a world where people live by a code of propriety and efficiency, "where every policewoman is a walking angel," will enjoy a type of narrative that is the almost exclusively specialty of John Ball, "the *restful* police story."[13]

"Restful" is what many people undoutedly find them, because the picture they present is comforting to readers worn out by the moral relativism of the present day, as reflected in the competing value-systems that agitate most crime fiction. The mood of the Ball story is one in which it is easy to be confidently partisan, to choose up sides with Our Team and cheer for the victory of efficiency and virtue.

Notes

[1] Chris Steinbrunner and Otto Penzler, *Encyclopedia of Mystery and Detection* (New York: McGraw-Hill, 1976), p. 18.

[2] The editions of Ball's novels used for this study are listed below, preceded by the original date of publication.

1965 *In the Heat of the Night* (New York: Bantam, 1967)
1966 *The Cool Cottontail* (New York: Harper and Row, 1966)
1969 *Johnny Get Your Gun* (Boston: Little, Brown, 1969)
1972 *Death for a Playmate* (New York: Bantam, 1972)
1972 *Five Pieces of Jade* (New York: Bantam, 1973)
1976 *The Eyes of Buddha* (Boston: Little, Brown, 1976. Book Club Edition)
1977 *Police Chief* (New York: Doubleday, 1977. Book Club Edition)
1980 *Then Came Violence* (New York: Doubleday, 1980)
1981 *Trouble for Tallon* (New York: Doubleday, 1981)
1984 *Chief Tallon and the S.O.R.* (New York: Dodd, Mead, 1984).

[3] *New York Times Book Review*, 2 May 1965, p. 32. Boucher's prediction came true in a literal sense. Virgil Tibbs was assigned a chapter in *The Great Detectives*, ed. Otto Penzler (Boston: Little, Brown, 1978), pp. 229-34.

[4] "One for Virgil Tibbs," February 1976, pp. 6-21; "Virgil Tibbs and the Cocktail Napkin," April 1977, pp. 6-15; "Virgil Tibbs and the Fallen Body," September 1978, pp. 96-104.

[5] Steinbrunner and Penzler, p. 389.

[6] "Three Key Questions," in *The Writer's Handbook*, ed. A.S. Burack (Boston: The Writer, Inc., 1976), pp. 67-9.

[7] Review of *The Eyes of Buddha*, *The Armchair Detective*, 11 (April 1978), 121.

[8] "Virgil Tibbs and the Fallen Body," pp. 101, 104.

[9] "One for Virgil Tibbs," p. 17.

[10] "John Ball comments," in *Twentieth Century Crime and Mystery Writers*, ed. John M. Reilly (New York: St. Martin's, 1980), p. 72.

[11]Jon L. Breen, "The Jury Box," *Ellery Queen's Mystery Magazine,* February 1978, pp. 89-90.

[12]For example: Newgate Callendar, "Criminals at Large," *New York Times Book Review,* 12 March 1972, p. 40; Jon L. Breen, "The Jury Box," *Ellery Queen's Mystery Magazine,* 18 August 1980, p. 90; Francis M. Nevins, Jr., Review of *Then Came Violence, The Mystery Fancier,* 4, No. 5 (September/October 1980), 37-8.

[13]Review of *Trouble for Tallon, The Mystery Fancier,* 5, No. 5 (September/October 1981), 31.

Hillary Waugh's Fred Fellows

Joan Y. Worley

"I'll be damned"—Chief Fred Fellows' frequent surprised remark at discovering the solution to a case—cannot, surely, be classed as the exclamation of choice for a Master Detective, nor does Fellows himself, at first glance, fit the mold. Tall and bulky, fighting an insistent paunch, Fellows is gray of hair and uniform, his voice often colorless and flat as he interviews suspects. Nor do his methods call to mind the eager sureness of Holmes on the scent. Fellows is often uncertain of the next step, and in *The Late Mrs. D.*[1] insurance investigator Burke feels compelled to chide Fellows for playing Cribbage on the job.

Needless to say, this picture of Fellows as a sleepy small-town policeman belies the energy and imagination that carried him through a series of popular novels from 1959 to 1968. Though Fellows' modesty causes many to underestimate his abilities, the reader is never fooled for a minute. That remains the distinctive charm of the novels.

Fellows operates in Stockford, Connecticut, a town of 8,000 with a police force of 18 and, as George Dove has noted, "a delightfully high homicide rate."[2] An amalgam of small New England towns, Stockford has its richer and poorer sections as well as a tourist/artist area, "Little Bohemia," situated on nearby Indian Lake. The generic small town setting suits Waugh's purpose in creating for the reader a common ground for exploring the foibles of human nature—murder being the foremost of those foibles.

In his rare time out of the station, Fellows becomes a generic small-town family man. He gets on well with his patient wife Cessie (Cecilia) and boasts four children—Larry, who wants to be a cop; Shirley, trained as a teacher; Katie; and Peter. Fellows' family is close-knit, and his worry over his children, especially his daughters, colors his concern for families in grief. Fellows has fewer eccentricities as a detective than Stockford has as a town, yet he commands respect from his men and his colleagues by an understated charm arising from the strength of his character. Though he is sensitive to the discomfort of others, making sure his men are regularly relieved on tiresome watches in freezing weather, he gives his own vacation up willingly to the task of trekking up and down the streets of Banksville in order to aid a man who claims to have been unjustly sent to Death Row. His detective sidekick and friend Sid Wilks sums up Fred Fellows:

Suspect is further known to be a bleeding heart with an overdeveloped sense of justice and a feeling of personal responsibility for righting all the wrongs in the universe... He's got a chip on the shoulder that has nothing to do with the lack of sleep since he can go thirty hours on duty at a stretch without forgetting his manners. The chip says he's mad at himself because he doesn't know the answer to a problem.

(*Plea*, 13).

Sid Wilks' freedom in this description clues us in to Fellows' modesty, his inability to take his own ego seriously. When cases do not break, Fellows is apt to chastise himself for the lack of results. Even when (as in *The Late Mrs. D.*) the chief has one of his flashes of inspired reasoning and breaks the case wide open, he regrets not having thought of it sooner. "I think I'm a stupid ape," he mutters, as he puts together the pieces of the puzzle.

Fellows' flashes of inspiration comprise as integral a part of his character as his modest good humor. Fellows never skimps on routine—that would be sloppy police work—but his imaginative approach to that routine makes the difference between his conduct of a case and the plodding investigations of lesser men. When, in *Sleep Long, My Love,* the search through rental agencies and other locators fails to turn up the identity of the victim, Fellows hits on the idea of questioning all the dentists in town, naturally prefacing the idea with "I really am stupid" (126). The secret of good police procedure, in Fellows' world, lies not in routine itself but in inspired use of routine investigation. This also gives the novels added charm, for Fellows, his light burning steadily under a bushel, flares up occasionally into the realms of the Master Detective. Fellows' inspired touches, however, are not out of character, for his whole approach to police work reveals openness to all possibilities. Wilks, who often refers to himself as "the facts man," occasionally wonders at Fellows' tendency to investigate the character of the suspect and the psychology of the crime as deeply as the physical clues. "That's more of your mumbo jumbo," he notes in the first novel of the series (*Sleep*, 67). Fellows defends his approach: "On the theory side of the ledger, the more you can find out what the man is like, the better chance you have of finding him." Wilks, however, continues throughout the series to bring the chief back to earth from what he always calls Fellows' "stratospheric" leaps of deduction. On most occasions, however, the stratospheric leaps prove valuable, and most of Fellows' cases are solved by the combination of routine drudgery and Fellows' psychological flashes. In *The Missing Man,* for example, Fellows gains a valuable lead to the murderer by estimating that despite her husband's order to contact no one, Mrs. Cooper would send flowers to a friend who had lost a child. In *Con Game,* Fellows even out-psyches a psychiatrist to bring the criminal to justice.

Fellows' brilliance never undercuts the procedural genre which Waugh helped to establish, for the starting point of each case, and its mainstay, remains police routine. Fellows may make stratospheric leaps, but those leaps generally come after all normal leads have been exhausted. Like any good cop, Fellows places his faith in autopsies, lab reports, and—most of all—dogged police canvassing and checking. Fellows has no qualms, despite pressure for quick results, about sending his men to interview employees of every store in town, or to seek out every blue Ford in a three-city area, or to comb passenger lists of every ship sailing out of New York in the past year. Often such drudgery brings results. If not, Fellows takes the lack of result as a sign that he has looked at the case from the wrong angle. There usually follows one of his stratospheric ideas to reopen the leads and bring on more routine checking.

One can readily see the challenge in presenting such an unassuming, reserved character as Fellows without making him dull. Waugh meets this challenge successfully, using secondary characters to draw out and reflect Fellows' rare qualities.

Sid Wilks is a case in point. Wilks, who rises from detective sergeant to lieutenant in the course of the series, is no dimwitted sidekick. His privileged position as both assistant and friend allows him to play devil's advocate, reviewing and criticizing Fellows' handling of an investigation at each step of the way. A man of precise and practical mind, "fact man" Wilks pieces together evidence as assiduously as he assembles model trains in his cellar. Wilks serves as sounding board for Fellows, often hearing the chief's weary tread on his cellar stairs when a case does not go well. Wilks' value lies in his ability to release Fellows' tension through humor as well as in his love of facts. His insistence on material evidence, however, often brings him to a dead end. When the leads in *Pure Poison* taper off, Wilks, trapped in fact, despairs: "I personally don't think the plot was aimed at anyone," he tells Fellows. "I don't think he's dead. According to everything we've found out, it couldn't have happened" (89). The gap between Wilks and Fellows, finally, is the gap between lieutenant and chief—Fellows' willingness to take responsibility for the case and his dogged search for the whole truth in the face of lies and concealment. It is no surprise that Wilks, good cop though he may be, never quite makes the promised rank of captain. Fellows' willingness to reopen his mind rather than close a case makes all the difference.

The character of Wilks is a masterful blend of confidant and foil to the character of Fellows. Other less subtly drawn contrasts to Fellows are found in his peers—the police chiefs of neighboring towns. First among these stands the irascible Chief Delbert Ramsey of Townsend. Symbolically as small in stature as Fellows is large, Delbert Ramsey finds his work a constant source of irritation. Called out to view a body on Sunday, Ramsey's response reflects his attitude toward his duties: "His first words were characteristic: 'Son of a bitch,' he said" (*Party*,12). Ramsey shows his lack of both breeding and training as he tramples the area around the corpse, destroying clues at every turn, disparaging his men when they quite rightly ask for orders. After harassing his only witness, Ramsey snarls for a subordinate to "talk to this Bakewell bastard" (16). Beside Ramsey's ramshackle approach, Fellows' careful thoroughness and polite questioning shine more successfully. A kind of courage needed to succeed in any important job is lacking in Ramsey. Fellows helps Ramsey with his case out of courtesy and professional interest. Ramsey, on the other hand, gleefully drops the case into Fellows' lap when he discovers that the body lies within the Stockford city limits.

Ramsey has earned his ulcers through his constant worry about how he will look rather than about how murder was committed. Afraid of appearing foolish, but with neither the training nor the desire to do his job properly, Ramsey takes his anxieties out on his men. Waugh shows us here the importance of leadership in the force, for the attitude of the man at the top influences the efficiency of the whole force. Under Ramsey's incompetent and querulous command, the Townsend police have become a particularly timid and inadequate group. Fellows, by comparison, worries only about the dignity of the law, not his own image. His easy-going style is backed up by an occasional well-timed reprimand, but the key to his efficiency is his own sense of what needs doing. The Stockford force is comprised of men who know their tasks and can complete them successfully, thereby earning the praise of their chief. Further, Fellows leads by example, willing to undertake the most difficult chores himself. He declares that he is "not the executive type" (*Sleep*, 46)—though he can delegate authority and command loyalty—because he itches to get out into the field and follow the leads on his own. In *End of a Party*, this tendency draws him into a near-fatal shootout.

While Ramsey provides an extreme example of the contrast Waugh draws between other police chiefs and Fellows, the character of Chief Acton of Banksville is drawn more subtly. Naturally concerned about Fellows' investigation of a "closed" case in his own district, Acton worries more about what the press will say than about the possible innnocence of a man on Death Row. He refuses to lend Fellows any aid or even allow him a look at the files, until Fellows' investigation becomes newsworthy. Fellows' own disregard for his image is obvious from his willingness to take on the nearly hopeless task of investigating an old murder. At the case's end, Fellows has brought out important new evidence, only to have it prove the state's original case. He warns sidekick Raphael Jones: "We've been double-decker fools and those who aren't going to be sore at us are going to be laughing fit to kill" (*Plea,* 173). Fellows then offers to take the whole blame on himself.

In addition to the lesser chiefs, private investigators like Raphael Jones help point up Fellow's good qualities. Throughout *Prisoner's Plea,* Fellows must slowly wean Jones from eagerness for glory to devotion to truth—and he succeeds. In *End of a Party*, matching detectives Gooch and Pennyworth play a Tweedledum and Tweedledee act that ends in an attempt to bribe the chief. All three operatives wish to ride Fellows' coattails to publicity and profit. None, of course, succeeds, but Jones does manage to learn what it means to detect. Like other police figures in the series, Gooch and Pennyworth dwell too much on image to risk finding the truth.

Despite his own unconsciousness of image, Fellows receives kind treatment from the press, for in several cases characters recognize him as famous in his area. The press's consideration of Fellows reflects his own fair treatment of reporters, whom he sees as people like himself with a job to do. Fellows' statements to the press contain all the known facts of the case, except those that might alert a suspect or threaten the privacy of the innocent. Fellows will not, however, speculate for the benefit of the press or draw hasty conclusions to impress reporters with his efficiency. He remains perfectly willing to admit being at a loss and will undergo the proddings of the press with equanimity, knowing his own methods to be thorough and successful. Fellows does not worry that the press will criticize him; he worries that he will deserve the criticism.

Though most reporters respond to Fellows' openness with respect, a few play the role of gadfly, chief among them Harrington, who seems always ready to sneer at the bumbling efforts of a small-town police force. In *Con Game* he tells Fellows, "You're not going to get a good story from the officials. If you want anything good, you've got to dig it out yourself" (167). In *Pure Poison,* Harrington launches a smear campaign against the chief, baiting him at press conferences and criticizing every aspect of the case. "The trouble with you Fellows, is you've had things your own way too long. You've got the press so buffaloed they only print what you tell them to print" (55). Later in the case, Harrington prints a scathing interview with a man who complains that his parents have been caused bitter grief by Fellows' probing into his sister's suicide. Fellows, interested in the background rather than his own image, finds clues in the interview to break the case, putting Harrington in the uncomfortable position of having run a bleeding-heart story on a fanatical killer. Like Burke, the insurance investigator who at first tells Fellows, "Maybe you're not used to crime" (*Mrs. D,* 34), most reporters come to respect Fellows, and he is content to let them discover his value as the case wears on. He can lay down the law, however, to maintain the dignity of the force—as when he runs poker-happy newsmen out of the station—or to protect his investigation. In *Sleep Long, My Love* he banishes a reporter from the station for having revealed the name of a woman through whom Fellows had hoped to lure the murderer to justice.

Waugh designs Fellows' cases as a combination of procedure and inspiration. Called in at the discovery of a body, Fellows gives complete attention to the immediate investigation of the scene, letting photographer Hank Lemmon, Medical Examiner Jim McFarlane, and the prints and lab experts compile as much physical evidence as possible. Meanwhile, Fellows sets his men to the preliminary questioning of those who were at the scene or knew the victim, beginning a search for possible motives. By the time Coroner Clement Avery holds his inquest, Fellows has usually uncovered enough to make the case intriguing to himself and frustrating to Avery. At this point Fellows must spread a net of men throughout the state seeking information on suspect and victim alike. As these initial leads begin to fade out, Fellows comes to fear he may lose the battle, as the reporters cry for action. Despair often leads him on a visit to Wilks' cellar where he can hash over the case and generate some of his "stratospheric" ideas. Using his inspirations, Fellows again spreads a net of inquiry, this time with a new angle. As the renewed investigation leads to a correct view of the case, Fellows must amass evidence to prove his view is correct.

The proof of a master series writer, of course, lies in variation on a successful formula. Waugh's twists on Fellows' cases keep the series from becoming stale. In *Con Game* Fellows must not only change his tentative solution; he must redefine the crime itself three times. In *Missing Man,* the prime suspect must be found amid a maze of false names. Most of *Sleep Long, My Love* is devoted to finding the identity of the victim, and, in a *Roger Ackroyd*-like touch, the murderer is hidden in plain sight. Waugh gives over most of *Death and Circumstances* to the plans of three criminals yet still manages to surprise us with the true nature of their crime. *Prisoner's Plea* takes Fellows out of Stockford, thereby placing him in an unofficial position without pull and with no aid save a publicity-hungry private eye. In *Con Game* and *The Late Mrs. D.,* Fellows spots the guilty party but must trap the murderer into an admission of guilt. In *End of a Party,* Fellows' trap nearly gets him killed. Through the kidnapping in *Death and Circumstances* and the imminent execution in *Prisoner's Plea,* Waugh adds the urgency of a race against time to the procedural format.

Along with these variations, there remains the continuing interest of Fellows' own devotion to a case and the intricacy of the searches on which he sets his men. The immersion in such investigation is a mainstay of the procedural genre, of course, but Waugh often manages to add the charm of the classic "train-schedule" murder, in which intricate studies of timing destroy alibis and trap murderers. Fellows indulges in such intricacy on a grand scale, as when he sends his men on the laborious task of cross-matching the travels of the victim with those of people only tangentially (or stratospherically) related to the case. The tenuous but logical relationship between the bits of evidence juxtaposed by Fellows often gives his deductions the fascination of a balancing act.

The Fellows novels thus yield a two-fold delight. There is always the satisfaction of seeing police routine in action, the thrill of watching prosaic investigation reveal the bizarre underside of life. This provides a sense of security in the ability of everyday common sense (personified by the cops and in this series especially by Wilks) to overcome the flashier but essentially unsound ratiocination of the criminal. Waugh often provides as well the twists of plot we think of as belonging to the classic "puzzle" mysteries, especially in *Death and Circumstances, Prisoner's Plea,* and *Sleep Long, My Love.* Waugh uses Fellows' stratospheric leaps, his inspired logic, to allow for these twists without destroying the procedural formula.

Hillary Waugh is no more trapped by the conventions of the detective novel than is Fred Fellows by conventions of thought. Aside from the twists of plot, Waugh also varies his handling of the structure of the novels. The procedural formula can change, but so can the whole shape of a "procedural" novel.

In *Death and Cricumstances* and *Con Game,* for example, we see more of the criminals than of Fellows. It seems as if in these two cases Fellows was modest enough even to surrender his novel to another cast of characters. Three quarters of *Death and Circumstances* is a fine hard-boiled study of the psychology of a baby-faced thief who becomes a killer in his pathetic need for friendship. *Con Game* spends many of its chapters chronicling the dissolution of four American marriages. The quarrels and mutual betrayal overshadow the murder, which seems to sprout naturally from this poisonous suburban garden.

Waugh's skillful handling of these two novels is not an aberration but an intensification of the dark themes that crop up in the whole series. Fellows' world is inhabited for the most part by those who have lost faith in each other and themselves. Marriages in these novels are traps and travesties. Adultery seems normal and murder more acceptable than a messy divorce. Almost more frightening are the couples who remain united, bound together in a slow mutual murder by habit, greed, or image, unable to communicate except through rages and taunts. Husbands are con-men or seducers; wives are shrews or doormats; children are "overprivileged juvenile delinquents" (*Party,* 88) or neglected waifs. The tragedy of Penny Gilmore, whose very humanity is threatened by her parents' self-centeredness, is more compelling than that of her murdered mother in *End of a Party.* The idea of love seems foreign to the milieu in which Fellows works.

Even strong traditional values undergo a sea change in the Fellows series. *Pure Poison* introduces us to a minister's family—a father who substitutes scripture for communication, a dominated mother afraid to show affection, a repressed daughter whose only out is suicide, and a Faulknerian son who defends his sister's honor with megalomaniacal fury. In *Missing Man,* Waugh draws a compelling portrait of a murderer's poverty-stricken mother, full of pathetic faith in her son and his goodness; this is skillfully juxtaposed with the character of a well-to-do physician who prides himself on his ability to judge men even as he gives his blessing to his daughter and a murderous con-man. The Partridges of *Death and Circumstances* are an upper-middle class family full of sweetness and light, but they are not close enough to their daughter to encourage the honesty that would keep her out of kidnappers' hands. In the Fellows series even the best of families are at risk.

Like many crime writers, Waugh has created in these often loveless lives his own picture of the gradual warping of the American Dream and the Puritan ethic. Adultery and betrayal permeate the middle class in *Con Game* and *End of a Party*, whose characters are rich enough to be happy, but empty enough to care nothing for happiness. The petty but murderous criminals of *Missing Man, Death and Circumstances,* and *The Late Mrs. D.* are small men of poorer background seeking wealth and status with no thought to character. Beside these types, Fellows' small-town sense of honor is refreshing, as we see in the following exchange between the chief and corporate lawyer Mills, who accepts that an innocent man may very well be on Death Row:

"You seem kind of naive to me, Chief. Stockford you're from? Pretty hick town, I imagine."

"Yeah," Fellows said. "It's a pretty hick town. We get a little bit concerned down there about the idea of justice going wrong. Especially when a man's life is at stake." (*Plea*, 37).

In the same novel, Fellows must introduce big-city private eye Raphael Jones to the art of detection and the burden of caring. This is not to say that the small town lives the American Dream, however, for the passions and greeds of human nature flourish there as well. We see that in many of Fellows' cases.

In fact, the only escape from such permeating corruption seems to be in the integrity of the individual and the community of the family. In Fellows' case, family includes his men and in some sense others with whom he feels rapport. Raphael Jones calls him "Dad" mockingly at first, but Fellows does become a trusted mentor to the younger man. In *End of a Party,* Richard Gilmore realizes his child's need for a parent by overhearing her childish prattling to a grandfatherly Fellows. The idea of caring for the whole family of humankind reverberates through *Missing Man,* as Fellows' men conduct an almost hopeless search for a husband who has strangled his young wife. Even in death the young woman's beauty prompts sympathy. Lieutenant Wilks notes that he'd like to have had a daughter like the girl. Officer Dzanowski vows that when the murderer is found, "I break his neck" (12). Among the maze of families who treat each other as strangers, then, Fellows and his men stand out in their concern for strangers as a kind of family.

Sympathetic and good-natured though Fellows may be, he does show a toughness in regard to the respect due the law. We see this partly in his occasional reprimand to his force or the press, but mostly in his insistence on the truth. Crime in the Waugh novels is community property, a shared sin that leaves everyone accountable and every man's private life vulnerable to questioning. Thus Fellows does not shrink from exposing the sad tale of Jean Sherman's one night of love in *Sleep Long, My Love;* nor does he hesitate to reveal the death of the Thurlows' beloved daughter as the suicide of an abandoned woman in *Pure Poison.* Willing to trade the privacy of these wounded creatures for the truth, Fellows will certainly not let the threats or protestations of the privileged deter him. He walks blithely in on Gilmore and his lover in *End of a Party*, exposing not only their guilty affair but also their ridiculous pretense of innocence. In Stockford one takes a chance in doing anything that he does not wish known. As Fellows stalks the big game of murder, he flushes coveys of smaller sins in his path. His attitude resembles that of a moral physician who has seen so many naked souls that very little surprises him except the constant repetition of the disease. Fellows is shocked only by the arrogance that lets one person buy his desires with another's life and by the false modesty of those who obstruct the law in order to avoid appearing foolish. Fellows remains always aware, however, that "People do funny things and murderers do funnier things than most" (*Mrs. D.*, 164).

Fellows' awareness of human foibles is nowhere more apparent than in his stream of stories. Wilks is the usual recipient of these gems, which Fellows tells with the insistence of any man unloading an unwelcome and only slightly funny joke. These tales, though Fellows must always explain them, do have a moral. The story of the missionary who carefully disguises himself to infiltrate the cannibal tribe, only to forget about his white skin, is used to illustrate the importance of looking for the one obvious fact that is out of kilter in a case. The steady accumulation of fact, on which Fellows puts so much faith, is the lesson of the man who shot B.B.'s into his ceiling for years and then expressed his shock when one B.B. caused the ceiling to fall in upon him. Fellows tells these tales to clarify his own stratospheric thinking, but he also uses them at times to explain the behavior of people in the case at hand. In *Sleep Long, My Love,* Fellows wonders at a woman's gullibility in letting a man set her up in an apartment with only a month's lease: "That's like the art collector who paid a thousand bucks to an Eskimo sculptor for a hunk of carving he fancied, only when it arrived at his house, it was nothing but a pail of water. I mean what's this girl buying?" (79).

At other times Fellows uses the tales to elucidate his thinking on the case and to spur Wilks on when the going gets tough. As the leads fade out in *Con Game,* Fellows tells a frustrated Wilks the story of the farmer who searched in vain all over town for a pet rabbit for his child but overlooked the rabbits who had been raiding his cabbage patch nightly. "The very thing you're complaining about," he tells Wilks, "may be the very thing you want" (154). Applied to the case at hand, the fable provides new leads for the two detectives.

Occasionally the stories even comment on Fellows' image as an infallible detective. When prosecuting attorney Metzger counts on Fellows "to pull rabbits out of hats," the chief responds with a story:

"It seems there was this very poor family and they had a little boy. Well, every Christmas they'd scrape and somehow or other they'd manage to get a little something to put in the child's stocking. Finally, though, there came a Christmas when the man was out of work and there was no food, no money, no anything. The little boy hung up his stocking but the poor parents couldn't get even the smallest gift to put into it. He opened it and he looked and he felt and then he realized that there was absolutely nothing there. He looked wistfully at his parents and said, 'Santa Claus let me down.' "

"It's kind of easy to sit back and have faith and maybe it's flattering to me that you have that faith, but the fact remains there isn't any Santa Claus."

(*Mrs. D.*, 143)

These tales of Fellows' illuminate the processes his mind follows in solving a case. Fellows does, as I have noted, depend on physical clues as far as possible. Unless, however, one is as fortunate as Chief Delbert Ramsey, whose only solved murder had thirty witnesses, then physical clues will seldom point unerringly to the criminal. Evidence generally points to at least two possible murderers in Fellows' cases, if it points anywhere at all. In addition, Fellows' cases often involve detection of the victim's identity as well as that of the murderer. Thus Fellows realizes that there are no laws of detection to tell him that if A,B,C, are true, then D is guilty. Fellows would, furthermore, reject any such laws as ephemeral. When asked for an opinion as to what a guilty man would do in a given instance, Fellows replies that he is unable to answer the question. He continues:

I told you what people in general would do, but you can't apply generalizations on human behavior to an individual. That's one thing police work has taught me... Knowledge of human behavior tells me what an individual is most likely to do, but it never tells me what he *must* do. It helps me but it doesn't prove a damned thing, and I can tell you that for sure."

(*Mrs. D.*, 64)

Fellows mistrusts generalization, the accepted fictions of human nature. Yet he persists in using fictions of his own to clarify the cases. For Fellows the prescriptive nature of generalization works only for the normal man, whereas he knows that "murderers do funnier things than most."

Fellows' own fictions work by analogy, describing what a person's behavior resembles rather than what it must be. And if Fellows can create an analogy for what a person does, he can spot the assumptions and motives behind that behavior. Most of Fellows' stories, in addition, have a catch to them which can, like the punch line of most jokes, be perceived only from an abnormal point of view. Thus the tales constantly remind Fellows to come at his cases from an unusual angle.

Waugh's novels in this series are very much like Fred Fellows' tales. They have a charm that comes from Fellows' folksiness and a wit that springs from the triumph of the small-town detective over such slick customers as reporters, prosecutors, lawyers, and murderers. They are filled with illustrations of human nature. Further, the solution to the crimes requires a twist of viewpoint and a leap of imagination. Fellows' greatest moments come not through routine, important as that is to him, but when such a twist of thought is needed to pull the case out of the fire. His special ingenuity is obvious at the end of *Sleep Long, My Love* when the murderer claims that he only panicked after an accidental death, the victim having struck her head in a fall, and that he purchased the implements to dismember her body the Monday after the Friday on which she died. Fellows is at a loss to prove premeditation until he remembers that the Monday in question was a holiday and the stores all closed. With admirable restraint, he sends one of his men to the prisoner with no other message than the relevant page of a calendar. "From the end of the hall," notes Waugh, "there came the sudden sound of sobbing." (192)

Waugh's handling of this scene suggests the economy of his style throughout the Fellows series. Waugh accomplishes a great deal in less than two hundred pages, adding social comment and vivid characterizations to a thorough description of police routine. Part of this economy Waugh owes to his skill at dialogue, for he can convey in a few lines not only the sense that a marriage is bad but also a feeling for what kind of bad marriage it has become.

Waugh's talent also lies in his refusal to insist on the sacredness of either his detective or the procedural genre. The Fellows novels do not merely follow the police chief on his rounds. Fellows often recedes into the background as Waugh rapidly shifts both scene and point of view, zooming in on the criminal's mind, then pulling back for a general overview of the case as Fellows sets his wheels in motion, and finally zooming in again on one cop discovering one bit of crucial information. The success of the novels depends on Fellows' *not* taking center stage at all times. Thus Waugh's creation of a self-effacing detective works as effectively to aid the structure of the books as it does in the characterization of Fellows.

The elements of classic puzzle mysteries—seen especially in Fellows' stratospheric flashes of inspiration—add a charm to the procedural formula Waugh employs. The novels also show the influence of the hard-boiled genre—especially in *Death and Circumstances*—with a healthy touch of the novel of manners—as seen in *Con Game* and *The End of a Party*. Just as the procedural formula provides ground for these influences, the solidly wholesome character of Fred Fellows provides a background against which the aberrations of others show up in bold relief.

Hillary Waugh's Chief Fred Fellows stands, in some ways, as the modest antithesis of a Master Detective like Sherlock Holmes, whose agile mind turned to cocaine in the lull between crimes. Fellows wants only peace and quiet; crime to him is a fearsome disruption of life. In other ways, however, Fellows is much in the Holmes tradition. With his incorruptible integrity and love of justice, he creates, like all the great detectives, a norm by which the reader can judge the failings of the world around him. At times Fellows' imperturbable dignity seems a calm center in a storm of greed and corruption. The slanted view of the world stems, of course, from the fact that Waugh is writing crime novels. The one drawback to the series is that there is a striking realism to the bickering couples, the sneaking adulterers, and the arrogant murderers, whereas Fred, Cessie, and the kids seem just too good to be true.

Notes

1The editions of the novels in Hillary Waugh's Fred Fellows series are listed below, preceded by the original date of publication. Quotations will be cited in the text, using, where needed, the abbreviation listed after each entry:

1959   *Sleep Long, My Love* (New York: Doubleday, 1959). (*Sleep*)
1960   *Road Block* (New York: Doubleday, 1960).
1961   *That Night It Rained* (New York: Doubleday, 1961).
1962   *The Late Mrs. D.* (New York: Doubleday, 1962). (*Mrs. D.*)
1962   *Born Victim* (New York: Doubleday, 1962).
1963   *Death and Circumstances* (New York: Doubleday, 1963). (*Death*)

1963   *Prisoner's Plea* (New York: Popular Library, 1963). (*Plea*)
1964   *The Missing Man* (New York: Harper and Row, 1981). (*Man*)
1965   *The End of a Party* (New York: Doubleday, 1965). (*Party*)

Dell Shannon's Luis Mendoza

Mary Jean DeMarr

Blessed with a large and enthusiastic group of readers, Luis Mendoza's creator, Dell Shannon, is also controversial, much criticized for the sometimes excessively obtrusive political content of her detective stories and for the often sloppy style, a result no doubt of the speed with which the novels are written.[1] Their appeal to their loyal fans is dual: sordid but original tales of crime and violent death and the contrasting healthy normality of the domestic lives of her large and likable cast of policemen and their wives and children and pets. A reader of Shannon knows exactly what to expect: an interlocking collection of crimes which occupy working hours punctuated by scenes of domestic lives of very ordinary middle-class policemen. We follow murders, robberies, muggings, rapes and other sorts of violence and at the same time we are refreshed by reading of courtships, marriages, pregnancies, searches for new homes, unexpected acquisitions of pets, and other details of daily life.

"Dell Shannon" is only one pseudonym of Elizabeth Linington, the author who, under several different names, makes her formula work effectively for her in her police procedurals. Under her own name, she writes about Ivor Maddox and Sue Carstairs of the Wilcox Avenue precinct in Hollywood; as Lesley Egan, she writes of Vic Varallo and Delia Riordan of the Glendale police and of attorney Jesse Falkenstein. As Dell Shannon, her concern is with Luis Mendoza, a lieutenant in Central Homicide (later Robbery-Homicide, after a reorganization) of the Los Angeles Police Department. In all three incarnations, the author uses basically the same elements: the contrast of police routines with normal daily life, stress on the sordidness and stupidity of criminal activity, creation of a group of characters, mostly policemen, who can be followed from novel to novel and who change and develop as their situations alter and as they learn from their experiences.

Luis Mendoza, the central character of the novels written under the Shannon pseudonym, is given a number of distinguishing characteristics that might have easily allowed him to become little more than a caricature or, perhaps, another in the line of eccentric detectives;

in some respects, he rather resembles Christie's Poirot—notably his prissiness, concern for neatness and order, and talent for reasoning out a criminal's motivation, although he at least avoids such cuteness as referring to "little gray cells." Of Mexican-American origins, he is independently wealthy, having inherited a fortune, much to his surprise, from a disreputable grandfather, a gambler and miser. His resentment of this grandfather, who had despite his wealth left Mendoza to grow up in slums, a street kid scrambling for cash to help support his much loved grandmother and himself, is repeatedly alluded to, especially in early novels when the adored grandmother is still alive. As a result of his deprived childhood, Mendoza knows the streets and alleys of Los Angeles thoroughly, a frequent help in his police work. Another result of his grandfather's ambiguous influence on him was his early learning to gamble: he, too, became a card shark and then put this special knowledge to work for the police in his first assignment as a cop, to Vice. By the time the series opens, with *Case Pending* in 1960, he has been a policeman for some twenty years and is well established with Homicide. Nevertheless, when puzzled, or needing to think a case through, he usually picks up a pack of cards and practices crooked deals.

Other characteristics which distinguish Mendoza are also related to his background. He sprinkles his speech with Spanish, constantly reminding readers of his ethnic origins. Perhaps because of his poverty as a child, he tends to be particularly fastidious about some aspects of daily life. His appearance is repeatedly mentioned: he is always "dapper" or "immaculate" in a gray suit, of either Italian silk or Dacron. He is an atheist, considering organized religion a con game. His grandmother had reared him in her Roman Catholic faith, but his experience on the streets led him to deny her beliefs, and through the early novels he is contemptuous of religious belief and worship, although this changes, as we shall see. He is also described as a "womanizer," a man of many women who fears entanglement, commitment to one woman. This, too, is beginning to change as the series opens, and we actually see little of this side of Mendoza. -

Mendoza became a policeman as a young man, before the discovery of his grandfather's great wealth. However, when he came into his inheritance, he nevertheless remained on the force. One reason, surely, is simply his personality—an active man, he would need socially productive work to keep himself occupied. What Shannon stresses, however, is his twofold commitment: to finding things out and striving to create order. His need for order and for understanding of how and why things happen is repeatedly illustrated. Sometimes, in fact, he even claims that he doesn't care much what happens after a case is over, if only he can satisfy his insatiable curiosity. Summing him up, Shannon tells us,

That was Mendoza: the orderly mind, place-for-everything-everything-in-its-place. Probably one of the reasons he had acquired a little reputation as an investigative officer: ragged edges worried him, the thing left all untidy, patternless. He might be and often was irritable at the frustration of continually being presented with another box of jigsaw pieces to put together, but he was constitutionally unable to leave them alone until every last little piece had been fitted in where it belonged. (*Ace*, 18)[2]

Even more crucial is his moral stance. He had tacitly taken a position when he became a cop, and his inheritance of a fortune, while it certainly eased his life, did not change his ethics and view of the world. As Shannon puts it, "The essential choice made when he took the oath. A cop made the conscious choice, white against black, good against evil, creativity against destruction" (*Kindness*, 98). So he remains a dedicated cop, donating his salary to the pension fund, driving an expensive car, dressing in specially tailored suits, living in homes well out of the reach of other cops—and coming in on his days off to put in overtime on what Shannon repeatedly calls the "thankless job."

All through his series, Mendoza is clearly the central figure, but his primacy is plainest in the first few novels. In those early novels, a number of his colleagues are introduced, sometimes with details hinting at what their characterizations will later become. But most of them long remain little more than names—Saul Goldberg of Robbery, John Palliser, George Higgins, Bert Dwyer, Tom Landers, Nick Galeano, Matt Piggott, and others seem in early novels to serve primarily as a backdrop for Mendoza, validating his life and work by their presence but not becoming of much interest in themselves. At first they tend to be characterized by one or two special qualities: thus Goldberg is always sneezing and blowing his nose as result of allergies; Hackett and Higgins are big and tough-looking, Hackett incongruously holding a degree in psychology and Higgins always the recognizable ugly cop; Landers looks younger than his years and is regularly irritated at having his cop's identity questioned because of his youthful appearance; Piggott is a fundamentalist Christian and his faithful attendance at church and regular ascription of blame to the devil for the evil surrouding them are treated both comically and sympathetically. Most of these details are early established, and then, bit by bit the portraits are fleshed out.

In acknowledging that the secondary characters are more realistic than Mendoza himself, Shannon points out that

over the years they have evolved, here and there, into three-dimensional characters, so that the whole crew is now, we might say, a cohesive cast frozen in time between books, taking up renewed life with each new one. The two senior sergeants Hackett and Higgins, ingenuous-looking Landers, earnestly religious Piggott, simple-minded Grace, the plodder Glasser, handsome Palliser, Schenke, Conway, and Galeano, and all their concerns and individualities gradually grow and emerge in one book or another over the years.[3]

And some are still available for development: Conway and Schenke, of those named here, have not yet been very fully characterized, while Dr. Bainbridge, of the coroner's office, and Duke, of the crime lab, appear repeatedly but are so far little more than names, and patrolman Bill Moss, a new figure in two late novels (*Exploit of Death,* 1983 and *Destiny of Death,* 1984) seems an obvious candidate for further and fuller use.

The earliest novels are very strongly centered around Mendoza, but the tendency has been for the focus to broaden, so that the other characters come to seem more and more nearly equal in importance, with the result that in later novels the group seems almost to take the place of a single protagonist. The one policeman who shares the stage with Mendoza in the earliest novels is Arthur Hackett. From the beginning, he and Mendoza have a special relationship. Mendoza affectionately calls him *Arturo,* and their friendship is clearly deep and of long standing. Hackett's function is that of sidekick to the main detective, the person with whom Mendoza talks out his discoveries and intuitions. Their personal lives follow somewhat similar patterns, introducing a kind of thematic paralleling of domestic events that Shannon has come to use very heavily in later novels. In the opening novel, *Case Pending,* Mendoza meets Alison Weir, who is destined to become his wife. But Mendoza, that notorious womanizer, has no intention of settling down, although he clearly allows Alison a place in his life far superior to what any woman except his grandmother has previously had. It is only after she is threatened with grievous harm, in the fourth novel, *Knave of Hearts,* that he realizes she has become so important to his life that marriage is the inevitable outcome. Similarly in the third novel, *Extra Kill,* Art Hackett meets Angel, daughter of a former film actress. Angel is an odd young woman, unkempt, antagonistic, resentful, and bitter, but Art finds himself strangely attracted to her. Both unconventional courtships end in marriage, Hackett's more quickly than Mendoza's and from then on we see both men in happy domesticity.

The female halves of these two couples at first seem about as different from each other as possible. An aspiring painter, Alison supports herself as owner-manager of a charm school in which she tries to teach ungainly young women the rudiments of grooming and manners. She had been reared by a widowed father, an engineer who built bridges throughout Spanish-speaking America and who loved her and whom she loved dearly. Angel is supported by her wealthy mother whom she hates when we and Art first meet her, knowing that she is little more than an embarrassment to that mother. And she seems pitiably helpless to Art outside that stifling home environment.

Both women quickly succumb to their suitors, and both are clearly representative of the conventionally feminine—as, indeed are all the women married to policemen in these novels. Angel is a gourmet cook, tormenting Hackett who must always watch his weight while she is able to eat all her rich concoctions without gaining a pound. Alison gives up her charm school with delight, for she had never enjoyed working for a living and she seems not to like her pupils very much. She continues to paint, occasionally, and retains her involvement in the art world, but her home and family are henceforth central to her life. Both women quickly bear children, to the delight of their doting husbands, and both make for those husbands homes which are refuges from the ugly reality with which they must deal in their daily work. Both families are more favored than most police families—the Mendozas because of great wealth inherited from his crooked grandfather and the Hacketts because of Angel's inheritance, less than Mendoza's but still substantial, from her despised mother.

Hackett and Angel remain prominent through a number of early novels, but then they tend to move to the background as other police families are developed more fully. George Higgins soon moves center stage, as he falls in love with and then humbly courts Mary Dwyer, widow of the first (of, so far, only two) important police character to be killed in the line of duty. And then, one by one, others fall in love, court and marry the young women whom they usually meet through police cases (Piggott, the fundamentalist, is in this as in many other ways an exception: he meets his Prudence through singing in the church choir).

Two significant police characters are policewomen. Philippa Rosemary O'Neill, usually called Phil, works in Records and Information while Wanda Larsen, assigned to Homicide, sees herself and is seen by the men as their secretary. In *Chance to Kill* Wanda is assigned to Homicide and there is a good deal of concern about what she will do until she makes it clear that she is eager to type the men's reports and tidy their desks. No friend to feminism, Shannon assigns her two women officers to essentially clerical duties—at least at first. Later, they too, "emerge" into fuller characters—and into more demanding activities. When Landers is accused, in *The Ringer,* of criminal activity, Phil takes it upon herself to investigate and, almost single-handedly, breaks the case and clears him. But she remains in R. and I., although she repeatedly refers to her work as "just a glorified clerk's job" and, after she and Landers are married, in *Deuces Wild,* she expresses eagerness to quit when they can afford it. More devoted to her career is Wanda. After her early self-effacing, humble behavior, she develops into an eager professional, desirous of street experience and hoping eventually to "make detective rank" (see, especially, *Cold Trail* and following novels). Unlike Shannon's other women characters she is not pining to give up work for matrimony; she seems to be resisting Glasser, who we know is interested in her.

The Los Angeles Police Department is depicted in extremely favorable terms in these novels. It is repeatedly described as the finest police force in the world, and the police are, almost without exception, people of integrity and dedication. When accusations of corruption are made, such as those against Landers in *The Ringer,* they invariably turn out to be unfounded. The cops often fail to solve crimes, which must be "shoved into pending" for want of evidence, and they sometimes express distaste for punishing criminals who have killed what they see as worthless individuals. So they are fallible. But this fallibility is a minor part of the gritty realism of the novels and coexists with the pride they take in representing order and goodness in an evil world. Interesting, however, are two very early situations which present the police in a more ambiguous light. In *Case Pending,* the very first novel, one character is a policeman who is plotting a murder. However, his motivation makes him a sympathetic character (he is desperately trying to keep the much-loved baby he and his wife have adopted), and when it comes to the point, he does not actually commit the act he had so carefully planned. More troubling is a situation presented in *Knave of Hearts.* It is learned that an innocent man has been executed; the cops seem regretful, but they spend little time worrying about possibly faulty police procedures, and they excuse this injustice by pointing out that there are various sorts of injustice (30-1, 41). This wrongful execution is hardly mentioned later in the novel; after being used as an inciting incident, it is forgotten.

The Los Angeles setting of the novels is repeatedly referred to. The city, however, could generally be any city, and elements of true local color are rarely used. Place names, streets, and communities within the Los Angeles area are often alluded to, but they usually function only to help the reader keep straight which of a number of concurrent cases is being investigated. Particularly noticeable by its absence is the world of films. While Hollywood appears as a place (the Mendozas' house on Rayo Grande is in Hollywood), it rarely appears as a film capital. An exception is *Extra Kill,* in which we meet the mother of the woman who is to become Angel Hackett, a faded film actress somewhat similar to the character played by Gloria Swanson in *Sunset Boulevard*, although Angel's mother had never enjoyed the success claimed by the Swanson character. In fact, Shannon makes quite explicit that the glamor and glitter popularly associated with Hollywood are irrelevant to the world of the Los Angeles policemen.

To people elsewhere, you said Hollywood and it conjured up an immediate vision of glamour. But Hollywood was just another city. A city within the big city, and it had more of the old, shabby, middle-class streets, and ordinary middle-class people, than it had the celebrities and mansions with swimming pools. (*Kindness*, 96)

The presence of large numbers of Mexican-Americans is always obvious, but we rarely enter their world. One exception, of course, comes in Mendoza's frequent recollection of his youth in a Mexican-American slum neighborhood. In *Extra Kill,* however, we are taken to Olvera Street, and a brief passage contrasts the old and the new, the genuine and the tourist attraction. This passage is unusual, though, and as a rule little true local color appears in these novels.

Shannon's formula, eventually so recognizable,[4] was rather slow in developing, three stages, or periods, being discernible. In the earliest books, there is essentially one narrative line, the central mystery around which everything revolves. Gradually, Shannon began making tangential mention of other cases which the detectives are presumably investigating, although in the early novels these are not developed or explained. From that beginning, the tendency is in the direction of ever more mysteries or concurrent plot lines, until as many as fifteen or more cases may be at least briefly described in a single novel. However, only three or four will be examined in any detail, and usually only one or two form the central interest of the novel. Often, in fact, what initially seem to be several separate cases turn out to be related—either because the crimes are committed by the same criminal or because one forms the motivation for others. By about 1965, this formula seems well established, and following novels intensify some of the tendencies of that formula.

In this formula of what might be called the middle period, we are introduced *in medias res,* the detectives already investigating some cases and doing paper work on others, although these cases usually are not fully examined. Mainly they establish the daily routine of the force. Then several more cases will be introduced, and among them will be the case or cases which are to be the major focus of the novel in question. As we follow the central plot line, occasionally other investigations will be mentioned, but these tend to pile up toward the end of the book. Near the end, as the primary case or cases are being solved, new crimes will be reported, and in fact the last lines of many novels deal with new cases, thus creating open endings. Many of the minor cases are not mysteries at all, reminding us that a Homicide Division deals with all sorts of deaths—suicides, accidental deaths, natural deaths lacking an attending physician, and so on. Many of these deaths require no investigation, only a certain amount of that paper work of which the detectives are always complaining. Their presence in the novels is of course one element of the books' realism. Another element of realism is the fact that not all cases are solved—although this is true only of minor cases; the major ones are always concluded by the discovery and punishment (actual or future) of the criminals. All these elements combine to make quite real the world in which the detectives work.

In the novels of the most recent period, the formula has become even more open, less structured. Less emphasis tends to be given to one or two central cases, and the primary sense is that of an interlocking network of cases in various stages of investigation. Thus these novels, dating from the late 1970s, become more difficult for the reader to follow; keeping in one's mind the details of up to fifteen or so cases is no easy task. But lessened form accompanies increased realism, and these late novels probably come closer to recreating the actual texture of the daily lives of big city policemen than do the earlier, more artistically structured books.

Shannon's detectives often comment scornfully on the contrast between fictional and real mysteries. For them the world of the detective story is simplistic and the work too easy. It is also neat, too neat. The form of Shannon's novels underlines the messiness of their lives. Work is constantly ongoing; the men's attention is always divided among a number of separate and unrelated problems. If one or two cases are solved, others remain open, and more are always coming in. Thus, unlike the closed form of most detective novels, with the tidy solution and cleaning up of details, with everything clearly explained at the dramatic conclusion, Shannon's formula calls for an open ending. Several mysteries will be solved, for without that much shaping, the novels would stray so far from the mystery form as to be unsatisfactory as stories. But the openness of life will be preserved, as we are reminded that the work goes on—and on—and on—as more details are reported. Occasionally, a plot will be continued from one novel to the next. One case is followed from its inception in *Felony at Random* to its fated conclusion in *Felony File*, as Shannon demonstrates how one violent act can blast the lives of many others, instigating further violence by a formerly good man.

This continuing of one plot line from novel to novel is another of the structural devices lending realism to the novels as is its reverse, the failure to follow a plot line to a conclusion (the unsolved cases). Frequent reminders that most of the work of the detectives is simply boring, that few cases are dramatic or even very meaningful, serve a similar function. The problem for Shannon is to make interesting and meaningful the depiction of what is by design dull and meaningless. For that, the introduction of the occasional case which is extraordinary or, in the favored term of the detectives, "offbeat," is essential. Thus Shannon repeatedly tells us how dull the work is but introduces into each novel (far more frequently than would be realistic) the dramatic, exciting case:

As a rule the kind of business occupying the detectives at Central Headquarters was very routine, not to say dull—because the violence they dealt with they were used to, and it was mostly irrational, random violence. Just now and then there came along the oddities, the queer things. And sometimes they could be very damned odd.

(*Spring*, 25)

Repeatedly cases are solved only because of some glaring coincidence, despite all Mendoza's intuitive brilliance and all the hard, slogging, detective work of the policemen. Shannon has often been criticized for her heavy use of such happy accidents. A case in point is *Root of All Evil*, in which Mrs. MacTaggart, just acquired as nursemaid to the twins (the search for an appropriate servant to take from Mendoza and Alison the bother of being wakened at night by the babies has been the running domestic motif of this novel), overhears Mendoza mention to Alison a name which has appeared tangentially in his investigation. She happens to know the person in question and to be aware that his baby son had possessed a very noticeable and unremovable birthmark. With this information, Mendoza is able to piece together an old crime and thus to solve his current one.

Such coincidences often seem incredibly convenient, bringing cases to happy conclusions after the requisite number of pages have been filled but without any sense of inevitability, and thus the reader may feel cheated. But for Shannon, chance itself is a central theme; while chance often works against both victims and police, it is only appropriate that it would sometimes work in their favor. Note how many titles stress the fickleness of life: *Chance to Kill, Unexpected Death, Whim to Kill* and *Felony at Random*. And repeatedly the detectives are struck by the randomness, the meaninglessness of the crime and the violence which they daily confront.

Shannon often uses scornful allusions to mystery novelists to buttress the claims to reality of her own fiction. Generally the detectives find crime fiction merely laughable, since it is so contrived, the crimes are so carefully planned and the criminals so clever. Hackett, citing a woman mystery writer to whose lecture Angel had taken him, says,

One thing stuck in my mind, because it shows how different books are from real life. She said in fiction you can't have anything happen by coincidence. Well, my God, we're always running into coincidences on the job. (*Deuces*, 15)

And he then goes on to mention several from their recent experience. Thus Shannon argues that her use of coincidence, far from being unrealistic, is actually an example of art copying life. Some readers may find this an easy excuse for her avoidance, especially in the more recent novels, of careful plotting. But it seems clear that for Shannon, coincidence is an essential element of plotting as of life.

One case solved by chance, despite all the best intentions of the detectives, occurs in *The Death-Bringers*. Here a promising black high school student has been shot to death in what is apparently an impossible crime, only one of the many times Shannon plays about with the devices of Golden Age crime fiction so antithetical to the tone and assumptions of her own work. The detectives work hard, going through what seem to them interminable but necessary lines of investigation, all of which eventually end in nothing. Then, unexpectedly, a woman and her young son come into the office, bringing the entire story with them. It turns out that Carol Coffey's death had been pure accident, in fact the culmination of a series of accidents. Their randomness is repeatedly stressed.

Mendoza said softly, "*¡Pares o nones!*" And who or what decided the throw of the dice? A one-in-a-million chance. Young Norman, curious to know how it felt to fire a gun. Firing a gun, at a tin can on a fence.

Sam Coffey taking off the screens to repaint the frames. Just then.

Carol Coffey, who got A's in English and wanted to be a teacher, dusting the living room. Standing in that doorway, facing it and the rear bedroom window—just the few moments when her mother was in the side yard...

The moment young Norman fired the gun. A nice well-brought-up boy, who never meant to hurt anybody.

The millionth chance. The wild bullet, wide of the innocent target, going across the narrow back yard there, into the open bedroom window, into Carol's heart.

At random. Death was so random. (*Bringers,* 217; ellipses are Shannon's.)

Note the use of the "dice" image in the beginning of this quotation. Here we are in Mendoza's point of view, and so this image is doubly suitable—because the gambler would think this way, and as a conventional image for chance. But Mendoza, for whom gambling is symbolic of the lack of order which he sees in the world and which he is always trying to set right, is an atheist who has deserted his Catholic upbringing and who views organized religion as a kind of confidence game. When his closest associate, Art Hackett, lies seriously wounded, he is contemptuous of his housekeeper's promised prayers:

Damned ridiculous, he thought. Superstitious... On her knees at the nearest one, the Church of Our Lady of Good Counsel, obeying the ancient meaningless ritual.

What happened or didn't happen, to Art or Luis Mendoza or anybody else, it was just according to how the hands got dealt round. (*Mark,* 152; ellipses are Shannon's).

But he now questions—or at least resists—the conception of a universe of pure chance. "Death was so very damned random," he thinks again. And then, "It would be nice to be able to think that—whatever arranged things—had some valid reasons" (*Bringers,* 218).

These meditations bring him to the idea of destiny. Do our lives follow paths determined by forces outside them? If so, then, what are those forces—the randomness he has long accepted or some kind of divine order? Alison, with whom he discusses these questions, rebels against the idea of destiny in general. "I don't like to feel that every last little thing that's ever happened to me or is going to happen is all—all blueprinted out already, and nothing I can do about it at all. It's not fair" (*Bringers,* 220). Mendoza replies, that life isn't fair—and of course all his experience as a police officer corroborates that belief. For him, fairness is not an operative principle. The conflict between order and chaos is of greatest importance:

"What *I* don't like is the—the untidiness of it all." He sounded angry. "All I can say is, if there is something making all these arrangements, it's being done in a very damned disorderly way." (*Bringers*, 220.)

Thus the obsession with tidiness which is characteristic of Mendoza and which is used to explain his motivation for remaining a policeman also becomes an expression of his philosophical stance. On the profoundest level, both his police work and his personal prissiness are simply evidence of his longing for order in a world that remains intractably chaotic. He keeps trying to push back the chaos—by arranging his possessions tidily, almost mathematically, on his desk, Poirot-like, and by seeking to find out what individuals have disturbed the social order by committing crimes, so that they may be removed from that order. His sense of futility about the general chaos, however, is also illustrated by his repeated assertions that he really cares more about knowing the truth than about acting upon it.

Two great moments of crisis, however, bring him to an acceptance of a principle of order, of destiny. Against his will, he returns to his mother church. When Alison, early in their relationship, is briefly seized by a rapist-killer, he finds himself repeating, automatically by rote, prayers learned in his Catholic boyhood:

Alison, Alison, *mi novia, mi hermosita, amada, querida—Madre Maria, te suplico—*Alison—*Dios te salve, Maria, llena ores de gracia, el Senor es contigo—es con—* God, I can't remember the words—Mary—salute you—of grace, of—help me remember—*Santa Maria, madre de Dios, ruega, Senora, por nosotros ahora y en la—*no, no, not hour of death— (*Knave*, 276).

This panic-stricken conversion, however, is short lived. Much later, a second personal crisis, this time involving his children, is needed to bring him back permanently to the Church. In *Deuces Wild,* during the long search for the twins and their kidnappers, he goes almost surreptitiously to an old Spanish church downtown to pray, and the results of this second near-loss are lasting. From this time on, he regularly attends Mass, but he seems embarrassed and refuses to talk about it with anybody, apparently even Alison. His conversion is a matter of emotion, of the strength of his love for these few others, his "hostages to fortune," as Shannon's policemen always think of their families.

These tensions between chaos and order, randomness and destiny, are thematically illustrated by Mendoza's police methods and by the ways the crimes are solved. For example, in *Knave of Hearts,* coincidence, hunch, and good police work combine to contrive the solution. The coincidence is the arrival in California of a small-town Illinois police chief, who, upon reading in the California press about Mendoza's serial murderer, recognizes similarities with an old case of his own. He had been morally certain of the criminal's guilt although unable to prove it, and he now accompanies Hackett on a long, tiring series of expeditions to look at the "possibles," to see if he can identify any of them as the young man from Mount Selah who had come to California several years earlier. Thus coincidence leads to tedious, painstaking police routine.

The major element of hunch, or intuition, is Mendoza's building up a theory, from very little evidence, about the personality and movements of the serial murderer. On little more than the evidence of where the victims' bodies were found and the fact that several of them were known to have met respectable-appearing young men shortly before their deaths, he builds up a profile:

Coming here—from a smallish place inland—thirty to thirty-six months ago. Liking the beach. Renting a cabin, even buying one, for weekends there—but holding a job in the city. That we can say, because if he'd lived in Santa Monica—anywhere west of Beverly Hills—he wouldn't have been at L.A.C.C. inquiring about evening classes, he'd have thought first of U.C.L.A., nearer him.... He has some kind of white-collar job—take your choice, banker, merchant, clerk, salesman—

(*Knave,* 171)

Such theorizing eventually leads him to ask a real estate agent with knowledge of beach areas to find out who owns a number of cabins of the sort his putative murderer would have. So here hunch also leads to dull but crucial investigative work.

When these three strands of chance, intuition, and investigation come together, at the climax of the novel, yet another element of chance is added. The serial murderer has a date with Alison, from whom Mendoza is then estranged (having feared any close or lasting relationship with a woman), and she is clearly intended as the next victim. But the Illinois police chief recognizes him, and the real estate agent's identification of the name under which his public California life is carried on leads Mendoza to him in time to rescue Alison and, of course, their reunion swiftly follows.

Such a resolution can easily be criticized as relying too heavily on the element of chance, and indeed many of Shannon's coincidences do seem farfetched, functioning only to bring the current novel to its close within the requisite number of pages. But these coincidences are also defensible on thematic grounds. Since chance, often reduntantly called "random chance," is such an important part of the world in which Shannon's policemen live and work, it should not be surprising that sometimes chance works to the advantage of the policemen, thus balancing out, to some degree, the cruelty of the random deaths and suffering which are the more obvious evidence of this chaos.

Shannon's narrative voice and her policemen are ostentatiously tolerant. Repeatedly stress is laid on the unfairness of stereotyping people as members of groups. Intolerant people tend to be treated particularly harshly. Thus, in *Root of All Evil,* when we learn that a particular character is a member of a group of bigots, we should be alerted that he may also be guilty of crime. And so it is. The strange dumping of a body in a Catholic schoolyard is thus explained; only a stupid bigot who actually believes some of the more outlandish accusations against Catholics would have acted in such a way.

I thought sure it'd work. Why, hell, everybody knows how *they* do! All those priests and nuns carrying on, and they bury the babies all secret in the convent grounds—anybody knows anything about *them* knows— I thought they'd hush it up! Natural thing. Wouldn't want the church connected, so they'd get rid o' the body like they do and—

(*Root,* 286)

But Shannon's tolerance has its limits. First, it applies only to those who have allowed themselves to be assimilated into what she clearly considers the mainstream of American life. Over and over again, she makes it clear that anyone can adopt good middle-class values, no matter what his or her skin color, ethnic background, or religious faith. And it is the adoption of these middle-class values that earns one the right to be accepted. Thus Mendoza, despite his background—his poverty, his Mexican-American childhood, the borderline-criminal activity of his grandfather—has become a bastion of society. Thus also has Jason Grace, a late addition to the team (he first appears in 1965 in *Death by Inches*).) Grace is black; he and his Virginia lead comfortably middle-class lives, which are not distinguishable from those of his colleagues. The only difference is that Grace is brighter than most, and his father is a prominent physician. The fact that blacks can succeed in our society is rather heavy-handedly underlined.

Grace, in fact, is made both to represent blacks, showing that they can succeed, and to express middle-class resentment of social programs which aim to help members of disadvantaged minorities. To him are given speeches that might be taken as anti-black if spoken by any other character. He claims special knowledge of the black community and culture, but he mocks black English and expresses contempt for those who do not have the gumption to get education and the strength or knowledge to be clean and live properly middle-class lives. Once Mendoza quotes the old counting-out rime so beloved by children: "Eeny-meeny-miny-mo—" and Grace responds,

"Why Lootenant, suh," said Grace, "you nasty old racist you, quoting that one!... Did you hear about that bunch of silly people agitating at the library to take *Little Black Sambo* out of the juvenile section? Fact. Just how ridiculous can you get?" (*Intent,* 116)

Through Grace, Shannon has it both ways; she demonstrates that blacks can make it in our society and she denigrates lower class blacks while avoiding the appearance of white racism. The problem is that Grace has not made it on his own (his father's professional status has enabled him to have every advantage), and that in making these speeches denigratory of people of his own race, he comes to seem something of an Uncle Tom, not as admirable a character as he is intended to be. Additionally, he is presented as something of a superman—too intelligent, too widely informed on too many subjects, too capable of doing whatever is needed—and thus he is less realistic than most of the other police characters.

The other limit to Shannon's tolerance is one specific group. Her acceptance does not extend to homosexuals. Any hint of homosexual activity automatically qualifies the character in question as a suspect and often brands him or her as a criminal. While Shannon is consciously alert to verbal slurs against racial, ethnic, or religious groups, linguistic abuse of homosexuals is accepted. The word "nigger" and other similar epithets are given only to bigots and are self-righteously criticized by her policemen, but these same policemen quite naturally and happily refer to "fags" and "queers" and have no qualms about stereotyping members of this group. Shannon seems to accept the theory that homosexuality is a chosen behavior, so that one may be anathematized for having chosen that lifestyle just as one may be credited with having chosen to adopt middle-class values.

The world inhabited by Mendoza and his colleagues is a bleak one. Whether chance or destiny governs our fate seems to make little difference. Much of what the detectives see is senseless, random violence. Some crimes are carefully contrived, either for greed or out of sexual lusts. Most, however, are simply unconsidered acts, the results of moments of impulse, because an individual wants something and someone else happens to stand in the way. Others result from helplessness—an individual thinks he or she is entitled to something—

and may well be—and strikes out against others when the expected rewards are not forthcoming. These latter tend to be helpless old people, misled to believe that Social Security would care for them in their old age or angered that neighborhood punks find their neighborhood stores, built up by the labor of years, ripe pickings for robbery so they can buy drugs.

What redemption there is comes in the lives of the policemen. Sworn to defend order and living by their concern for others, Mendoza and his colleagues form a slim but essential line against chaos. They battle the thoughtless "louts" (in a favorite word of theirs) and strive to uphold their old-fashioned standards of decency and concern for others. But mostly in their private lives—in their day-to-day concern over their children's development, over their changing neighborhoods, over the welfare of the pets they are always adopting or being adopted by— they represent an ongoing attitude of ordinary but admirable citizens. And the citizens who insist on cooperating with them because it is the right thing to do represent a continuing civilization, forces of good which continuously battle against the forces of evil. In Shannon's modern morality play, the forces of evil often seem predominant, but there is always the balance. No matter how many unsolved crimes are outstanding, no matter how horrible the criminality and brutality confronting the policemen, there are still at home their wives and children, their ordinary concerns, which contrast and which remind us that daily life can nonetheless be good. George Higgins, after he marries his beloved Mary Dwyer, widow of his slain friend, with his concern for "Bert Dwyer's good kids," Mendoza and his Alison with their frustration over teaching the twins the difference between Spanish and English, Jason Grace and his Virginia's long struggle to be allowed to adopt a baby, Palliser's years of caring for his elderly mother and then his courtship of the woman he marries—all these are but a few examples of the ordinary, decent lives of Shannon's policemen. Their daily concerns, often trivial but very representative of ordinary life, are balanced against the pain and suffering they see in the course of their work. And the dichotomy of these two lives—work, which takes them into the heart of darkness, and home, which gives them stability and proves that order and goodness can exist in this world—creates the texture of Mendoza's world.

Notes

[1] In addition to the consistently good sales of the novels written under all three of the author's names, other evidence of the strength of their appeal is the recent foundation by Rinehart S. Potts

(1223 Glen Terrace, Glassboro, New Jersey) of a quarterly newsletter, *The Linington Lineup,* devoted entirely to the work of this prolific author. For a representative negative view, see Marvin Lachman, "People, Philosophy, Politics, and the Policemen: Elizabeth Linington's Louis Mendoza," *The Poisoned Pen,* 5, No. 3 (1983), 19-22.

²Listed below are the titles of all novels in the Mendoza series, preceded by the original dates of publication. All were published in New York by William Morrow and Company; this information has been omitted from the individual listings to save space. All quotations will be cited in the text using, where necessary for clarity, the abbreviations given after the entries:

1960 *Case Pending.*
1961 *The Ace of Spades. (Ace)*
1962 *Extra Kill.*
1962 *Knave of Hearts. (Knave)*
1963 *Death of Busybody.*
1963 *Double Bluff.*
1964 *Root of All Evil. (Root)*
1964 *Mark of Murder. (Mark)*
1965 *The Death-Bringers. (Bringers)*
1965 *Death by Inches.*
1966 *Coffin Corner.*
1966 *With a Vengeance.*
1967 *Chance to Kill.*
1967 *Rain with Violence.*
1968 *Kill With Kindness. (Kindness)*
1969 *Schooled to Kill.*
1969 *Crime on Their Hands.*
1970 *Unexpected Death.*
1971 *Whim to Kill*
1971 *The Ringer.*
1972 *Murder with Love.*
1972 *With Intent to Kill. (Intent)*
1973 *No Holiday for Crime.*
1973 *Spring of Violence. (Spring)*
1974 *Crime File.*
1975 *Deuces Wild. (Deuces)*
1976 *Streets of Death.*
1977 *Appearances of Death.*
1978 *Cold Trail.*
1979 *Felony at Random.*
1980 *Felony File.*
1981 *Murder Most Strange.*
1982 *The Motive on Record.*
1983 *Exploit of Death.*
1984 *Destiny of Death.*

³Dell Shannon, *First Four by Dell Shannon* (Garden City, NY: Nelson Doubleday, Inc., 1960), p. x.

⁴For an enlightening discussion of Shannon's view of her formula and of her working methods, see Margaret J. King, "An Interview with Elizabeth Linington," *The Armchair Detective,* 13 (Fall 1980), 299-307.

Collin Wilcox's Frank Hastings

Frederick Isaac

Collin Wilcox is a soft-spoken man whose books have spoken powerfully about the life and work of big-city policemen. An intensely personal writer, he has nevertheless retained his privacy, allowing only dim reflections of his own life to show through in his novels. Born in Detroit, he moved to San Francisco in the late 1940s, and has lived there since. His first success came as the developer and creator of a well-received line of designer lamps, which he sold under his own name. By the mid-1960s, when divorce made him the single parent of two sons, the business allowed him to begin a second career as a writer of mysteries.

His first two published novels featured a reporter on the fictitious San Francisco *Sentinel.* Stephen Drake, the hero, solves crimes through the use of extra-sensory perception in *The Black Door* and *The Third Figure.* After these two appearances, though, it became clear that Drake's ability made suspense practically impossible without resorting to tricks or making the character seem ridiculous. As a result, Wilcox attempted to develop a more complete and emotionally satisfying protagonist. The result of this search was Frank Hastings, S.F.P.D.

Since his first appearance in 1969, Hastings has appeared in thirteen novels, including one a year through most of the 1970s. In addition to growing respect among readers and critics of the police procedural in the United States, the detective has an international following, especially in Japan. One result has been a book written specifically for that audience and sold directly to the foreign publisher. As of this writing (1984), it has not been contracted for release to the American market.

In conversation, Wilcox tends to see difficulties and loose ends in his novels, rather than his sizable achievement. But Hastings' longevity as a series hero has derived from a combination of elements which do not appear in mystery novels as frequently as one might hope. What the writer has created, in fact, is a policeman who challenges our expectations. Through his cases he has turned into someone about whom the reader cares deeply and sincerely. Hastings has both a past and a present which create currents and conflicts as he performs his job. The stories not only differ in plot; they present fundamentally different plot types and styles, developing and resolving problems according to different sets of rules within the traditions of the detective story. There is a cast of continuing characters that is large enough to be realistic, each having traits and quirks that engage the reader's involvement. We care about them all because Wilcox has told us about them. As a corollary, the books are enlivened by minor people whose strong impressions give the conflicts and cooperation still more life. Finally, there are several social and moral concerns which Wilcox addresses repeatedly, and which gain insights with each repetition.

As the first-person narrator, Hastings is at the center of all of these currents. His background, which becomes a litany to readers, forms a framework under which the series' structures can be seen and around which the emotional and ethical content has been built. Born in the Bay area south of San Francisco, Hastings grew up fatherless after his mother was deserted. Frank starred in football through high school, and won scholarships to college. After military service (various books identify World War II) he returned home and attended Stanford, playing linebacker while ostensibly majoring in Business.

After graduation he was drafted by the Detroit Lions, and played for them for several years until a progressive series of knee injuries forced him into retirement. While playing, he met and married a local socialite and began working for her father in the family business. Thus, at age 30 Frank's future seemed assured. At the end of his football career he began working full-time for his father-in-law in the Public Relations Department, where his name and reputation attracted clients.

Over the next few years, though, Frank became disenchanted with the situation and angry with his life. He became an alcoholic in his role as glad-hander for the company. He found himself depressed and frustrated as he acted as drinking companion and occasional pimp for visitors. Finding his life and sense of propriety in disarray, and his wife and two children increasingly distant, he agreed to a divorce and moved to San Francisco. There a superior from Frank's army days offered Hastings a chance to start over.

While Hastings passed the requirements, learned the law and became a beat cop (the oldest rookie in his class), his drinking continued unabated. One night, however, the man who had convinced him to join heard of a particularly bad drinking bout and went to Frank's apartment. Waking to find his mentor, Hastings received a personal message: "I know you have troubles, but you must put them behind you. And if you can't stop drinking, get off the force. I won't have a drunk in my squad endangering the lives of his fellow officers." Having said this, the man left. Sobered by the concern he had been shown, and by the threat he posed to himself and others, Hastings stopped drinking that night.

When we meet him for the first time in *The Lonely Hunter* (1969) Hastings has been a cop for about seven years and is still a sergeant.[1] For his work in that book, though, he is promoted to Lieutenant, where he has worked since with Pete Friedman, his best friend and conscience. Over the years, Frank has become somewhat uncertain about the prospects for further advancement, in part because of Friedman's cynical attitude toward departmental politics. Even so, Hastings continues to find the work challenging (especially in the street) and believes that he is a valuable part of the system.

The Hastings books have several intriguing aspects, among which is the unpredictability of design. While the series format demands that some elements be repeated, the books display a surprising range of emotion and interplay between Hastings' public and private life. Two of the novels, for example, include Frank's children. *The Lonely Hunter,* in fact, uses Hastings himself as the title character. While investigating a murder among the hippies in the Haight-Ashbury district, he also goes in quest of his daughter Claudia, who left home with a high school boyfriend and has buried herself among the runaways and outcasts in the late '60s city of love. The poignancy of this divorced father searching for his estranged offspring counterpoints the cop uncovering a murderer among the same flower children. An important emotional point in this novel comes when the reader realizes that although Claudia is recovered, Hastings does not find her. He is the recipient of good will from the people he has met and become involved with in the community; they show their gratitude by returning the girl to her father. In fact, Hastings forgets her entirely during the climactic chase and capture (which takes him through the fog over the Bay to Angel Island in a helicopter), and only remembers her the following morning when told that she is waiting for him. The understanding that, just as Frank has focussed on his present life and neglected his past, the reader has been pulled along and also forgotten Claudia, is a powerful one. Additionally, there is the fact of Hastings' having left his wife and children before. How can he reenter their lives without relinquishing a part of himself in his new, successful life? The fact that Hastings does not— perhaps cannot—reach deeply enough inside himself to tell us is some measure of his uncertainty.

The partner to this excursion into Hastings' private past is *The Watcher* (1978). This time it is the son, Darrell, who joins Frank for two weeks on a vacation. Their attempts to break the barriers of time and distance never wholly succeed, even though they experience a life-threatening adventure. Getting out of the city to a cabin near the mountains, they must chase a quartet of squatters who have set up in the house, and fend off a madman whose son's death in prison has turned the father's love to a violent hatred for Hastings, the cop who arrested the young man. During this series of crises Darrell comes to understand his father better, and Frank finds himself closer than ever before to the boy he never really knew. The process shows promise, and communication has begun, but the time is short. Darrell returns to Detroit before the two can secure their relationship. Even so, it is clear that each of them has gained insights which they can use in future encounters.

Family relationships are one of Wilcox's most important themes in the series. Hastings' attempts to revive and solidify his tenuous contacts with Claudia and Darrell, while only marginally successful, highlight the hero's desire (and that of his creator) for families to build and maintain trust. Not knowing his daughter, Frank's task as a parent is essentially impossible; how can he find someone whose actions he cannot predict? As a cop he might find her, but not as a father. Only the people of the Haight can bring her to him. With Darrell the circumstances are different. Their similarity binds them, though they are wary at first. Their adventures in the woods emphasize their likeness, even though their time together is limited.

The other family which is portrayed in detail displays another vision of unsuccessful marriage, but with a happier ending. Frank meets Ann Haywood in *Dead Aim* (1971), when her eldest son is temporarily a suspect in a murder. Ann is a schoolteacher, recently divorced and raising her two sons alone. Dan, the teenager, is at first hostile and then wary, but finally tells the truth that eventually leads to the real killer. The younger boy, Billy, has isolated himself after the divorce and needs a positive male to bring him out of his shell. The problem for all of them is Dr. Victor Haywood, Ann's ex-husband. A society psychiatrist, he has used his professional techniques to browbeat his wife and sons, depriving them of their self-respect. When Hastings falls in love with Ann he provides some strength with which they can fight Victor's emotional attacks. The books show a progression as Ann and the boys regain control over their lives, and come to respect and love Frank. When he is injured at the end of *Mankiller* (1980) Hastings goes to live at Ann's where he has remained through *Stalking Horse* (1981) and *Victims* (1985) as a buffer against Dr. Haywood and the world at large. It is clear that Frank's position as Ann's lover has not diminished him in the sons' eyes. They have come to see him as a second, better father, both compassionate and strong.

Family relationships have a large role in almost every novel. James Biggs in *Aftershock* (1975) and Charles Keller in *The Watcher* have each lost relatives and blame Hastings for the deaths. Their mourning has turned to an obsessive fury as they attempt to murder Frank as compensation for their grief. *Hiding Place* (1973) employs the relationship between an uncle and nephew who were the last to see a murdered woman. Only by breaking through their commitment to each other and gaining their trust can Hastings solve the case. *Doctor, Lawyer...* (1977) involves Chief Dwyer and his son Irving, a late version of a hippie whose confused life enmeshes him in a serial murder. *Stalking Horse* (1982) portrays the life and surroundings of a political figure and his associates, a pseudo-family whose in-fighting and in-breeding lead to intrigue and eventual disaster. And *Victims* contains a successful man whose fierce desire to hold his family close to him ultimately destroys him. These, along with several murders committed by family members, form a continuing focus for Wilcox. Families, he seems to say, are at the core of our society. Their breakdown, for whatever reasons, must be averted whenever possible.

Wilcox's plots offer another aspect of the novels worth exploration. Almost all writers employing series characters can be identified as following one of the three recognized styles of detection, exposition and solution: classic detective, hard boiled, and police procedural writers are well known to all readers, and while authors may employ some of the aspects of all, a hero may be legitimately placed in one of them without fear that the books or their methodology will change. In the event a writer wishes to change styles, a new detective is created. (Thus Ed McBain, in introducing Matthew Hope, has a classical hero to complement his masterful 87th Precinct novels.) The rarity of such crossing by authors, however, suggests the public's devotion to established forms and expectation of similarity.

Collin Wilcox, though, has proved something of an exception to this set of assumptions. Although Frank Hastings is a policeman, and draws upon practices of real police departments and the fictional formulae of the procedural style, his cases cannot by any stretch of imagination be placed together among the procedural books. As has already been shown, the tension in *The Lonely Hunter* between fatherhood and duty takes the book away from the strict focus on the job which many writers have used. Similarly Hastings' off-duty life has been shown in *The Watcher* and *Aftershock*. These novels employ known villains, and thus might be said to be in the "hunter-hunted" tradition, with a police protagonist. In much the same way *The Disappearance* and *Doctor, Lawyer,...* with their last-chapter endings, least-likely murderers, and explosive conclusions, might seem more in the tradition of Agatha Christie than that of Maurice Procter. Red herrings and reversals are not unknown in police stories, but are unexpected and underutilized tools.

In other books there are multiple cases, including both simultaneous and successive problems for Frank to tackle. *Long Way Down* (1974) begins with a call for him to divert from the scene of a murder to an attempted assassination of the governor. This takes only 45 pages to resolve, but makes clear that Hastings is a cop, always ready to do what comes up. *The Disappearance* (1970) contains two cases besides the central problem: the murder of a servant in a posh home and a single chapter devoted to a deaf-mute who has killed his father. Most dramatic is *Aftershock*, which joins the "standard" case of murder with the bizarre challenge of James Biggs and the threat he poses to Ann Haywood and Frank. These books highlight two factors about the Hastings novels. In one way they examine the constant pressure on the protagonist to perform in quickly changing environments. Concurrently they broaden his range of response, heighten the reader's respect for his humanity, and create in doing so a more complete (and more plausible) individual than either the perfect amateur or the totally dedicated working policeman.

Beginning with *Power Plays* (1979) Wilcox has taken Hastings in still another direction. Three of the books since then have used politics, influence, and the abuse of power as the theme. In *Power Plays* the F.B.I. intrudes on what at first seems a local murder when the victim is discovered to be a journalist who has uncovered information regarding a major scandal in Washington. Hastings, along with Pete Friedman, finds a bag man, a two-bit hood who was hired to drive the victim while he was killed, and an out-of-town hit-man who does not know who hired him. At the top of this pyramid is an industrialist, whose money and prestige insulates him from their investigation. Throughout their search the police must constantly ward off federal interference, as others try to stop their work or usurp their authority. Both Special Agent Richter and Assistant Director Forbes unsuccessfully attempt to deflect or to cow Hastings and Friedman, suggesting the insiduous nature of higher authority when improperly used.

Stalking Horse (1982) concerns at first not murder but a series of threats directed at Senator Donald Ryan. Because of the wall built by his aides and confidants, Ryan does not know about them, and a recent heart attack has weakend him. Hastings' first task is to identify the person who has sent the letters. In this book Frank and Pete find not corruption but lies and intrigues which have isolated Ryan from reality and ended by perpetuating both his secrets and those of his allies. Ultimately the network crumbles as Hastings digs out its hidden past, finally destroying the man whom it was designed to protect.

In *Victims* (1985) Hastings once again faces a man of influence. This time it is Alexander Guest, a wealthy lawyer. When an ex-cop is killed and Guest's grandson is taken, Guest accuses his son-in-law. Frank once again needs all of his skill to find answers, as Guest has established control over those around him from which they cannot escape. Guest's treatment of the police as stupid and arrogant adds to the un-flattering portrait and turns the case into a fight by Hastings to free the lawyer's iron grip. Success for Frank comes through his assertion of the power of the law and his own prerogatives in spite of Guest's assertions and objections.

In all three of these books Hastings discovers the guilty parties, yet in none of them can he bring a charge. Each of the villains is morally culpable, and in one case personally guilty of murder. Their importance and the power they wield, though, allows them to elude justice. In this respect Wilcox differs from some of his colleagues who have strong beliefs in the abilities (or the inability) of the system to adequately punish wrong-doers. Instead, Hastings' partial success highlights the problems faced by police, and their need to work toward the proper ends even when those results escape them.

Throughout the books Hastings has shown himself a man who cares deeply for others. From his first meeting with Ann Haywood he has been concerned about her emotional state, and this has continued as the relationship has blossomed. He has tried to show her his dual role and in so doing has exposed her to danger, as when he takes her to Emile Zeda's cult temple (in *Long Way Down*). In that episode Ann is almost killed by Zeda's crazed assistant Leonard. When the couple is trapped by James Biggs in *Aftershock* Frank makes her safety his highest priority, in part because he takes responsibility for their danger. This selflessness is reciprocated by both Ann and her sons as they look to him for guidance, and when they take him into their home after his injuries in *Mankiller.*

But Hastings feels sympathy toward many of the people he meets. Throughout both *Long Way Down* and *The Watcher* he attempts to make contact with his enemies, and is pained by Biggs' and Keller's unwillingness to take his suggestions and leave him alone. He is also not too proud to accept suggestions from others. In *The Lonely Hunter,* when a young woman on a bad drug trip takes a baby to the roof of a building and threatens to jump, Hastings accepts a suggestions from Charlie Vanucchi, the Haight's local guru. Since the woman obviously fears the cops, Vanucchi says, why not take all of them away; maybe she will come down of her own accord. With no better options available, Frank and the others withdraw. Some time later footsteps descending the stairs tell them that Vanucchi was right. As has been noted, the Hippie community repays this by returning Claudia.

This pattern of sincerity and emotional exchange is a compelling theme in Hastings' cases. He is both a man of action and a person who can see and respond to others' pain. His ability to communicate with the young people in the books is still another demonstration of his caring. From the first he has related well to both Dan and Billy Haywood. In *The Disappearance* he disarms a youth in Golden Gate Park, in a situation which could destroy valuable property and injure dozens of people. *The Hiding Place* and *Victims* find Frank serving as confidant for boys whose information is vital to the discovery of the killers. And elsewhere Hastings simplifies his work by refusing deviousness, choosing instead to try to understand and relate to the people with whom he deals. By serving as a silent confessor he allows the suspects to tell what they know uninterrupted. He knows that judging others only returns him to judgment of his own unhappy past, and thus chooses silence.

Of course, this does not work at all times. James Biggs and Charles Keller, with their warped minds, challenge Hastings in ways that are diametrically opposed to his best instincts. Their deaths are, to some extent, his own failures of communication and empathy. In addition Frank's occasional involvements with offbeat religious movements bring him into confrontation with other forms of fanaticism. Emil Zeda and his mesmerized assistant in *Long Way Down* try to kill Ann. And in *Mankiller* Frank almost dies while trying to find a killer at Aztecca, the weird cult established by the original victim's step-brother.

While Hastings is clearly the star of the books, he demonstrates a somewhat surprising lack of individual heroism. As narrator, he of course takes the splotlight. But he does not take unrealistic credit for the work. In fact the two books which turn out worst for him are those in which he disobeys orders and takes matters into his own hands (*Long Way Down* and *The Watcher*). In these novels the villains' passions become Frank's own. And even when he overcomes them there is no victory; his rightness does not relieve him of responsibility of their deaths.

In other situations, however, Hastings uses the equipment and manpower of the department whenever he believes it necessary. The climax of *Dead Aim* (on the Golden Gate Bridge) may be overly picturesque, but it demonstrates the point well. Beginning as a stakeout of the killer, the capture develops into a multi-car tailing maneuver, and ends with a cordon of police and a sharpshooter. This dramatic example is repeated several times as Hastings calls for back-up and assistance in all phases of his investigations. It quickly becomes clear that he is no longer a beat cop, and does not care about the reputation he might gain by taking criminals single-handed. From *The Lonely Hunter,* when he commandeers a traffic helicopter and speaks to Friedman, to *Victims* and its capture on Telegraph Hill, two points are repeatedly made clear. The reader never questions the hero's bravery, and at the same time recognizes his dedication to police policies and processes rather than individual glory.

Additional evidence of Hastings' willingness and abililty to work with others comes from *Twospot* (1978). This novel, co-authored by Wilcox and Bill Pronzini, alternates Hastings and the S.F.P.D. with Pronzini's series character, the 'Nameless Detective'. While the two men begin warily, their collaboration leads them to recognize each other's sympathies, abilities, and sincerity. In successfully completing the case they come to realize that they are similar, both worn down by the job and the lack of respect they receive. But while the private operative must work alone, Hastings has the department. The thought that if he is killed in the line of duty his funeral will be attended by fellow officers is a bleak one, but a grim satisfaction for Frank nevertheless (215).

Twospot, however, is only the most dramatic display of Hastings' ability to relate to and join with others. In all of the other books his co-workers perform as much more than background. Several of them have faces that are recognizable over the period: there is the worn and angry Culligan, whose tense face reflects his bitterness toward the public and its lawless behavior; and Markham, Frank's co-Sergeant in *The Lonely Hunter,* who will rise as fast as his demanding ego and polished shoes will take him. Krieger, the man who brought Hastings into the police, is something of a godfather for Frank, but he is killed in the line of duty between novels. Following him as Chief is Dwyer, the "Masked Man's" final target in *Doctor, Lawyer...* But aside from his rank he has no claim of loyalty or any shared past with Hastings. His direction of the Homicide office to date has been benign. He will allow his men to do their work with as little interference as possible, but he is also prepared to counsel or intervene in times of trouble.

There are two police characters, though, who help to define Hastings' character and reinforce the series as a police drama instead of another form of mystery. One of them is Lt. Pete Friedman, Hastings' supervisor in *The Lonely Hunter* and senior co-lieutenant since then. He is in many ways a balance for Hastings. Where Frank is tall and slender (about 6'1", 215 lbs.), Pete is obese. Weighing nearly 250, he claims that the only chair that will properly fit him is the visitor's chair in Frank's office. As a result Friedman visits every morning, elaborately unwrapping his first cigar, searching for matches and settling in before the daily discussion of pending cases can begin. At one time an aspiring actor in Hollywood, Friedman became a cop years before because the work was steady. Since then, however, he has found moral satisfaction in solving crimes and personal enjoyment from unravelling the puzzles they occasionally present. Sitting back in his favorite chair, eyes nearly closed as he works through the cases in his methodical yet curious ways, Pete reminds Frank of a pensive Buddha.

At the same time he proves himself to be a good cop and a worthy partner for Hastings, Friedman remains surprisingly cynical about the job. He insists to Frank at various times that while they have risen to their present eminence almost entirely on merit, they will go no higher. He has also suggested that Frank's success (and media attention) have both assisted Hastings' promotions and have hardened resistance at the top. For himself, Friedman says that aside from his weight (which he refuses to do anything about), he is stuck because of his religion ("I'm a Jew") and his ability ("I'm a smart Jew").

The two men are alike, however, in their dislike of political infighting. While battles over turf and the withholding of information for personal gain feed men like Jerry Markham, both Hastings and Friedman have a moral sense which makes it difficult to lie simply for the sake of expediency. Ironically, though, Pete is an artist at the use of policies and political conflict when they suit his ends in a larger cause. In a finely written scene in *Power Plays* (Ch. 16) Pete directly challenges the Feds and makes them back away from their assertion of rights over the case. Later, in both *Stalking Horse* and *Victims*, Frank wins by attacking privilege and promoting his place as the officer of the law. It is important to note, though, that such attempts to gain standing can have several ends. Sometimes they are used to identify and catch the criminal; at others they can be employed to gain leverage or power. Neither Hastings nor Friedman, however, wishes to retain such authority, and they are quick to relinquish it when the need no longer exists.

The third cop with major duties in the series is Hastings' driver and assistant, Inspector Canelli. He has never had a first name (Wilcox says he never really thought of it), but it never seems to matter. Canelli is the antithesis of both of his superiors in ways that make him the laughing-stock of the books and one of the most lovable cops around.

Canelli is described by Hastings in almost every book as "suety", a mass of body that comes perilously close to flabby and threatens to become a problem. He has none of Frank's athleticism, and seems incapable of losing weight. He has been engaged to the same woman for several years, and at twenty-eight may have forgotten that he should propose marriage. When driving he seems possessed by a demonic angel who repeatedly saves him and Hastings from collisions by inches and sheer good luck. An electrician before entering police work, he says that cars and people are complicated, but wiring is easy because it always works the same way.

On the job Cannelli is even more confusing. Hastings comments on his sensitivity, saying that he is "the only cop I'd ever known who could get his feelings hurt" (*Aftershock*, 16). On the telephone or at the scene of a crime, Canelli is as eager to please as a puppy. He apologizes to Frank for disturbing him, gives far more information than is needed, and discusses background data before Hastings knows the basics of the situation. Even in the office, he always knocks before entering Hastings' office.

In spite of his flaws, Canelli is a good cop. He is dogged, even when ordered to retreat. In *The Disappearance* he stays all night at a taxi company trying to discover which cab took the victim to her death. His singular success is partly attributable to the fact that he looks less like a cop than anyone else on the squad. "The entire homicide detail could be searching for a suspect while that same suspect was tapping Canelli on the shoulder, asking for a match," is the way Frank puts it once (*Hiding Place*, 7).

This last element is directly related to Canelli's unbelievable string of good luck. In *The Disappearance* Canelli stumbles on a stolen taxi as he leaves the company early in the morning. The operation Hastings mounts pays off with the capture of the killer. In other books Canelli almost literally steps on vital information: a weapon, an inadvertent question, or a person he finds makes the difference in quickly ending the cases. In his guileless innocence Canelli allows his superiors to take advantage of those who take advantage of him.

What emerges from analysis of the work of Collin Wilcox, then, is a realistic portrait of a policeman. The books do not dwell on the intricate work of laboratories, or the drudgery of the routines, though these are part of the job. Instead they concentrate on the hero, his personal life, and his interactions. Frank Hastings is neither a saint nor a hero in the traditional mold of detectives. He is not creative, leaving much of the thinking to Pete Friedman. He does not have inspired insights, tending to work things out carefully and through his self-knowledge and subsequent awareness of other people.

At the same time, he does not spend all of his time on the job. His past life, which has had believable problems and a personal redemption, influences his present behavior. In the same way, his current happiness with Ann Haywood has a direct effect on his stressful job.

Finally, his co-workers have made the books more than the story of a single cop's success. Canelli and Friedman, with the others, expose the inner workings of police work in its demands that people cooperate. In watching Hastings we can understand what a good policeman is made of, and how he makes the everyday quiet of our lives possible.

Notes

[1]The following are the novels of Collin Wilcox featuring Frank Hastings:
1969 *The Lonely Hunter* (Random House)
1970 *The Disappearance* (Random House)
1971 *Dead Aim* (Random House)
1973 *Hiding Place* (Random House)
1974 *Long Way Down* (Random House)
1975 *Aftershock* (Random House)
1977 *Doctor, Lawyer,...* (Random House)
1978 *Twospot* (with Bill Pronzini) (Putnam)
1978 *The Watcher* (Random House)
1979 *Power Plays* (Random House)
1980 *Mankiller* (Random House)
1981 *Stalking Horse* (Random House)
1985 *Victims* (Mysterious Press)

Tony Hillerman's Joe Leaphorn
and Jim Chee

Jane S. Bakerman

In his excellent novels featuring Joe Leaphorn and Jim Chee, members of the Navajo police force, Tony Hillerman[1] addresses the problems common to fictional law enforcement officers, thereby enhancing the realistic tone and intense impact of each plot. As scholars,[2] sociologists, television dramas, and police procedural novels have all taught us, the lot of the police officer is hard, lonely, and taxing; his life itself is sometimes endangered, and he frequently works in an atmosphere of tension and distrust. Conflicts and jealousies between various law enforcement agencies, whose jurisdictions sometimes overlap or whose goals sometimes seem to be at odds with one another, engender further complication. Officers' keen awareness of the prevalence of lawlessness, their periodic resentment of the laws designed to protect the rights of the criminal, and their inability to gain final victory over crime (despite triumphs over individual criminals) are also intensely unsettling as is the public's frequently expressed, widely felt distrust of the police force. Any of these factors is debilitating; taken together, they can create an attitude of cynicism or despair keen enough to threaten the integrity and commitment of all but the strongest individual dedicated to preserving the peace.

Several—if not all—of these complications appear in each Leaphorn and Chee novel to date, as even a few examples illustrate. In the course of two of his investigations, Leaphorn is subjected to extreme violence; he is shot with a hypodermic dart designed for stunning animals in *Dance Hall of the Dead* (1973, winner of the Mystery Writers of America Edgar Allan Poe Award for best novel), and almost burned then buried alive in *Listening Woman* (1978), displaying great heroism in the face of both attacks. In *The Blessing Way* (1970), Leaphorn must not only conceal many of the true facts of his case but also must persuade a good friend to keep silent because the jurisdiction of military intelligence prevails over that of his own agency. Similarly, Jim Chee destroys evidence in *The Dark Wind* (1982) because he distrusts (for good reason) federal agents on the scene, and in *People of Darkness* (1980), he refuses to be warned off a case by the local sheriff.

Indeed, Leaphorn and Chee struggle with problems of jurisdiction that increase exponentially. The territory they cover overlaps New Mexico, Arizona, and Utah as well as several Amerindian reservations and "checkerboarded" areas granted to the Atlantic and Pacific Railroad in the 1880s. Cases may, therefore, involve officers of various tribal police forces, state or city police, county sheriffs' patrols, the F.B.I., or drug enforcement agencies. Furthermore, a suspect's race may also complicate the question of jurisdiction (*People*, 22-23).

Both officers are well aware of the laws of evidence, and both take steps to overcome what they perceive as the limitations of those laws. Leaphorn, realizing that a perpetrator is beyond the reach of civil authority, takes steps to see that justice is nevertheless served (*Dance*). Chee, in like fashion, pays attention to testimony which would be laughed out of any city, state, or federal court, and, as a result, is able to solve two crimes, one current, one hidden deep in the past (*People*).

All of these complications serve Hillerman and his plots very well— as they serve other writers of police procedurals. The frequent danger as well as the extreme violence to which Leaphorn and Chee are exposed enhance characterization by revealing their bravery and resourceful-ness, and the officers' willingness to circumvent the law in order to serve it indicates plainly that they are neither defeated nor wholly limited by the legal system. By thinking and acting independently and honorably, they demonstrate that despite moments of cynicism, they are far from despairing.

Like many of their urban colleagues both real and fictional, Leaphorn and Chee interact with people whose backgrounds vary widely. Because the novels are set in Arizona and New Mexico, on and around Navajo, Hopi, and Zuni reservations, racial, social, political, and geographical circumstances require that these officers not only come to terms with the dominant Anglo culture but also deal effectively with a host of other Native American and Hispanic cultures and peoples. This situation results in a superabundance of paperwork, that ubiquitous complaint in police procedurals, which thrives especially well in the multi-ethnic society in which Leaphorn and Chee function, and in this fashion, as with the jurisdictional tangles, the setting underscores the social commentary and the realism of detail.

Social commentary is indeed a key factor in these novels because for Hillerman's protagonists, the problems shared by all fictional law enforcement agents are exacerbated by the fact that both Leaphorn and Chee are Navajos, members of a minority group. They contend daily with the racist thinking of others and also strive to avoid engaging in it themselves. Joe Leaphorn, for instance, is well aware that he distrusts Zunis because he believes they feel superior to Navajos, but he overcomes his bias when honor and justice require him to do so (*Dance*), and once, in a bitterly ironic twist, Chee's life is saved because an Anglo murderer mistakes a Chicano for the Navajo cop (*People*).

A tense, uneasy interview between Jim Chee and Sheriff LAWrence Sena reverberates with racial overtones. Sheriff Sena spells his given name as he does in an unsuccessful attempt to override the "insulting" nickname, "Gordo," which has followed him throughout his career (*People*, 18). To him, Chee, a young, eager officer presently inquiring about an old crime and a new puzzle involving Sena's long-term enemy, represents not only another agency but also another generation, most importantly another race. Though both cases Chee and Sena discuss involve Navajos, the earlier one also involves an Hispanic—and Sena wants Chee out of his political, racial and personal territories; he simply doesn't trust him, and he resents him (18-24).

The setting of the Leaphorn-Chee novels (particularly the vastness of the territory the officers must cover) interacts with the problems of jurisdiction and the multi-ethnic backgrounds of the various characters to establish an important difference between these plots and those of most police procedurals. Generally, Leaphorn and Chee work alone rather than as members of a close-knit team of investigators; neither has a regular partner. Though each officer does once (to date) work closely with another investigator—Leaphorn's old friend Bergen McKee, a temporary amateur sleuth, is actually more involved in the central action of *The Blessing Way* than is Leaphorn himself, and Jim Chee's Hopi friend, Cowboy Dashee, conducts a parallel, usually cooperative, investigation in *The Dark Wind*—the Navajo policemen are far more apt to have companions (who often require help, protection or rescue) in their adventures rather than colleagues. This pattern is apparent in *Dance Hall of the Dead*, *Listening Woman,* and *People of Darkness* and affects readers' perceptions of Hillerman's protagonists markedly. Their caretaking attitude toward their companions demonstrates Leaphorn's and Chee's empathy and their willingness to assume personal as well as professional responsibility. But the fact that they must often work in isolation, amidst an alien culture, without the support of other officers elevates the quality of heroism Hillerman assigns to his Amerindian central characters, especially in the case of Leaphorn who undergoes horrific trials of courage and endurance in *Dance Hall of the Dead* and *Listening Woman.*

Yet a further complication arises from the Navajo policemen's racial identity. Even though they work for their own people's law enforcement agency, they must also, of course, uphold and enforce the laws of county, state, and federal governments, so their sense of themselves as Navajos could readily be undermined in the course of fulfilling their duties, and this factor intensifies the problems of self-concept common among lawmen. On the one hand, police officers know they are performing an important public service; on the other, they realize, as has been mentioned, that many citizens resent their best efforts even as they need and *want* those efforts. Any officer may find himself upholding laws he believes to be silly, stupid, useless, unfair, or downright disruptive and doing so in the face of tacit public disapproval or open disdain. Far too often, Leaphorn and Chee find themselves upholding such laws (the legislation enabling checkerboarding, for example) which have been imposed upon their own people by outside agencies, laws which have little to do with—or frequently conflict with—Navajo sensibility, tradition, belief, or culture. Thus, just as they are constantly exposed to racist behavior, they are constantly exposed to the threat of violating their most personal identity, their unity with the People.

This threat seems to be rather less of a problem to Joe Leaphorn, though Hillerman notes at one point that almost all of the lieutenant's professional decisions are colored by his concern for the People (*Dance,* 108). Leaphorn is, however, keenly aware that his race can persuade the unwary Navajo witness to say, perhaps, too much, and at one point, when interrogating a child, he backs off from this advantage, refusing to exploit either his own identity or the vulnerability of his young witness. In fact, he even goes so far as to remind the lad that he will have to share information with Zuni investigators and so reaffirms not only his loyalty to a fellow Navajo but also his compassion for the suffering (*Dance,* 18).

Possibly Leaphorn seems somewhat less threatened with the loss of his racial identity simply because readers know relatively little about him: he is married; he has children, and he retains at least one friendship from his undergraduate days at Arizona State—but beyond that, few details of his biography are clear. Still, one prime factor in his family background (a Navajo's most important means of identifying himself) may also explain why Joe Leaphorn carries few grudges and bears the burden of his dual roles—as lawman and as private, *Navajo* citizen— with grace and poise.

Reared according to custom in the heart of his mother's clan, Leaphorn was nurtured by his grandfather, Hosteen Nashibitti, a ritual singer revered by the Navajo for his skill, wisdom and understanding. Singularly untouched by the anger and resentment which defined the thinking of many of his peers and which resulted from generations of betrayal by whites and other Amerindian peoples, Nashibitti seems to have concentrated on the original teachings of the Navajo rather than on the lessons of political exploitation. Accordingly, his instruction of the young Leaphorn centered on beauty as humankind's only proper "goal" and emphasized beauty's only source, the intricate harmony of nature (*Dance*, 51-52). Like his grandfather, Joe Leaphorn also seems to have learned little bitterness. Hardly a dreamer, never a fool, he recognizes the complexities of coping with a multi-ethnic society and does cope, just as he avoids exploiting and thereby violating his identity as a Navajo.

Though he is a good bit younger than Leaphorn, Jim Chee shares a common background with him, being also the product of traditional Navaho upbringing among his mother's people, of reservation schools, and of a state university, the University of New Mexico. But when readers first meet Jim Chee, he is at a major crossroads of his life, one of many similar decision-points which will, apparently, turn up again and again as they have in the past.

Like Leaphorn, Jim Chee comes from a family of singers, most notable among them, perhaps, his mentor Hosteen Frank Sam Nakai, "who performed the Night Chant and the Enemy Way and key parts of several other curing ceremonials" (*People*, 61), but unlike Leaphorn, Chee himself was early recognized as a potential singer. Despite his family's interest in developing Chee's talent, however, Hosteen Nakai initially refused to teach him until the youngster had undertaken an important task: he insisted that Jim first "understand the white man" by studying Anglo habits and values in order to make an informed, conscious choice between white and Navajo life styles (*People*, 62). Eventually, Jim Chee, having studied the white man's way, opted to become a singer, a man who will perform an important service to the People.

In *People of Darkness*, Chee is deciding yet again whether or not to follow the white man's way, in this case, whether or not to attend the F.B.I academy to which he has been accepted. Already well aware of the difficulty of preserving his integrity as a Navajo while doing police work, Chee is even more keenly aware that he would no longer *be* a Navajo in the East: "you couldn't be both a Navajo and an F.B.I. agent.

You couldn't be a Navajo away from the People" (78). Readers share most of Chee's thoughts as he struggles with this decision, as he thinks of leaving Dinetah even while practicing his chants, and this process dramatizes very effectively the tension both Leaphorn and Chee feel, leaving readers with a sense of knowing Jim Chee quite well, at least during the action of *People of Darkness*. Though in *The Dark Wind*, Hillerman does not refer either to Chee's decision about the F.B.I. or to his relationship with an Anglo woman in *People of Darkness*, we see Chee working at his initial job and assume he has chosen to remain with the People, remain, in effect, a Navajo. This omission diminishes the intimacy readers felt with Chee during his first adventure, but the assumption that he is indeed in his proper place intensifies the importance of his heritage to the tone and thrust of the plot and deepens his characterization.

Other elements of characterization are also enriched by Hillerman's mastery of his protagonists' background which, for example, lends a different dimension to the familiar concept that the lawman upholds public law but often also follows a special code of ethics. Certainly their Navajo code informs their thinking about conventional legal justice and occasionally frees them to take the law into their own hands.

When a parcel of land is arbitrarily transferred from Navajo to Hopi control, for instance, Jim Chee keeps his peace about the propriety of the change in ownership, but his sensitivity to his own faith makes him responsive to a Hopi's dedication to a nearby shrine endangered by the windmill which has been built on the reassigned property (*Dark*, 141). In return for the Hopi's cooperation in his investigation, Chee, extralegally but properly, finds a way to protect the shrine—the windmill is only a white man's device; the shrine, like Chee's own chants and charms, belongs to the area.

When he decides to pursue his first case, Chee also acts extralegally, infringing, as we have noted earlier, on the jurisdiction of another agency. But in this instance also, it is his personal code, his identity as a Navajo, which gives him the insight and the will to do so. A member of a dead man's family, a Navajo like Chee himself, explains that a witch has stolen the corpse from a New Mexico cancer research center. Chee knows that no functionary at Albuquerque's police headquarters would give an instant of serious attention to such a complaint, and that many might not even bother to be courteous to the complainant who, conditioned by a lifetime of racial and religious discrimination, would not press his case (*People*, 71). Angered that the system should thus have denied Tomas Charley's personhood and dignity as well as the validity of Navajo belief, Chee does pay attention and solves the case. By doing so, he obeys his uncle's precepts and also becomes—as Hillerman fully intends—the paradigm for a modern American operating independently but sensitively in a multi-ethnic culture.

Just as their Navajo heritage affects Leaphorn's and Chee's motivations, so it also colors their professional methodology, further enhancing their characterizations. Both men are expert trackers, and Hillerman makes clear that their skill results from tutelage by older members of their families. At the outset of a deadly chase, for instance, Chee recalls specifics of his training, controlling his impatience for the hunt by reviewing portions of the Stalking Way:

> *I am the Black God, arising with twilight,*
> *   a part of the twilight.*
> *Out from the West, out from the Darkness*
> *   Mountain, a buck of dark flint stands*
> *   out before me.*
> *The best male game of darkness, it calls to*
> *   me, it hears my voice calling.*
> *Our calls become one in beauty.*
> *   Our prayers become one in beauty.*
> *As I, the Black God, go toward it.*
> *   As the male game of darkness comes*
> *   toward me.*
> *With beauty before us, we come together.*
> *   With beauty behind us, we come together.*
> *That my arrow may free its sacred breath.*
> *   That my arrow may bring its death in*
> *   beauty.*

When the song has replayed itself in his mind, Chee is fully prepared for the confrontation (*People*, 180-181).

For Leaphorn, solving a case is a matter of discovering the underlying pattern; to do so, he remembers the words of his grandfather:

'When the dung beetle moves,' Hosteen Nashibitti had told him, 'know that something has moved it. And know that its movement affects the flight of the sparrow, and that the raven deflects the eagle from the sky, and that the eagle's stiff wing affects you and me, and the flea on the prairie dog and the leaf on the cottonwood.' That had always been the point of the lesson. Interdependency of nature. Every cause has its effect. Every action its reaction. A reason for everything. In all things a pattern, and in this pattern, the beauty of harmony. Thus one learned to live with evil, by understanding it, by reading its cause. And thus one learned, gradually and methodically, if one was lucky, to always 'go in beauty,' to always look for the pattern, and to find it (*Dance*, 52).

Invariably, in solving his cases, Leaphorn looks for a pattern of behavior—why does the perpetrator behave as he does? How has the harmony of spirit and of the social order been disarranged? Generally, the "how" reveals both the "why" and the identity of the perpetrator so that beauty can be restored. According to the thinking of Leaphorn and Chee, criminals operate against the harmony of nature as well as against that of the social order; ascertaining the true pattern of original harmony and the counter-pattern of evil becomes thereby a method of operation as well as a metaphor for interpreting ordinary clues. Clearly, though the Navajo policemen's relatives have yet to appear actively in their adventures, their family heritage plays a key role in each plot. This treatment of jnfluence rings a change in one important structural element of the police procedural.

Their ethnicity, then, informs the characterizations of Joe Leaphorn and Jim Chee at every turn. Hillerman himself is keenly aware of the centrality of Native American belief and custom to the Leaphorn and Chee series, and he has commented about the attention he pays to this motif:

To play the game as it should be played, I think the setting must be genuine—the reader must be shown the Indian reservation as it is today. More important, my Navajo tribal policeman's knowledge of his people, their customs, and their values must be germane to the plot. More than that, the details must be exactly accurate—from the way a hogan is built, to the way a sweat bath is taken, to the way it looks, and sounds, and smells at an Enemy Way Ceremonial at 2:00 A.M. on a wintry morning.[3]

In his examinations of cultures which exist within the umbrella culture so casually dubbed "American," Hillerman is following the advice and methodology of a noteworthy predecessor, Ross Macdonald, who believed that the good social critic has to understand at least two cultures in order to comment wisely. Macdonald also pointed out that conflict between cultures often results in criminal behavior:

"Most people in trouble are people caught between two...gradations [cultures], and in order to explain what the trouble is, you have to define both sides of the pincers, so to speak."[4]

Here, too, Hillerman follows Macdonald's strictures, for his novels are filled with characters caught between two gradations of culture, people in danger of losing their identities—or dangerous people who have already lost or abandoned them.

Like all police officers, the Navajo lawmen are hunters (and for these skilled observer-trackers, that metaphor is particularly apt). In pursuing their prey, the villains caught in "the pincers," they seek to restore beauty—harmony—to mend the social fabric, again like their colleagues in other branches of law enforcement. But perhaps because of their awareness of the difficulty of maintaining one's balance within this nation's social structure, and certainly because of their conscious efforts to find and understand both the harmonious and the disruptive patterns in social behavior, Leaphorn and Chee seem less prone to the bitterness and vengefulness of some contemporary heroes of popular culture (filmdom's Dirty Harry comes immediately to mind). Hillerman's Navajo officers seem able to hate the sin but to understand the sinner even as they exorcise him.

It follows then, that one of the most important elements in the Leaphorn and Chee series is the organizational pattern which undergirds each exciting plot and which grows out of the central characters' efforts to understand the patterns. Invariably, Hillerman compares and contrasts his protagonists, successful at balancing their racial identities against the pressures of other cultures, with characters who do not know who they are or who have redefined themselves in ways which violate their tribal codes. Some of these characters are bewildered, questing for identity and definition; others are lost, intent upon evil ways; the first group are portrayed sympathetically; the latter are depicted with insight but without sentimentality. Hillerman's ability to convey sympathy and understanding without descending into maudlin philosophizing or sociological invective lends impact to his social commentary and keeps the vigorous action of his plots dominant in readers' minds.

Several of Hillerman's characters in crisis are also companions who accompany the protagonists during their investigations. All are men and women who have lost their identities and who cannot—at least temporarily—cope with either their own or the dominant culture. One of the most appealing of these figures is Susanne, an adolescent who has fled her home, sought refuge in a commune only to learn that it is a cover for drug-smuggling, then discovered that her lover values upward mobility more than her safety or their love (*Dance*). In the course of Leaphorn's investigation, Susanne observes him closely, absorbing, readers hope, something of his strength. Capable of bravery and loyalty, aware that she must function alone in a confusing, dangerous world, Susanne leaves the reservation still a wanderer, uncertain of her destination. With Susanne as with most of his characters, Tony Hillerman indicates that there are no easy answers, that one cannot simply assume an identity as one slips into a new blouse, but that the groundwork for self-definition should be inculcated early so that the individual can hone and refine it throughout his life.

Hillerman extends his pattern of comparison and contrast a bit further in *Dance Hall of the Dead* by comparing and contrasting Susanne with George Bowlegs, suspect and fugitive. Because George's best friend has been murdered and because he fears that George may also be endangered, Leaphorn searches for the boy, gradually discovering George's personality and interests as he investigates. What emerges is a moving portrait of another child who does not know who he is but who, like Susanne, undertakes desperate measures to acquire a workable identity. Deprived of the guidance of his mother's people, George, a Navajo, has made do, caring as well as he can for his alcoholic father and his younger brother—and seeking the light. Not well versed in the Navajo Way, George has explored Roman Catholicism but finally determined that he will become a Zuni. The impossibility of this "conversion" seems not to have registered with George Bowlegs, to whom a sustaining faith means everything; especially, it means he will know who he is, how he should behave, what he should believe.

Through his characterizations of Susanne and of George Bowlegs, Hillerman makes some of his most pointed social criticism as Leaphorn reflects that neither George's father, a Navajo, nor Susanne's, an Anglo, has nurtured his child effectively. Neither has established rules or ethics which his child finds useful; neither has enabled his offspring to formulate a serviceable identity. Susanne is a victim of a failed family and of the generation gap; George is a victim of a failed family and the void within which many deracinated Native Americans live. Though both youngsters try hard to define themselves, George is given too little time to do so, and Susanne departs strengthened but still uncertain of herself and her goals. This indictment of familial failure and its high cost to the young puts Hillerman firmly in the company of many fine contemporary American crime writers, perhaps most notably Ross Macdonald, Robert B. Parker, Joseph Hansen, and Jonathan Valin, whose novels about tough urban private investigators tend to explore this theme rather more frequently and in more detail than do most police procedurals.

George Bowlegs' preoccupation with religion is an interest shared by many of Hillerman's characters in crisis. Tomas Charley (*People*), for instance, is another whose faith exiles him even as, apparently, it sustains him. A man of mixed Navajo and Acoma blood, Charley is a member of the Peyote Church, a cult frowned upon by Navajo and Anglo alike. Aware that the customs of both his mother's and his father's people conflict within him, Charley also believes that a witch is decimating his church—but because of his mixed blood, because of his religious practices, and because of racism, there is no supportive social structure to which he can really appeal. He is a man trapped within a multitude of conflicting cultural pressures.

Benjamin Tso, member of the Order of Friars Minor, is a Navajo who has chosen the white man's way and for many years, apparently, has found peace and identity as a Franciscan (*Woman*). A relatively minor but pivotal character, Tso contrasts with Leaphorn and with the antagonist. When Leaphorn meets him, Tso has retreated to the reservation in an attempt to sort out his beliefs, his commitments, and his identity, for he has fallen in love with a possessive woman incapable of understanding his obligations or his torment. Ultimately Ben Tso takes extreme measures to "save himself," as Leaphorn puts it (200), and in doing so saves others. His story is a vivid reminder that in the Leaphorn-Chee world, no answer is definitive; the quest for self is unending; the struggle to balance one culture and one obligation against another is constant.

When we meet them, these questors are persons without functional identities, people who agonize (but with considerable dignity) over their roles, caught as they are between cultures. They are not, however, evildoers; their intentions are uniformly decent, and they are sympathetic characters with whom many readers identify. The extreme difficulty— or failure—of their attempts at self-definition emphasizes Hillerman's social criticism, strengthens the novels' realistic tone, and enhances the characterizations of Joe Leaphorn and Jim Chee, who are capable of retaining their poise and identities in the face of almost overwhelming cultural pressure.

Still other characters, the villains, have ceased agonizing and have invented deadly new personal identities which are informed by neither familial nurture nor cultural training and which free the villains to serve their own ends, to behave wickedly, even murderously. According to Hillerman's symbolism, these destructors are Navajo Wolves. By denying their true identities, they deny their own humanity, and in the plots, they function not only as generators of action but also as the chief elements of comparison and contrast with Leaphorn and Chee.

Throughout each of Hillerman's novels to date, there is talk of Navajo Wolves; other terms for them are "witches" and "skinwalkers."[5] These people are genuinely evil, and Jim Chee explains that witches invert the concept of beauty, spreading "sickness" or disorder instead of seeking harmony. Possessors of magic powers, skinwalkers need little or no motive beyond the inherent wickedness of their acts (*People*, 139). In one fashion or another, each murderer Leaphorn and Chee confront is a metaphorical Navajo Wolf; each has forgone beauty and harmony in favor of ugliness and discord. Each has abandoned any attempt at balance within his birth-culture or between the cultures active in his environment in favor of exploiting society and any individual who gets in his way.

Although all the murderers are Navajo Wolves, all are not Navajos. Some are Anglos. In an important passage in *People of Darkness*, Jim Chee and a young woman introduce themselves to each other. She, an Anglo, defines herself by what she does (75-80). Here Hillerman suggests that many Americans of European descent base their identities upon their roles as workers; fellow-workers are, in a sense, then, their tribes. In *Listening Woman* and *People of Darkness*, Hillerman depicts villains who violate professional codes (thus abdicating tribal as well as personal identity) for gain. One abandons name, family, and profession to pursue riches and wreak havoc upon almost everyone whose life he influences. The other uses his professional skills to formulate an intricate lie designed to misdirect North American cultural history—and to corrupt another man—in order to gain esteem. In keeping with the traditions of crime fiction, these Anglos, like their Amerindian fellow destructors, begin with a motive, but like Navajo Wolves, most also descend to doing evil for evil's sake, all sense of proportion disappearing.

People of Darkness, is an inverted mystery in which the murderer is literally a man without identity. Abandoned by his mother when only a child, Colton Wolf has never been nurtured; he has no roots, and his desperate search for his mother and his heritage is unsuccessful—and far too tardy. The prototypical Navajo Wolf in the canon, Colton Wolf is dehumanized, a killing machine, and his extended contest with Jim Chee, his pursuer, is one of Hillerman's most obvious and successful studies in comparison and contrast, neatly uniting that motif with the nurture/failure-to-nurture theme.

Colton Wolf is a Navajo Wolf because he has no identity except evil. A hired assassin, he is, in effect, one "illness" his employer, another Navajo Wolf, inflicts upon others. According to Hillerman and Jim Chee (*People*, 188), the way to restore harmony is to turn the Wolf's magic against himself, and in the bloody climax of *People of Darkness*, this is exactly what happens. Indeed, the Navajo Wolf's magic works against him in each novel through a smooth blend of realistic circumstance and careful, honorable attention to the concept of the skinwalker, yet another example of Hillerman's regard for his subject matter and of his authorial skill.

All of the Navajo Wolves are vicious; some, like Colton Wolf and two of the Amerindian Wolves, are also pitiable. Neither Hillerman, his protagonists, nor readers excuse these criminals, but because of Leaphorn's and Chee's capacity for introspection and because of the careful search for the pattern which readers share with the detectives, these villains are understandable. Having abandoned beauty, they live in ugliness, wickedness, and destruction. And generally, their deeds and attitudes reflect the flaws in the cultures they have rejected—and which rejected or exploited them. In these characters, Hillerman joins the Navajo Wolf motif to his examination of racism in contemporary America, firmly uniting action, theme, and social criticism.

Just as Colton Wolf is Jim Chee's opposite number among the ranks of criminals, so Goldrims, a Navajo who appears in *Listening Woman,* may be considered the character who contrasts most obviously with Joe Leaphorn. Like Leaphorn, Goldrims functions in both the Anglo and the Amerindian cultures, but his goals are antithetical to the lawman's. Playing upon the pain, bitterness and anger felt by many native Americans (and venting his own), he is active in a quasi-religious, quasi-political underground, the Buffalo Society, "as militant as they get" (23), whose goal is to punish Anglos for past crimes against Native Americans. The movement is funded by a brilliantly planned and executed series of crimes, and the kidnapping which generates the action of *Listening Woman* is also presumably a means of serving the cause.

But irony informs this characterization as it does many others in the Hillerman canon, and Goldrims is a true Navajo Wolf, who "turned from harmony to chaos" (66). He has no loyalty. Scornful of Anglo culture, perfectly willing to violate an area profoundly sacred to the Navajo, willing to sacrifice his own relatives, Goldrims is also exploiting the Buffalo Society and its members for his own gain. Wholly evil, he is a powerful symbol of the modern American caught between cultures, both of which have failed him, both of which he fails because he is strong enough to strike out in fury and destructiveness, yet too weak to avoid bitterness.

The element of sacrilege in Goldrims' scheme also appears in other plots. One Navajo Wolf disguises himself as a Salamobia and violates sacred rites of the Zuni (*Dance*); another turns treasured amulets into weapons (*People*); a third intrudes into a secret Hopi ritual to cover a murder plot (*Dark*). Obviously, these descretions contribute to the suspense of Hillerman's excellent plots. Furthermore, the Navajo Wolves contrast not only with the protagonists but also with other characters who revere their heritage, yet again serving Hillerman's useful organizational pattern. Most importantly, however, these plot complications show readers various Amerindian peoples' structures of belief and social order functioning and enduring despite the incursions of outsiders, the corruption of insiders. Thus, Hillerman teaches members of the dominant culture a good deal about several minority cultures, but he avoids pedantry, opting instead for fully dramatized scenes, fully realized characterizations.

By comparing and contrasting Joe Leaphorn and Jim Chee with sympathetic characters, questors caught in a crisis of identity and spirit, and with Navajo Wolves, people who have abandoned all spiritual concern, Hillerman enhances the stature of his protagonists and intensifies the impact of his police procedurals. By extending the organizational pattern of comparison and contrast to include other pairs of characters, the author suggests very effectively that in a multi-ethnic society, each individual must define his identity carefully, guard it closely. To lose it is to surrender a vital link with one's ethnic culture and to diminish or to relinquish one's ability to function healthfully in the dominant culture. To deny the power of self-definition to another person or culture is sheer wickedness—Navajo Wolfishness—whether practiced by an individual, by a social institution, or by one culture toward another. These are Hillerman's messages. They are not new, but they are important. And because they are presented in skillfully crafted novels by means of exciting plots and fully realized characterizations, they are effective.

The exploits of Joe Leaphorn and Jim Chee, courageous, enduring, decent men, offer readers armchair danger, adventure, and heroism. But because Hillerman's characters reflect the truth of the human heart and because his social criticism speaks directly and forcefully to the problems of modern American society, his novels not only entertain us, but they also make us think and feel. The Leaphorn-Chee adventures are escapist fiction in the highest sense of that term: though they provide relief from the daily routines of most readers, they also heighten our awareness, enriching as they entertain.

Notes

[1]The editions of Hillerman's novels in which Joe Leaphorn or Jim Chee appears and which are cited in this essay are listed below, preceded by the original date of publication. All quotations will be cited in the text, using where necessary for clarity, the abbreviations given after the entry:

1970   The Blessing Way (New York: Harper & Row, 1970). (Blessing)
1973   Dance Hall of the Dead (New York: Harper & Row, 1973). (Dance)
1978   Listening Woman (New York: Harper & Row, 1978). (Woman)
1980   People of Darkness (New York: Harper & Row, 1980). (People)
1982   The Dark Wind (New York: Avon, 1983). (Dark)

[2]For a detailed, useful discussion of the attitudes, strengths, weaknesses and problems of the fictional policeman, see George N. Dove, The Police Procedural (Bowling Green, OH: The Popular Press, 1982).

[3]Carol Cleveland, "Tony Hillerman," in Twentieth Century Crime and Mystery Writers, ed. John M. Reilly (New York: St. Martin's, 1980), pp. 774-775. Dr. Cleveland's discussion of the Leaphorn novels is cogent and useful. Other sources include Ellen Strenski and Robley Evans, "Ritual and Murder in Tony Hillerman's Indian Detective Novels," Western American Literature, 16 (Fall 1981), 205-216; and Bruce Taylor's interview with Tony Hillerman, The Armchair Detective, 14 (Winter 1981), 93ff.

[4]Jane S. Bakerman, "A Slightly Stylized Conversation with Ross Macdonald," Writer's Yearbook 1981, 52 (1981), 111.

[5]Hillerman's definitions of the Navajo Wolf are used for this paper; scholarly discussions of the Wolves include Clyde Kluckhohn, Navaho Witchcraft (Boston: Beacon Press, 1944); Clyde Kluckhohn and Dorothea Leighton, The Navaho (Garden City, NY: Anchor, 1962); and William Morgan, "Human Wolves Among the Navaho," Yale University Publications in Anthropology, Numbers Eight to Thirteen (New Haven: Human Relations Area Files Press, 1970), No. 11.

Constables

Edited by
Earl F. Bargainnier

Henry Wade's John Poole

Leah A. Strong

In one of Henry Wade's novels the arrival of a Scotland Yard detective is imminent. The local officials are, of course, apprehensive, and the Chief Constable has been "conjuring up imaginary pictures of the C.I.D. detective. Tradition allowed a variety of types: the 'ferret'; the 'bull-dog'; the 'paternal'; the 'muddle-headed idiot'—..."[1] Presumably in the novels in which Inspector John Poole appears, local authorities are also waiting with similar concern and speculation. Their emotions are, undoubtedly, mixed as they resent the intrusion into their world of the outside expert, while at least some of them recognize the advisability of having assistance. But still there must be the question, "Will he be a muddle-headed idiot?"

Their first look at John Poole shows them a gentleman who is five feet, ten inches tall, with straight hips, a small waist, the broad shoulders of an athlete, quietly firm mouth, and grey eyes. Gradually, his poise, his ability at this job, and his courtesy and respect allay their apprehensions. Never in his cases does he have any serious difficulty caused by resentment or resistance. In his younger years, Poole could even win the "locals" over to the point of their feeling paternal toward him and wanting this fine young man to succeed, rather than feeling resentment at his role in the case.

The creator of Inspector Poole, Henry Wade, a pseudonym of Henry Lancelot Aubrey-Fletcher, 6th Baronet, was well aware of the awkwardness of the relationship between local police and C.I.D. men. After graduating from Oxford, he served in the Grenadier Guards, 1908-1920 and 1940-1945. More relevant to his novels was his participation in local government in Buckinghamshire. He served as Justice of the Peace and County Alderman for Buckinghamshire, becoming High Sheriff in 1925. This background gave him the varied experiences which intensify the realism of his portrayal of policemen, rural and metropolitan, their procedures, and their relationships as they work together. His novels include rural policemen whose entire careers are spent in one local area, as well as metropolitan policemen who do or do not succeed in being assigned to the C.I.D. and then moving up in rank.

Throughout all his novels and short stories, Wade seems to be interested primarily in plot, a mystery to be solved. Police procedures, fortuitous occurrences, and/or discoveries (luck), thinking, analyzing, planning—all these contribute to the central purpose of a Wade tale, that being the telling of a story, the unraveling of a plot.

Ideas about society, the law, or taxation contribute primarily to the atmosphere of suspense and reality. Any messages, whether about the nature of man or the injustices of taxation are genuine, but of secondary importance to the tale being told. Whether a crime is solved by the policeman's skill, by a chance event (a book falls to the floor with the fly leaf giving Poole the essential clue in *Gold Was Our Grave*), by the thinking that puts the pieces of evidence into a pattern, or by straight police procedures leading to a solution, Wade is primarily holding the reader by means of suspense. His mysteries are to be read because the reader wants to know what will happen next, and, of course, who did what.

In the Poole novels, nevertheless, Wade also creates an interesting person whose career is covered through several decades. Even though Wade, perhaps unfortunately, does tell the reader more about Poole than the action of the novels illustrates, the reader does come to view him as a person.

John Poole is first introduced in 1929 in *The Duke of York's Steps*.[2] At that point in his career, he has recently been promoted to the rank of Inspector, recommended ("put up") by Sir Leward Marradine, Assistant Commissioner, in charge of the Criminal Investigation Department of Scotland Yard, who had become aware of his abilities in an earlier case. Marradine, a soldier without previous police experience, apparently, like his creator, Wade, recognizes the value of the combination of educational background and police experience.

Poole is not the typical policeman of his day. His father is Dr. Ned Poole, a graduate of King's College, a country doctor with a practice that has made him financially very comfortable. Dr. Poole had been disappointed when his son showed no interest in a medical career. Above-average intellectually (even above the family average), young John was sent to one of the smaller public schools (never named in the novels) and then to St. James College, Oxford University. (In one of the short stories, "The Missing Undergraduate," the college is identified as St. Peter's.) His father had decided that his son's study should be directed toward a career at the Bar, second best, apparently, in his opinion, but acceptable.

John's characteristics as a youth, in addition to his intellectual ability, made this career choice an extremely logical one. He was intelligent, expressed himself well, and was willing to work not only diligently, but even doggedly, toward a goal that was important to him.

As an undergraduate, he did work diligently, as had always been expected of him, but he also participated in assorted undergraduate activities. He developed an interest in theater, accepting a small part in *The Winter's Tale* for the Oxford University Dramatic Society; he found, however, that it took too much of his time and gave it up. More to his liking were political and debating societies. A major event leading to his ultimate choice of police work as a career came at one of these debating societies when the debate dealt with the handling of a well-known criminal trial. "...Poole, rising as a comparatively unknown member when the discussion had reached a stage of considerable confusion and imminent collapse had reviewed the evidence for the prosecution from so original a standpoint and with such logical precision that the 'jury' had returned an enthusiastic and overwhelming majority for the defense" (Duke, 65).

As a result of this effective presentation, Poole was elected to membership in the Criminologists Club, a distinguished organization to which old members often returned and spoke. There he met people involved in crime detection as well as those interested in the law itself. More and more, he became interested in police procedure, investigative techniques and, basically, in the solving of a crime and capturing the perpetrator even more than in the legal prosecution or the defense of the accused. One speaker, not a member, at a club event was the Chief Commissioner of the Metropolitan Police, and young Poole's career decision began to take a definite direction. At this stage he could still not envision abandoning the kind of legal career for which he had been preparing, and so he decided to be a private detective, and do legal work on the side. Thoughts about the Commissioner's remarks kept recurring to him; he also read books on police work. His final decision to become a policeman was based on this conclusion that "the powers and machinery of the official police gave them such an overwhelming advantage over the 'amateurs' that in the Force itself alone lay the prospects of really great achievement" (*Duke*, 66).

Setting his goals high, Poole becomes a man aware of his own abilities, neither humble nor conceited. He is capable of significant personal honesty in his self-evaluation. This attitude, or outlook, permeates his career choice, career goals, and everyday performance. He decides almost simultaneously with his decision to become a policeman that his ultimate goal is to become the Head of the Criminal Investigation Department of Scotland Yard.

Although current officials had often come into police work after a military career, Poole feels that army or navy training is not sufficient preparation for police administration. Nor does he feel that legal education alone is adequate background. Analyzing the current recruitment practices of the police also convinces him that policemen who have come up through the ranks do not necessarily have the qualifications for police leadership. His conclusion is that the best preparation must include a combination of educational background and practical experience. These two ingredients give the policeman the ability to fulfill his assignments, and from this successful accomplishment will come advancement. With his own willingness to work, his dogged determination, plus his intelligence—all those characteristics which his wise father had found in him when he was a youth—Poole then sets out to become his own ideal policeman.

The first step is to finish his formal education at Oxford, where he takes a Second Class in Law at the end of his third year, 1921. He is called to the Bar, secures a place in the chambers of a well-known criminal lawyer, Sir Edward Floodgate, and stays there for a year, gaining experience and increasing his legal knowledge. At age 23 he leaves the law chambers of Sir Edward and joins the Metropolitan Police as a recruit. He serves for fifteen months as a Constable in "C" division. The quality of his work is excellent; this is recognized, and he is then transferred to the Criminal Investigation Department of Scotland Yard. At age 27 he is promoted to Sergeant and is lucky enough to be involved in two noted cases where his service is as might be expected, superior. One of these cases, called the Curzon case, causes him to be noticed by the Assistant Commissioner, who recommends the Detective-Sergeant for accelerated promotion.

These early years of John Poole's life precede his introduction on page 61 of *The Duke of York's Steps,* but are presented to the reader in all of the Poole books in varying detail. While, for example, some of the details of his undergraduate years appear in one volume and different ones in another, the result is cumulative, a consistent, but everwidening view of the man Poole.

A picture, then, of the young John Poole develops which is, in many ways, relatively unremarkable. He is a young Englishman participating in the educational and social activities of his time and place, but with a genuine dedication for police work developing.

Always he is seen as, if not a typical, at least an ordinary sort of person. While he was making these serious career decisions as a young man, he was also living as any other undergraduate. He was interested in sports; his athletic accomplishments include his earning of two Blues, in boxing and rugger, playing cricket for his College, and serving as second string in the low hurdles. Both at Oxford and later as a young barrister, his social life includes some mild stage-door flirtations and other romantic events.

Throughout these early years—as an undergraduate, a barrister, a police recruit—he becomes more and more convinced that for successful police work a combination of background and experience is needed. The young university graduate without police experience, he feels, is never really qualified to start a police career at a higher level than recruit. The recruit, on the other hand, needs more background and education to be qualified to handle greater responsibility. This idea, often expressed, is obviously Wade's position on police qualifications based on his own experience.

Wade, unfortunately, very often tells the reader about Poole without providing any opportunity of observing the reality of this description of the man. Poole chats with people throughout the novels on assorted artistic topics (he is a man of culture), but is never described as attending concerts, the theater, or reading books, or participating in sports, except in very isolated references. That he does all these "cultural" things is to be taken for granted or assumed.

His family consists of his father, who never thoroughly approves of his son's choice of profession, but accepts it; his sister, about whom all that is known in the novels is that she is widowed and, in the latter novels, that her brother makes his home with her in Battersea. The most interesting relative mentioned is his Aunt Joan, his father's younger sister, who thinks it is delightful to have a nephew who is a policeman. Poole spends one weekend with her which is described. On Saturday they go shooting, read Mary Webb and Henry James, entertain guests for dinner, and play bridge. On Sunday they go to church, play golf, read, and gossip about relatives, politics and neighbors. This weekend is the only time that Poole is seen in any kind of family situation.

The man himself, then, remains constant in many ways throughout the fourteen works, seven novels and seven short stories. He is occasionally lonely, particularly in the early novels when he returns to his empty apartment with its windowbox of mignonettes. In several tales, he is temporarily attracted to a woman whom he meets during a case, but he never falls deepy in love, seeming to prefer his adopted life-style of detection and occasional cultural activities.

He ages normally during the time covered by the novels, with his assurance growing as he becomes older. He always wants to succeed. He wants to earn the next promotion, though talking about it or even thinking about it is, for him, inappropriate. Solving the present case is the all-consuming goal of the moment. He always needs quiet time to think, and makes use of time in travel to analyze, to go over the aspects of the case again, and to plan.

In his first recorded case, his Chief Inspector, obviously unhappy about the young Poole's very rapid advancement, thinks that a failure, or a fiasco, might help him. Chief Inspector Barrod does not like Poole's type: his education, what he considers a suspected softness, and a swelled head. The softness and swelled head are not true. Barrod does not even like his appearance, his good looks. But Poole, who will meet this kind of resistance on other occasions, shrugs it off and gets to work on the case. The ability, plus hard work and luck which had started Poole's rapid career rise, continues, though the luck is often a result of his considerable ability. Good luck, or at least not having bad luck, seems important.

In several non-Poole novels, the competition for advancement is more apparent and casts further light on Poole's career. Wade's treatment of the advancement of other policemen emphasizes his recognition of the various routes to advancement as well as his awareness of the elements that can handicap a young officer, often the element of luck. In *The Hanging Captain* (1933) Detective-Inspector Herbert Lott is forty years old, has a good record, but a slight check is referred to because a man he was arresting (*The Dying Alderman* 1930) committed suicide, something he should have been able to prevent. Now, several years after this "bad luck," Lott, it is felt, is in competition with the younger Poole for a promotion to Chief Inspector. In *Here Comes the Copper* (1938) another policeman in the uniformed branch, Police Constable John Bragg, combines hard work and ability with a conscious plan to improve himself as a policeman. He, fortunately, does not become handicapped by any bad luck and in the next-to-the-last short story in the collection, is promoted to the C.I.D. In the last story he is Detective Constable Bragg and is doing well. Thus, Poole is not the only recruit described by Wade as rising, by merit and a lack of bad luck, to higher positions.

One of Poole's chief characteristics is his ability to deal with various kinds of people. While he is often assigned to routine cases that might have been handled by any one of a number of qualified officers, he is often used by his superiors when it seems as if someone of his educational and social background will have a greater chance of success in dealing with the people involved in a specific case. The most obvious illustration of this is in "The Missing Undergraduate" in *Policeman's Lot,* when he is sent to his college at Oxford. Two factors are considered by his superiors. His understanding based on his own experience of undergraduate life there, his local knowledge, should be helpful. Presumably, also, he and the people there will be able to work together comfortably. Poole, arriving at Oxford, finds that he must consult first with Mr. Luddingham, the dean, who had been his lecturer in Constitutional law. Then, of course, he must interview faculty and students who had known the missing young man. All goes well in his investigation, and it is obvious that an Inspector with police training only would have had a much more difficult time understanding the scene and atmosphere and being accepted as easily by the Oxford men. With his usual combination of work in the field, interviewing, and thinking, Poole is successful. Poole always thinks and thinks, while he travels on the case and at other quiet times. A very happy ending results when his routine procedures, his analyses, and a little luck lead him to the missing student in time to save his life. Poole had felt a little coolness between himself and the dean at first, but the dean's remark at the conclusion of the case pleases Poole:

"I knew you would prefer to be treated purely in your official capacity while the case was in hand," said Mr. Luddingham, "but I had great difficulty in not remonstrating with you when you asked me 'to approximately estimate' the amount of young Catling's debts. You must be a changed man indeed, my dear Poole—and probably a better one—calmly to split an infinitive in the presence of the Dean of St. Peter's" (Missing, 46-47).

In dealing with other kinds of people, Poole is equally successful. The author's first-hand knowledge of rural policemen makes his presentation of them and their frequent lack of enthusiasm about accepting help from the Yard very clear. In these novels, the attitude of the local constabulary is more often passive resistance than outright resentment. The typical reaction of the local man is apt to be polite, officially informative, but nothing more. Poole, however, understands this feeling and is not personally offended if someone seems less than cordial. He recognizes the difficulty of an experienced local man who must accept the assistance of a much younger man from the Yard.

As a result, he does his job, shows his genuine respect for them and their work, and is inevitably eventually accepted by them as a man, like themselves, doing his job. Some are originally even amused by his "thinking" when they might prefer to run around doing something. Usually they come to see that thinking can also be helpful in solving a crime.

In *No Friendly Drop*, Superintendent Clewth, aged fifty, self-confident, dedicated to duty, is very quickly interested in Poole's thinking. "You keep on suggesting theories and then when you've convinced me that they're sound, you knock 'em down again." In his response to this remark, Poole gives a direct statement of his "thinking" methods, one of his reasons for needing time for his mental process:

"That's only a trick, sir,—a method of working; set up all the possibilities in turn, make out the best case for each and then pull it to pieces. It's a good way of cleaning one's mind of prejudice. If one has a favourite theory and tries to prove it, one is inclined to turn one's back on anything that doesn't fit in."

"Well, I suppose you've got to justify your reputation for brains at the Yard," said the county policeman with a grin. (Drop, 60-61)

Clewth does help Poole, and even makes him feel at home. Gradually, he finds that this man Poole is not only a personable and conscientious young officer, but also that his methods work. Toward the end of the novel when Poole has offered to do some of the regular procedural work. Clewth says: "No my lad, I'll do the dirty work; you go on with the thinking" (Drop, 239).

Poole's background, while generally helpful to him in his career, also gives him one weakness which he becomes aware of and tries to overcome. On occasion his ability to evaluate people is too much influenced by his feeling that a person of good background could not possibly be a criminal. Intellectually, he knows that murder, for example, is a crime that might be committed at any level of society. But in *Lonely Magdalene* (1940) Poole is now forty years old, no longer the young, new investigator. He has had many cases and has dealt with many people, both victims and criminals, from many classes of society. But Wade says:

Poole shuddered at the horror of that thought. Was it possible that a man or woman of the birth and tradition of these two could plot such a foul crime, to murder a poor woman who was the wife of one, and the half-sister of the other (Lonely, 286)

Even though he reminds himself that murderers do not run true to any type, twelve pages later in the novel he is still concerned with the same idea: "Murder of a wife by her husband and his mistress was no new crime, but that people of gentle birth should do such a thing was terrible beyond Poole's experience" (Lonely, 298).

Perhaps it is the author, also, who cannot accept the possibility of such behavior on the part of people of gentle birth because Poole finds that they are not guilty. It might have helped him to overcome this weakness if they had been guilty.

This particular weakness, perhaps Poole's only significant one, never causes him to fail in an investigation, but it continues to handicap him. He recognizes the problem, wants to guard against it, but continues to err. In *The Duke of York's Steps* when he is in his late twenties, he finds that he has known the murdered man's secretary at Oxford and asks him to help in one aspect of the investigation. Poole, explaining this to his Chief Inspector, says, "I can trust him, I know; we were at. . .I knew him before I joined the Force." The Chief Inspector replies, "That's no reason for trusting anyone" (Duke, 220).

Several decades later, in the final novel of the series, Gold Was Our Grave (1954), a much older Poole, now fifty-two, still makes the same mistake. "Poole realized that by accepting the drink [sherry] and the apology, he had weakened his position; he could not now press his questions as inexorably as he would do to a hostile—a palpably hostile—witness. He had had hastily to reconstruct his plan of action" (Gold, 241).

At the beginning of his career he made the mistake; at a much later career time, he does it again. This weakness, wanting to be friendly with people he trusts, is life-long. In mid-career, in his thirties Poole receives the "most severe telling off that had come his way since he had received his sergeant's stripes" for the same weakness. Sir Leward points out that it is not to be considered a formal reprimand and thus a matter of record. Poole needs continuing reminders by others and by himself to keep under control that one weakness of making friends with people in his cases, his continuing failure to recognize that gentle, well-born people are not necessarily innocent of crime. That the weakness does not produce any failures in his work or cause any bad luck is indeed fortunate. It is a weakness, but it does add warmth and charm to his personality.

Discussing police work, Poole on one occasion says: "Most of it's dull routine work and quite a lot of it is unpleasant." Poole describes the presentation of detection in books as not always wrong, but too much "concentrated." He says, "You couldn't put in a book all the routine work that makes up nine-tenths of modern detection" (Bury, 56). He may speak that way, but as he is presented, he himself, while devoting much time to police procedures and routine work, does spend more than one-tenth of his time thinking. "For an hour he remained motionless, twice filling and lighting a disreputable pipe and occasionally referring to the file" (Soon, 96).

Although human—making occasional mistakes, wanting cases that will bring him to his superior's attention, too conscious of gentle birth—he is a believable policeman, on the verge of becoming ideal. From his appearance in 1929 to the final novel in 1954, he represents Scotland Yard at its best.

Poole, then, is a detective whose adherence to police procedure, the dogged following of routine methods, is constant. After all, it has been his recognition of the powers and machinery of the Force that made him select police work and to become a recruit in the first place rather than to pursue a career in law or in private investigation. Add the ingredients of his educational and cultural background, hard work, and a little luck—the result, an impressive Scotland Yard man.

His ultimate goal, set when he was still at Oxford, was to become Head of the Criminal Investigation Department of Scotland Yard. In the final novel, he is fifty-two years old; he is one of sixteen Chief Inspectors, with eight Superintendents and a Chief Superintendent ahead of him. Did he make it? The reader does not need the additional novels that the author never wrote to be confident that he did indeed make it. Educational and cultural background, police training and experience, diligent work, the application of routine police procedures and some thinking, with the addition of a little luck, must have been sufficient to bring John Poole to the position he wanted.

Notes

[1]Henry Wade, *The Dying Alderman* (New York: Garland Publishing, Inc., 1976), p. 85. Originally 1930.

[2]The editions of Henry Wade's novels and short stories in which Inspector John Poole appears are listed below, preceded by the original date of publication. All quotations will be cited in the text using, where necessary for clarity, the abbreviation given after an entry:

1929　*The Duke of York's Steps* (New York: Payson & Clarke, Ltd., 1929). (Duke)

1931　*No Friendly Drop* (New York: Brewer Warren & Putnam, 1932). (Drop)

1933　*Policeman's Lot* (London: Constable & Co., Ltd., 1933).

The first seven stories in this collection of 13 are titled "Cases of Inspector Poole" and include:

"Duello"

"The Missing Undergraduate" (Missing)

"Wind in the East"

"The Sub Branch"

"The Real Thing"
"The Baronet's Finger"
"The Three Keys"
1934 *Constable Guard Thyself!* (London: Constable & Co., Ltd., 1934). (Guard)
1936 *Bury Him Darkly* (London: Constable & Co., Ltd., 1936). (Bury)
1940 *Lonely Magdalen* (London: Constable, 1940). (Lonely)
1953 *Too Soon To Die* (New York: Macmillan Co., 1953). (Soon)
1954 *Gold Was Our Grave* (New York: Macmillan Co., 1954). (Gold)

Christianna Brand's "Cockie" Cockrill

Liahna Babener

Traditionally, detectives of the classical school of English mystery fiction are portrayed as advocates of the laws and conventions of an ordered society. Although their methods, motivations, and professional circumstances may differ, amateur sleuths and police detectives alike serve as agents of the moral norms of their culture and practitioners of its values. Because crime represents both an affront to civility and a resurgence of irrational impulses, it must be defeated by those who have made the primacy of order and rationality their business. As W.H. Auden has argued in his seminal essay, "The Guilty Vicarage," the detective's task is "to restore the state of grace in which the aesthetic and the ethical are as one."[1] Hence, reason and law constitute the province of the fictional policeman, governing the ethical world inside the story as well as the aesthetic dictates of the genre itself.

Christianna Brand's serial character, Inspector Cockie Cockrill, the chief constable of the rural hamlet of Heronsford, Kent, and the protagonist of six novels and a number of short stories,[2] is a consummate example of the police hero as arbiter of order and moral accountability. Despite his eccentricities of manner and comical demeanor (dwarfish stature, bird-like movements, an out-sized head topped by an ill-fitting and unstylish hat which accentuates the disproportion), Cockrill is consistently depicted as a formidable authority and a stable person in an unbalanced world. In virtually every one of the stories in which he appears, Inspector Cockrill is thrust into a milieu of passion grown perverse, a Freudian swamp of obsession, jealousy, lust, and envy, where normative values are buried and vice festers. To this primal chaos, the Inspector brings his analytical mind and his conventional loyalties.

Though Brand occasionally allows us to watch Cockrill in his professional domain—consulting with fellow investigators, utilizing forensic facilities, supervising underlings, and manipulating the levers of law enforcement—more typically she positions him as a lone analyst in a world deranged by evil. Her interest is less in police methodology than in the moral and mental contest between the discipline of society and the profligacy of crime. Cockrill's official credentials underscore his adherence to the state and to the civilizing authority it represents, but his exercizes in detection resemble more the feats of ingenuity practiced by the gifted amateurs and solitary police protagonists from an earlier literary tradition than the practical methods of the cops in modern procedural novels.

As Cockrill's originator has herself acknowledged in an essay on her detective:

He is not a great one for the physical details of an investigation: 'meanwhile his henchmen pursued their ceaseless activities' writes his creator, not too sure herself exactly what those would be; and he is content to leave fingerprint powder and magnifying glass to the experts, using their findings in a process of elimination to get down to the nitty-gritty from there on.[3]

The "nitty-gritty" is the systematic unriddling of the crime and an affirmation of the mandates of the community. Because moral imperatives and the dictates of law are made more compelling in these stories than demands for strict verisimiltude, Brand stresses Cockrill's incisiveness and his ethical discernment rather than his technical expertise. The Inspector becomes a social healer whose resolution of the mystery and restoration of lawfulness constitute a kind of medicine for the body politic. Not surprisingly, in fact, Brand reveals to her readers that the imaginative model for the Cockrill character was her own father-in-law, a country doctor whose humane wisdom and shrewd diagnoses she long admired.[4]

Indeed, the medical metaphor is appropriate to describe not only the detective in Brand's stories, but the crime as well. In each of his cases, Cockrill is drawn into a diseased world which must be washed of its deep-seated pathology. All of the stories feature domestic settings and focus on a small circle of intimates—close friends, associates, blood relatives—in whose midst resides a hidden enemy, one afflicted with some skewed passion, some twisted compulsion which has grown monstrous in its secrecy and now culminates in a *crime passionnel*. This central villainy is often disguised by the disturbed behavior of other characters whose troubled psyches demonstrate how deeply and pervasively the contagion has taken hold. Cockrill's task is not merely to identify the murderer, but to cleanse this soiled world. To do so, he must penetrate through the matrix of deception and desire, holding firm against its dark tides. It is this victory of moral order over the anarchy of passion which constitutes Cockrill's personal and professional achievement in each tale, from his first recorded case, *Heads You Lose* (1942), to his later ventures in detection.

Most often, the problem of deviant emotion is evidenced in the familiar love-triangle, an age-old manifestation of the potential dangers of passion. The detective himself is exempt from such dangers. Abstemious by nature, he is also beyond the age of sexual temptation. We learn in *Heads You Lose* that the romantic impulse left him long ago with the death of his wife and infant in child-bed, and his attractions to female characters are regularly portrayed as avuncular rather than romantic. Cockrill is thus fit by his emotional disinterestedness to unravel the twisted compulsions of others.

And of these, there are many. Episodes of infidelity, displaced affections, and sexual jealousy abound in the novels in complex and convoluted patterns. In *Heads*, the key to the solution of the murders of two women at Pigeonsford, the estate of the local squire of a small community in rural Kent, is to disentangle a Gordian knot of romantic interrelationships and sort them into their correct configurations. Cockrill learns that both victims were in love with men who did not return their affections, but rather competed themselves for the love of a third woman, the young beauty Francesca Hart. To ferret out the motive for the double deaths, Cockrill must identify the person whose jealousy has turned homicidal. The process of discovery requires both insight and stability on the policeman's part: he must educe that Stephen Pendock's frustration has transformed him from a failed suitor into a deranged killer, and he must withstand the inclination toward sentimentality which might lead to a misguided amnesty for the man. The novel exposes the peril inherent in romance. Pendock, insecure and self-effacing, cannot bear the burden of his own *grande passion*. Believing himself too old, too stodgy, and too paternal to win the love of Francesca, he converts his repressed yearnings into murderous lust, killing her symbolically through other female victims and then rationalizing these deaths as acts of chivalry to protect Fran from her rivals. Pendock's sick fury culminates in the near murder of Fran herself.

To make sense of this emotional morass, Cockrill must counterbalance psychological empathy for the murderer (whose age, loneliness, and honorable past invite an affinity between the two) with moral restraint (he cannot allow pity to hinder duty). In the climactic scene, he stands aside while Pendock, struggling to overcome his murderous frenzy, points the revolver at himself, thus saving Francesca through his own suicide. Cockrill ceremoniously pronounces benediction over the corpse, "God rest his soul" (237), thus presiding over a purgation of the deviant passion and a return to normalcy. Significantly, the novel closes with the marriage of Francesca to her more suitable beau while Cockrill's presence at the wedding reinforces his role as the champion of convention.

Rivalry in love also figures prominently in *The Crooked Wreath* (1946), which interweaves two romantic triangles, one from the past and one contemporary. Inspector Cockrill has been called in to investigate the death of Sir Richard March, a member of the local gentry. Although Lady Bella March, his second wife, is the nominal mistress of Swanswater, the March home, she enjoys no prerogative until her husband's death because Sir Richard has turned the memory of his deceased first wife into a kind of perverse adoration, converting the family estate into a shrine to the long dead woman to the neglect of the living Bella. This original romantic triangle is revisited in the form of a more modern entanglement in which March's grandson, Philip, is torn between a wife and a mistress. Sir Richard's selfishness in manipulating the competitive affections of two women is echoed in the behavior of Philip March, a better man than his grandfather, but one whose vanity is flattered by the contention for his heart.

The many jealousies inspired by this romantic strife overspread and infect the entire March clan. Cockrill's task is to trace the venom to its source and identify the character whose envy has become lethal. Brand describes the murderer's disturbance as a "bitter grievance [which] flowed like poison through her veins, bursting out in a hundred ugly little sores" (128). While Cockrill's police procedures help him to discover how the murder was accomplished, it is his moral insight rather than his methodology which brings about his recognition that Claire, the other woman in Philip's life, has killed in a vain attempt to win his love. The moral character of the novel's resolution is underlined by the language of the final passage, which describes Claire's death and the destruction of Swanswater in sacramental, or rather, apocalyptic terms, as a "cleansing by fire" (181).

Ruinous passion is also central to *Death of Jezebel* (1948), in which a series of London murders is linked to the suicide, years before, of a wronged lover whose romantic disillusionment had precipitated his death. The victims in the current plot include those originally culpable in the betrayal of Johnny Wise: Perpetua Kirk, his unfaithful sweetheart; Earl Anderson, a handsome cad whose brief affair with Perpetua is the original sin from which all subsequent injury follows; and Isabel Drew, the "Jezebel" of the title who had fostered the intrigue between Perpetua and Earl for her own cynical amusement. Seven years after the event, the three principals are still tied to each other by the emotional after-effects of Wise's suicide, and all three have fallen into dissolute and purposeless lives.

Cockrill, who is attending a law enforcement conference in London, is called into the case in an unofficial capacity when Isabel is murdered after receiving a note prophesying her death. Since the other figures in the old scandal receive similar warnings, Cockrill infers that she has been killed in a belated revenge plot. The problem facing the Inspector, however, is hardly as simple as it appears. Either of the remaining members of the original trio might be the slayer; both Perpetua and Earl bear the burden of that festering guilt. And the circle of suspects is wider than initially assumed. There were others damaged by Wise's suicide: a bereft brother, a former consort; there were others who might welcome the death of Jezebel: a scorned suitor, a troubled adolescent. Cockrill must sort through these involuted feelings of resentment, vindictiveness, and shame to ascertain the true motive, but first he must tear away the veils of deceit behind which several of the suspects have hidden their true identities. The challenge is one of the most aggravating in his career. Cockrill is misled repeatedly and a second murder occurs before he finally exposes the killer.

Though the process of inquiry is pertinacious and thorough (witnesses are examined and reexamined, the killing is restaged several times, the crime scene is scrutinized meticulously), the solution is once again reached as much through moral perceptivity as through methodical analysis. The inspector's crucial insight is that in the killer's fury is the same strain of unbridled violence that had earlier prompted Johnny Wise to self-murder. The recognition that the link is fraternal—that it is Johnny's brother who has become his avenger—is not far behind:

Johnny himself—how delicately balanced between madness and sanity, that at the sight of his girl in another man's arms, he goes out and kills himself without waiting for an explanation or regrets!. . .It was 'in the family' as they say, to be just a little mad—delicately balanced on the borderline between the normal and the abnormal. (199).

The line between normal and abnormal is almost imperceptible, but Cockie discerns that Bryant Wise, unmasked as Johnny's brother and defender, has crossed it.

Cockrill's acuity and dispassionate nature guide him through the sexual and familial turbulence which he encounters recurrently in his police duties, but in *Green For Danger* (1944)) Brand's most celebrated novel, the cauldron of passions spills over and threatens to engulf the detective before he finally contains the flow. The story is set in a Kent military hospital during the Blitz, and its chief characters (and suspects) are a team of doctors and nurses who struggle to administer medicine under almost constant enemy bombardment. War-time stresses exacerbate the already dire emotional tensions among the group, and the agitation culminates in the murder of a patient during surgery and later of a nurse in the operating theater.

It seems initially that the trouble stems from romantic conflict, since the first victim had witnessed a series of compromising flirtations and quarrels among the hospital staffers, and the second had participated in them. The intrigue centers about the hospital's chief surgeon, Gervayse Eden, a middle-aged bachelor who has promoted himself by enticing, exploiting, then spurning vulnerable women. Several of his staff nurses are vying for his attentions, and the acrimony between them permeates the working atmosphere. Cockrill himself is initially fooled into believing that the homicides are byproducts of this romantic turmoil, and this misconception—that sexual feuding accounts for the two murders— is reinforced when subsequent attempts are made on two other victims, both principals in the various entanglements. Cockrill's challenge is to clear the romantic fog which obscures the puzzle, and to disclose the other more primal motive which actually provokes the killings: the vindication by a daughter of her mother's needless death.

Nurse Esther Sanson, whose young fiance is one of the near victims and whose elderly suitor is one of the suspected doctors, seems herself to be in the center of a lovers' tug-of-war. Cockie hits upon the truth when he discovers that Esther's compulsion is filial, not sexual. Having defied her mother's selfish hypochondria to assume volunteer duty at the hospital, Esther is rankled with secret guilt. When her mother is killed in an air raid, Esther's self-blame is redirected irrationally against members of the local rescue squad who had failed to save the woman, and they become the victims of the daughter's ingenious design for murder. When Cockrill observes in another context that "there is nothing like just indignation for fostering unreasoning hate" (159), he unwittingly offers the formula for solving the mystery, revealing again the psychological insight that equips him for detection.

Repeatedly, Brand thrusts her detective inside a chaotic world where he must confront psychic maladies which might deter a less stable man. The pattern is reiterated in *Fog of Doubt* (1953), an aptly titled novel which again features the Inspector winding his way through a maze of thwarted libidos and seething jealousies. The disturbance begins when Raoul Vernet, a Continental swain who has romanced several of the female characters in the story, makes a trip to London and stirs the desires of his former devotees and the anxieties of their respective mates.

When Vernet is murdered, Cockrill is invited to assist the London police by the Evanses, old Kent acquaintances. Acting unofficially as advisor to the case, the Inspector must determine which member of the Evans family, in whose Maida Vale residence Vernet is clubbed to death, fears the agitation he has aroused enough to kill him. Is it Mathilda Evans, once Vernet's partner in adultery, now reconciled to her doctor husband Thomas, whose resentment of the past might motivate him? Could it be Rosie Evans, Thomas's sister, whose schoolgirl adventures abroad left her pregnant by an unnamed lover who might be Vernet? Or is it solid and dependable Ted Edwards, a family friend and fellow doctor who fancies himself Rosie's protector and beau? All of these characters are linked to the fatal event by the skewed logic of passion. Even the secondary constituents of the household—an elderly grandmother who has foresworn life's tedium for steamy fantasies about romance and seduction, and a mother's helper who hankers after Rosie's fast life—are similarly implicated. Whoever killed Vernet acted out of some sexual compulsion, but this might be anyone. Indeed, Cockrill fathoms the how of the crime before he knows the why of it, and it takes a second killing to cut through the detective's fog of doubt and a murder trial to validate his recognition.

If the title alludes to the detective's bafflement, it also describes the private anguish of Ted Edwards, "Tedward" to young Rosie, who views her longtime friend as a confidant and brotherly mentor, while he nurtures secret dreams of romance between them. Cockrill, in whom both characters confide, comes progressively to realize the ominous edge to Ted's stifled yearnings:

It was true that it made Tedward mad: mad with that ravening hunger of his for something more tender from her, or something less—better that she should be cold and disregarding altogether than torment him with her innocent coquetries, her little, offhand pet names and dabbing caresses that proclaimed aloud that to her he was no more and never would be more than dear old, tubby old Tedward Bear, comfortable and kind... I *must* get over it, he thought; I *must* shake it off. A fat cross-grained, hard-up old buffer like me, slavering over a girl half of my age... It was disgusting, it was absurd. (126)

When Rosie herself becomes the next corpse, Cockrill connects Ted's private pathology to the two murders. Drawing upon his expertise in the psychology of deviant emotion—knowledge amplified and refined over the course of five novels—the Inspector reinterprets both killings, in light of Edwards' obstructed desire, as expressions of carnal envy.

Vernet is, in Ted's eyes, a "vile, seducing rat" who is "better off dead" (9), while Rosie's offense is even more heinous. Promiscuity not ravishment explains her pregnancy, and her fatal error in Edwards' Victorian mind is the fall from idealization. When Rosie was his "broken lily," he had killed Vernet to avenge "her shame," but when the truth behind his misguided chivalry is revealed, he kills Rosie to avenge what he now thinks of as his own shame at the hands of "the slut who had trampled his lilies of illusion into ugly little fragments and handed them out to every casual . . . passerby" (250). Cockrill has engineered Edwards' confession by the end of the novel, but it is left to the reader to reckon with the knowledge that three deaths have resulted from the man's maniacal prudery.

Tour de Force (1955) repeats the familiar pattern of the detective caught up in a psychological morass, this time during a vacation to the Continent. Here too, Cockrill acts as an impromptu investigator who assists the designated authorities, a device Brand uses frequently to foster her portrait of a detective whose intelligence and moral wisdom— rather than his official status—comprise his crime-solving credentials. The teeming passions in this novel again boil over into murder. Cockrill has planned a quiet touring holiday, but finds himself enmeshed in the troubles of a group of discontented travelers. When one of the party is murdered, Cockrill must work his way through an imbroglio of hidden guilt, romantic feuding, and false identity to find the killer.

Cockrill's challenge is almost insurmountable in this particularly ingenious tale. The hothouse atmosphere of torrid emotions is accentuated by the tropical climate of the Mediterranean island where the crime has taken place. Adding to the tension, Cockrill's investigation is nearly thwarted by an inefficient and corrupt local government whose officials are more concerned with frivolous displays of power than with expediting the criminal proceeding.

The murder victim is Vanda Lane, an unpleasant woman who seems to stand in the way of everyone's happiness. She challenges a rival's affections for a married man, managing to alienate the other woman, the man, and his wife in the process, and she appears to blackmail several characters with their guilty secrets, magnifying small misdeeds into grand transgressions. Again, the Inspector keeps his balance in a sea of tumultuous passions. Since all of the characters nurse some private anguish or antipathy, Cockrill must single out the one whose buried emotions constitute grounds for murder. He proceeds by measuring the impact of Miss Lane's death upon the survivors. Suspicion turns readily to Louvaine Barker, Vanda's competitor for the attentions of the errant husband. A series of revelations discloses that the two women were not the strangers they had seemed, but had actually been cousins, secret business collaborators, and, behind superficially different exteriors, nearly alike in face and physique.

Cockrill wrestles with the contradition between his fondness for Louvaine, whom he has considered a kindred spirit and an admirable person, and a strong instinct that she is a murderer. As it turns out, both feelings are vindicated. Louvaine Barker is indeed worthy of Cockrill's faith and friendship—it is she who is in fact dead. Vanda Lane is actually the killer who has assumed the identity of her victim, a ruse made possible by the hidden relationships between the women. Once again Cockrill's triumph is the sureness of his moral impulses. As implausible as it might seem, the only way that Louvaine Barker can be both commendable and culpable is if she somehow becomes a different person in the course of the events. Despite the apparent absurdity of the proposition, it is the one that the Inspector pursues, and it provides the solution to a deftly conceived and ruthlessly executed murder.

Cockrill's instinctive partiality to Louvaine Barker proves to be as sound as his natural aversion to Vanda Lane, whose love for Leo Rodd is described as the perverse idolatry of a sufferer for an oppressor:

'I'm the slave type,' she thought, 'and he's the master type; and he's the only person in the world that I would want to be my master.' After all the years of existing upon vicarious romanticism, barren of personal relationship, suddenly...out of the blue had come fulfillment—to worship like a dog at the feet of a man....(16)

The Inspector is not privy to Vanda's interior mind, but he senses something horribly amiss about this secretive, repressed woman, and when she is apparently dead, he senses that her destructive influence persists. The intuition leads to a scheme to expose her, and Cockrill watches as "Louvaine" degenerates into Vanda, grovelling before her horrified lover and other characters:

A door slammed in her mind, slammed-to with a crash and a clatter that shattered the last vestiges of her tormented self-control: and she was on the floor at his feet, weeping and gibbering, sobbing, shivering, whimpering, at last falling silent, crouched there at his feet in the stony ring of their horror and recoil. (254)

At the end of the novel, the touring company returns to England where, thanks to Cockrill's maneuvers, Vanda Lane will face British justice. Whether his purpose is compassion (he knows the misery of a San

Juan el Pirata jail) or retribution is left unspoken, but the Inspector does not challenge Leo Rodd's final words: "I want to see her condemned to die for what she did to Louvaine; and when the Judge says, 'may God have mercy on your soul,' I want to be there, and not say Amen" (270).

The Inspector's success in each of these episodes is the result of his acuity in matters psychological. While the suspects wallow in emotional excess, Cockrill, dispassionate and canny, uses their own volatility against them. His usual strategy is to foment discord, creating apprehension and enmity among them until the guilty one panics and shows his hand. Often, this effect is achieved by a relentless barrage of questions, accusations, and conjectures fired at a targeted suspect until his composure is shaken or her determination broken. Cockrill is a "master at the art of prodding into flame damped-down fires of nervous irritability, of fanning to a blaze the embers of shock and restraint and strain" (*Wreath*, 129) until an explosive revelation occurs.

In *Green For Danger*, this tactic of vexation is particularly effective, since the characters under suspicion are confined to the grounds of an army hospital under constant threat of enemy attack, and nerves are already taut. The Inspector intensifies the pressure by ordering the suspects to remain in their cramped sleeping accommodations where, pressed together night and day, they grow increasingly tense, rankling each other with imputations and picking at old wounds:

They returned disconsolately to the cottage, and the first little murmurings of uneasiness began; the first strange sense of being always watched, of being never alone, of being dogged and harried and badgered, that was to drive them to desperation in the next few days; the first creeping faint irritation of the nerves that was to arise to a hideous crescendo in Cockie's process of 'breaking the criminal down.' (208)

Ultimately the criminal does break under the siege. Esther Sanson's latent hysteria, which has surfaced previously in bouts of sleeplessness, fitful laughter, and unprovoked weeping, now culminates in a kind of martyr's ecstasy as she is finally cornered. Despite being found out, Esther is oddly grateful to the Inspector who has freed her from her obsessional guilt.

A related Cockrill stragey is to "deputize" the implicated persons, recruiting them to act as his unwitting agents, questioning each other and offering their own speculations about the culprit and mode of the crime. Building upon the animosities and anxieties of the closed circle of suspects, the detective sets one against the other, sowing mistrust and inviting inadvertent self-betrayal. Such a method works in *The*

Crooked Wreath. While his police assistants are busy "coming and going and fingerprinting and photographing and measuring" (126), Inspector Cockrill concentrates on a plan to trick the killer into a misstep by subjecting her to the recriminations of the others accused:

> He liked to get his suspects talking; if they all discussed the case, the murderer was obliged to join in or remain conspicuously silent—and sooner or later, among the innumerable intricacies of time and place, of lies told, of reservations made, of apparently careless suggestions deliberately put forward, was liable somewhere to take a false step. (126)

Claire March's insecurity and self-doubt, which prompt her crime in the first place, render her susceptible to the kind of scheme which involves shattering the killer's complacency. Claire kills Sir Richard March because she feels unappreciated and unworthy. Conscious that she is a granddaughter out of favor, a failed journalist, a cast-off mistress, and a disinherited heir, she strikes back at her private disgrace through murder. When the verbal assaults of her fellow suspects commence, her fragile self-possession begins to crumble, and the detective's plan both exposes a killer and clears another who has been falsely charged.

Occasionally, false charges prove useful stratagems for snaring the real murderer. At the end of *Death of Jezebel*, Cockrill interrogates the suspects one at a time, conjuring up a series of hypothetical scenarios of the crime, each with a different culprit. When he turns to Perpetua Kirk, however, his tone shifts from speculative to accusatory. " 'What was anybody's desire for revenge compared with yours?' " he demands to know (203), thus setting up Perpetua as an unwitting decoy to elicit the gallantry of the real killer, Bryant Wise. The Inspector anticipates this turn of events, appealing to the same chivalrous motive which first compelled the man to avenge his brother's death and later to spare Perpetua's life. Cockrill knows that Wise's sense of honor will oblige him to exonerate Perpetua (" 'She was as much injured as Johnny: she was to be pitied—not blamed,' " 206), and his gamble pays off.

Again, in *Fog of Doubt,* the Inspector deftly extracts a confession by turning the killer's own chivalry—a drive which precipitated the murder in the first place—against him. Ted Edwards is on trial for the death of Raoul Vernet, but just as Edwards has planned, the evidence appears to vindicate him. It seems likely that the accused will be freed, until Cockrill, who knows Edwards is guilty, plays his trump card. He allows the testimony of a final witness in the case who confesses to the murder herself in a misguided bid to save a man who is in effect already saved. Her martyrdom is of course needless, and Edwards, who cannot in conscience exploit the opportunity, is compelled to divulge the truth. The resolution is a tribute to Cockrill's tactical proficiency and psychological acumen.

The same assets are called into play when the Inspector avails himself of another of his favored devices to entrap the guilty. Apparently drawing inspiration from his fictional forebear Hercule Poirot, Cockrill often maneuvers the key figures in a given case into a recreation of the crime, hoping in the process to incite anew the murderer's frenzy and thus provoke a revealing emotional display or to shake loose a telling detail which has heretofore escaped notice. A series of reenactments of the second murder in *Heads You Lose* properly directs suspicion away from peripheral suspects to the true killer, Stephen Pendock, and enables Cockrill to discredit unfounded hypotheses about the criminal's method which have diverted the investigation. The recreation of "Vanda Lane's" murder in *Tour de Force* serves metaphorically to suggest the truth behind the crime. "Louvaine Barker," who is really Vanda Lane, acts the part of herself in the restaging. The pointed resemblance between the victim and the woman now playing the victim does not escape the Inspector's notice. Applying the analogy of the drama, Cockrill ultimately perceives the murder itself as an ingenious masquerade. To unmask the performer and put a stop to her, he employs a theatrical ruse himself, feigning his own death and setting in motion the mock suicide of Vanda Lane's unresponsive lover, all for the purpose of disturbing her psychological equilibrium and elicting an admission.

Reenactments of the murder of Isabel Drew, who dies in a fall from a tower in full view of the audience at a charity pageant, are conducted so many times in *Death of Jezebel* that the story borders on tedium. Brand risks her readers' boredom in order to facilitate her detective's plot to force a slip-up by the killer who must relive the crime repeatedly, each time concealing his true role in Isabel's death. As it turns out, it is not an oversight by Bryant Wise so much as it is an insight by Cockrill which finally points to the culprit's identity. The Inspector realizes that Earl Anderson, whose disappearance has made him the chief suspect, was never actually present at the death scene. If Earl is now missing, he is more likely a corpse than a fugitive, and this recognition shifts suspicion to the true slayer, Bryant Wise.

All of these tactics—fostering discord among the suspects and exploiting their enmity to advance the inquiry, hounding the accused with incessant questions, leveling false charges to smoke out the real malefactor, and restaging the crime to provoke the killer's blunder—

depend upon psychological subterfuge. But Cockrill also relies on informed speculation and outright guesswork. The old-fashioned hunch is an integral part of his investigative arsenal, as when he grasps that Rosie's death in *Fog of Doubt* is deliberate: " 'I'm old,' he said, straightening himself with a hand to his back. 'I get feelings in my bones. I've got a feeling in my bones that this thing's murder....' " (173). The intuition prompts him to consider that Ted Edwards is Rosie's doctor as well as her dismissed suitor, thus adding opportunity to a list of incriminating factors. The Inspector's instincts are often almost clairvoyant, as in *Death of Jezebel* when he surmises the correct explanation long before the actual resolution is achieved and confronts the killer with an imagined reconstruction of the crime that proves uncannily accurate. Likewise, in *Heads You Lose,* he fathoms the importance of a critical clue—the untrodden snow surrounding the victim's body—because a long-suppressed childhood memory surfaces to trigger his recognition.

Cockrill's sure instincts are supplemented by a sensitivity to nuances, which enables him to recognize a small particular running counter to a suspect's explanation or a subtle pattern that emerges from a farrago of contradictory evidence. While his assistants are more pedestrian in their handling of minutiae, the Inspector's antennae are finely tuned. Cases turn on such discrete details as a carelessly placed brooch on a corpse's chest (*Heads You Lose*), a pair of tinted sunglasses *(Tour de Force)*, and a speck of black on a surgical gown (*Green for Danger*). When the disparate item shows itself, Cockrill ponders it until he discovers its place in the criminal design, or he reconceives the design until it accommodates the item. In *Death of Jezebel*, he cannot account for the blue eyes of Earl Anderson visible behind a knight's visor worn during the pageantry, since Anderson had actually been killed before the event. The enigmatic detail vexes him, resisting elucidation, until he discovers the answer rather by divination than deduction. The disclosure which follows is almost too bizarre for credence—that Earl Anderson's severed head, concealed beneath the knight's helmet and held in place by the rigid armor, has been used by the real culprit to feign his presence at the spectacle and thus to implicate him falsely in a murder. Like his mentors Dupin and Holmes, the Inspector often succeeds through his inventiveness and his willingness to credit the outre solution.

Despite a repertoire of artful tactics and a history of canny discoveries, Cockrill's record is not impeccable, a fact which has endeared him to readers and reviewers who find him "a relief from more infallible sleuths."[5] Brand herself argues that his propensity to error humanizes him, makes him more capable of empathy, and checks a counter-tendency to vanity: "often he *is* wrong—till the last hour. He is by no means cocksure—surely the greatest weakness in [a] detective."[6] Sometimes the Inspector's erroneous conjectures even detour the inquiry or lead to a mistaken arrest. For example, his supposition that Brough, the gardener in *The Crooked Wreath*, has poisoned Sir Richard March and then killed himself is both false and misleading, since for a time it doubly exonerates the murderer and camouflages the true motive behind the crimes. Ironically, it is not Cockrill but Brough's untutored wife who reads the scheme correctly when she ascertains that "this was a woman's murder....No man killed Brough—no man would have thought of that trick' " (142), alluding to the evidence of suicide and the dying confession which Claire March has fabricated to divert the police.

Another misjudgment by Cockrill almost dooms the case in *Green for Danger*. Hoping to goad the murderer into a second attempt, he risks the life of a surgical patient who is made a lure to trap her. But the Inspector miscalculates the security of the procedure and the craft of his opponent and nearly loses the patient while failing to snare the killer. In the operating theater where the patient struggles to survive, Cockrill upbraids himself for staking the case on a fallible plan:

His mind, usually so keen and clear, was a dark confusion of terror and self-questioning and hideous anxiety. He had made an experiment, thinking it was all so safe; he had taken a terrible gamble with a man's life; and suddenly everything was going wrong. (177)

The detective's rare loss of composure is abated when, in the next moment, he fixes upon a telling detail which eventually leads him to the unriddling of the crime. Despite his quick reassertion of control, the episode provokes a bout of self-doubt and professional humiliation which haunts Cockrill long after the mystery is brought to a conclusion. His dealings with the London police in subsequent cases are encumbered by their skepticism about his competence, as when one officer remembers, "It was you who made such a muck of that hospital case down in Kent" (*Jezebel*, 56). In fact the *Green for Danger* affair is neatly resolved in the end, but the onus of past error remains.

It also impedes the working association between Cockrill and Detective Inspector Charlesworth of Scotland Yard, who heads the inquiries in two London cases, *Death of Jezebel* and *Fog of Doubt*, into which Cockrill has been called at the behest of friends. Charlesworth conceives of himself as a master of modern investigative technique and Cockie as a bumptious fool from the provinces. As Brand notes, Charlesworth, prejudiced by the accounts of Cockrill's apparent bungle in the Kent mystery, "is a little inclined to Kindly Pity" for the old fellow,[7] who, as it turns out, bests him rather soundly in both episodes.

Their antagonism surfaces in their first encounter and evolves over the course of the two cases from mutual resentment to "armed neutrality" and eventually to a kind of grudging alliance. Initially, Charlesworth takes umbrage at what he considers Cockrill's unwarranted intrusion into his London domain and finds the Inspector's eccentricities grating and his meticulous approach to detail "hairsplitting." Near the end of *Death of Jezebel*, he dismisses Cockrill's interrogation of Perpetua Kirk as an example of provincial ineptitude:

Charlesworth could not help grinning a little. He wondered how Inspector Cockrill liked being called an old image. Poor little man—building up this wonderful fairy story about poor Peppi Kirk!... But these old boys oop from t'country, they doddered on and on and never seemed to know when they were beat. (208)

As the story's resolution makes clear, however, it is Charlesworth who doesn't know when he is beat, since the accusation against Perpetua induces the real criminal to confess his own guilt to clear her, just as the Inspector had anticipated.

Nevertheless, Charlesworth later greets Cockrill in *Fog of Doubt* with subtle condescension: "He wrung the old man's hand, asked after Crime in Kent, rather as though it were the routine of general misdemeanor in a minor preparatory school, and referred with great jocularity to that Jezebel case...apparently blissfully forgetful of where the ultimate credit for its solution had lain" (81). During the course of the investigation, he watches Cockrill systematically decipher each facet of the mystery: imaginatively reconstructing Raoul Vernet's murder, hypothesizing how it could have been accomplished by someone seemingly distant from the scene, and finally deducing that the crime was executed by a doctor whose special knowledge of physiology assures the victim's vulnerability to death.

All of these conjectures prove accurate—Cockrill has actually fathomed the truth almost from the beginning—but Charlesworth continues to deprecate his unwelcome partner, deeming "the old boy...past his prime" (232) when he misunderstands Cockrill's scheme to jog a confession from Edwards. As in the Jezebel case, Cockrill's plan succeeds and his unorthodox approach is vindicated. This time, however, he is denied the satisfaction of Charlesworth's audience at his triumph, since the full truth is revealed in a private exchange between the accused and Cockrill in a jail cell. It remains for the reader to congratulate the Inspector and chide his smug cohort; they do not collaborate again.

Cockrill is also leery of Charlesworth, not so much out of narrow-mindedness as wounded vanity. Smarting from the stigma he bears due to the *Green for Danger* episode and feeling out of his element on the London turf ("Cockie detested London: a lot of hurrying, scurrying people and not one of them to nudge his neighbor and say: There goes the Inspector—a fair old terror *he* is," *Jezebel*, 31), Cockrill regards the younger officer as an upstart who needs bringing down a notch. Nursing his injured pride, he vacillates between sullenness and showing off, sometimes withholding information to trip up Charlesworth "until...he, Cockie, the despised, the rejected, stepped in to put things straight for him" (*Jezebel*, 107), and at other times showing up his rival with a conspicuous display of deductive skill.

Though their competition persists through the two cases, Charlesworth and Cockrill achieve a kind of working affiliation which leads to the successful resolution of both. Each man, we learn, though he belittles his counterpart on occasion, harbors a guarded respect for the other, and their common mission to subvert a killer draws them together. In both novels, the cooperative accord is achieved in a neighborhood pub where the two men share a friendly pint, exchange confidences about the investigation, and shed some of their preconceptions about each other. Brand uses the figure of Charlesworth both to underscore, by contrast, the merit of Cockrill (whose incisiveness is sharper and whose overview is broader), and to gently spoof her vain Kent constable.

Petty pride notwithstanding, however, and analytical intelligence granted, it is finally neither of these attributes which best commends Inspector Cockrill to generations of affectionate readers. Rather, it is his humane heart, his capacity for empathy, which makes Cockrill both a worthy man and an admirable representative of the law. As a policeman, he is dedicated not only to the disclosure of fact but also to the pursuance of justice, and no triumph of discovery is more compelling to him than the larger claims of humanity. At the heart of virtually every one of the six novels is a critical moment when the search for truth and the interests of compassion converge—a point at which Cockrill's soundness of judgment and goodness of heart command precisely the same action.

While it goes without saying that the Inspector's consideration for the innocent propels his quest to unveil the guilty, it is the guilty whose plight awakens his deeper sympathies. As I have argued, Brand's murderers are those caught up in the vortex of fatal passion, as much victims of ungovernable drives as they are wrongdoers, figures of pathos more than evil. To his credit, Cockrill understands this moral mixture. He laments the self-inflicted death of Stephen Pendock in *Heads You Lose,* though he knows it is both fitting and inevitable for the killer to meet his own end. Pendock's violence invites retribution, but his loneliness and unreciprocated love for Francesca Hart invite pity. Cockrill's commiseration with the unhappy man is best revealed in the final scene where he retrieves a blood-spattered photograph of Francesca which has fallen from the pocket of Pendock's corpse, wipes it off, and "puts it back gently into the lifeless hand" (244), a private gesture of kindness toward a man who has paid for his folly with his life. The suggestion is made that Cockrill, himself an aging and solitary man, identifies with Pendock's suffering.

The sly and venomous Vanda Lane of *Tour de Force* is perhaps the least sympathetic of any of the murderers in the six novels, but even she wins Cockrill's compassion. When she masquerades as Louvaine Barker, the detective is moved by what he perceives as her dejection and vulnerability: "She was terribly white; for once she wore no rouge and he was smitten with pity for her, pity and fear" (188). At this point in the story, Cockrill believes he is offering condolence to a heart-broken Louvaine, but the combined fear and pity in his reaction implies that, subconsciously, he has seen through the imposture. Yet later, when the ruthless Vanda Lane steps from behind the mask and her crimes are revealed, the Inspector abstains from the bitterness which overtakes the other characters, explaining her villainy as the consequence of "bad heredity" instead of depravity.

As a police detective, Cockrill might be expected to act as the culprit's nemesis, but compassion rather than vengefulness defines his attitude. At the close of *Fog of Doubt,* he consoles a distraught Ted Edwards, promising the condemned killer that "They won't hang you.... You'll go somewhere quiet; and forget all this and your mind will be peaceful again" (253). Edwards is of course a multiple murderer, but Cockrill is not unmoved by the man's guilty torment, nor is he punctilious in judgment. He understands and finally forgives human error. Otto Penzler has written that Cockie is "one of the kindest and gentlest of detectives whose irascibility tends to conceal a genuine humanitarianism,"[8] but it is the latter quality which most impresses the reader.

Though he is the chief inspector of the Kent County police force, Cockrill belongs more to the literary tradition of the idiosyncratic amateur detective, and Brand herself conceives of him as a singular sleuth rather than as the head of a unit. As if to underline the solitary nature of his craft, she almost always places him in residence at the crime scene, separated from colleagues, facilities, and police department bureaucracy. Three of the six novels, in fact, are set outside of Kent where Cockrill must act *ex officio* as an advocate of the accused or as *amicus curae* rather than as a police functionary. Detached from the constraints of officialdom, but not from the symbolism of authority, Cockrill acts as an independent investigator whose moral wisdom, finesse, and empathetic heart make him one of the most memorable of British detectives.

Notes

[1]W.H. Auden, "The Guilty Vicarage," in *Detective Fiction: Crime and Compromise*, ed. Dick Allen and David Chacko (New York: Harcourt, Brace, Jovanovich, 1974), p. 406.

[2]The editions of Brand's novels featuring Inspector Cockrill are listed below, preceded by the original date of publication. All quotations will be cited in the text, using, where necessary for clarity, the abbreviation given after the entry as follows:

1942 *Heads You Lose* (NY: Dodd, Mead, 1942). (*Heads*)

1944 *Green For Danger* (NY: Perennial Library, 1981). (*Green*)

1946 *The Crooked Wreath* (NY: Dodd, Mead, 1946). (*Wreath*) Alternate title: *Suddenly at his Residence.*

1948 *Death of Jezebel* (NY: Dodd, Mead, 1948). (*Jezebel*).   1952 *Fog of Doubt* (NY: Charles Scribner's Sons, 1953). (*Fog*) Alternate title: *London Particular*

1955 *Tour de Force* (NY: Perennial Library, 1982). (*Tour*)

Two collections of Brand's short stories have also been published which include stories featuring Inspector Cockrill.

1968 *What Dread Hand* (London: Michael Joseph, 1968).

1984 *Buffet for Unwelcome Guests,* ed. Francis M. Nevins, Jr. (Carbondale: Southern Illinois University Press, 1984).

[3]Christiana Brand, "Inspector Cockrill," in *The Great Detectives,* ed. Otto Penzler (Boston: Little, brown, 1978), p. 63.

[4]Brand, "Inspector Cockrill," p. 63.

[5]Review of *Death of Jezebel, The New Yorker,* 4 September 1948, p. 76.

[6]Brand, "Inspector Cockrill," p. 64.

[7]Brand, "Inspector Cockrill," p. 65.

[8]Otto Penzler, "Christianna Brand," in *The Great Detectives,* p. 58.

Colin Watson's Walter Purbright

Earl F. Bargainnier

When Colin Watson (1920-1983) wrote *Snobbery With Violence*, his critical study of British crime fiction and its audience, he had already written six of the twelve novels featuring the cases of Detective Inspector Walter Purbright.[1] A comparison of that study and the novels makes evident that Watson set out to avoid in his fiction the many faults he considered present in such major writers as Agatha Christie and Dorothy L. Sayers, as well as many lesser ones who imitated them. Nevertheless, though his novels contain much satire of such fiction, they remain in the same tradition. His novels have come to be called "The Flaxborough Chronicles," after the town in which Purbright is chief investigative officer. Flaxborough is the true protagonist of the novels, but as Julian Symons has noted, "the inconspicuous Inspector Purbright runs like a vein of common sense" through them.[2] It is his common sense— in contrast to the lunacy, chicanery, and sheer bloody-mindedness around him—which forms the basis of his personality and gives a point of stability against which to measure the zany actions of the Flaxborovians. Purbright's various assistants and the townspeople of Flaxborough who create the havoc he must not so much solve as clean up demand as much attention as his personality and methods in considering his cases and the comic-satiric nature of Watson's novels.

In *Snobbery With Violence* Watson states that "The detective is traditionally a somewhat priestly figure, utterly reliable, incorruptible and socially unsmirched," but that he may be baffled occasionally or even "stand a round of drinks, in order to show himself related to humanity."[3] Inspector Purbright is no exception to such a description. Similarly, Watson's comment that an "over-clever detective grows as tiresome in the long run as the most uninspired plodder" has direct application to Purbright, for he is neither over-clever nor an uninspired plodder (182). Also, in an imaginary interview with Chief Constable Harcourt Chubb, Purbright's superior, for *Murder Ink,* Watson makes other statements about his policeman (and himself). One of these is "Watson claims that his police characters are based on officers he has known."

Then follows this exchange on Purbright's not being a tough policeman:

Isn't that being rather out of fashion?
    Possibly. But it wouldn't do, you know. Not in Flaxborough. The last really aggressive officer we had was nearly thirty years ago.... Purbright is a very conciliatory chap in comparison.[4]

An author's statements about his works may lead one into the trap of the intentional fallacy, but, all in all, Watson's are helpful guides in approaching Purbright as man and policeman.

One of Pubright's assistants describes him as "a conscientious gentleman," but adds that "you mustn't go thinking he's Scotland Yard or something" (Coffin, 20). On the other hand, a London newspaper presents him to its readers as the "golden-haired seven footer known by the criminal fraternity of this remote area of rural England as Apollo" (Covens, 98). Purbright is somewhere between these humble and exaggerated views. He is fifty-one in *Charity Ends at Home,* happily married to an almost invisible Ann and living at 15 Tetford Drive, Flaxborough. Aside from his having been a prisoner of war near Vienna during World War II, nothing else is known of his private life. He is tall, over six feet, without being intimidating, rather having "the endearing ungainliness of some outsize domestic animal" (4122, 10) or looking "like some big Viking who'd missed the boat home and gone soft" (Nuns, 106). His springy hair is his most noticeable feature, being called variously corn-colored, flax-colored, and king-cup yellow. His eyes are gray, and his face is either mild, benign, bland, pleasant, good-humored, or slightly diffident. His easy-going manner is matched by his somewhat shabby office. Essentially, to use one of Chief Constable Chubb's favorite words, Purbright is a "nice" man.

His official position seems rather anomalous. He is Detective Inspector, but his "immediate" superior is Chubb. In Flaxborough the five ranks between their two positions—from Detective Chief Inspector to Deputy Chief Constable—are unfilled or at least unmentioned. Also, Purbright has had no promotion in more than twenty years and has asked for none, which pleases Chubb. Apparently position means little to Purbright: when he is saluted by a constable, he makes a face at him.

Purbright's personality can almost be summed up by one short phrase in *Lonelyheart 4122:* "He was a kindly man" (54). His kindness appears in numerous forms: his mild temperament; his magnanimity to others, including breakers of the law; his refusal to be ruffled no matter the snub; his diplomacy, illustrated by his repeated use of "as you know" in discussion of a case with Chubb, subordinates, or witnesses; and his lack of show, which he finds embarrassing in a policeman. However, this quality can disturb the more austere Chubb: "A good policeman, not a doubt of it. But...A reluctance to accept and apply straightforward moral rules. A strange deficiency of indignation. And always that skepticism" (Nuns, 154). Two aspects of Purbright's kindness are seen in *Charity Ends at Home* when he has to interview the married mistress of a suspect:

Look, I'm sorry, but we cannot talk usefully until we acknowledge this basic situation. Don't think that I'm bothered about people's notions of what's moral or immoral; I'm not. There isn't time for that sort of nonsense when one's trying to get at facts. Now then, never mind that awful police-court word "intimate." You're fond of each other, you like to make love together when the chance offers—that's the situation, isn't it?
*****
He hated this game he had to play by rules that insisted on his pretending to be an umpire. The rules gave him not only protection but power as well—the power to use every trick of legal casuistry and intimidation from the safe balk of official propriety. Oh, to hell...(154 & 158).

Kindness is generally a combination of innate qualities and the ability to empathize with others. Purbright's empathy is illustrated in *Bump in the Night* as he watches a fellow officer who is also a suspect interrogate another: "This embarrassing parody of Hollywood third-degree, Purbright knew, was simply Larch's way of taking reprisal for the destruction of his own self-confidence" (170). His knowledge of the weaknesses of others and his own kindness to them as a result make him an unpretentious but powerful moral force.

In spite of his kindess and his rarely feeling "annoyed with himself—or anyone else, for that matter" (Hopjoy, 178), Purbright's wit prevents his being too saintlike; as his sergeant says, "Very dry, is my boss" (Blue, 131). This view is supported by the authorial voice in *Lonelyheart 4122*: "his mild manner contained a seam of shrewdness against which many a specious or blustering argument had splintered. It was Purbright's 'sarcasm', as those who failed to impose upon him called it, that made stupid people nervous" (93). Purbright is not really sarcastic, but he continually uses irony, paradox, and understatement and enjoys punning. In *Hopjoy Was Here* he thinks of a snobbish waiter serving wine as "a well-bred dog owner awaiting the conclusion of his animal's defecation in a neighbor's gateway," considers a young woman as looking like "a bed-hopping Sunday school teacher," and floors a security agent by saying, "time wounds all heels...as Marx so succinctly put it," and then slyly adds, "Oh, not Karl...Groucho" (96, 118, 192). In *Bump in the Night* his comment on Chalmsbury is that "this little township deserves to be administered by the Sodom and Gomorrah Joint Sewage Board" and on a series of bombings, "High explosive...is the apotheosis of un-Englishness" (124 & 123). He puts down a pompous author in *Lonelyheart 4122* by saying he thinks John Buchan is "awfully good," but immediately feels that he has been malicious. He asks an American gangster posing as an olive oil salesman in *Six Nuns and a Shotgun* if he has come to Flaxborough for the East Anglian olive crop. Such examples number in the dozens, but as with Ngaio Marsh's Roderick Alleyn and his Sergeant Teddy Fox, most of Purbright's sallies take place in private with Sergeant Sidney Love. Two examples from many are found in *Coffin Scarcely Used:*

> 'Nothing round here, Sid?'
> 'What had you in mind, sir?'
> Purbright looked at Love from under his brows. 'Clues,' he said. 'Cloth fibres. Nail parings. Dust from a hunch-backed grocer's shop. You know.'
>
>   *   *   *
>
> Sid, we might stretch a point and let you borrow an o-fficial ve-hicle. Take the Hillman, and for heaven's sake don't scratch it or park it without lights or anything; the police are bastards in this town. (30-31 & 114)

Watson carefully balances the kindness and wit of Purbright so that he is neither too dull nor too clever, but an easy-going, engaging man who carries out his duties as police detective with common sense and compassion.

    Cyril Hare has noted the dangers of "the stodginess which is almost inseparable from official procedure" and the "quiet sober manner" expected of the British policeman and has further commented that writers may be excused if they "streamline police routine fairly ruthlessly" and if they surround the principal policeman with contrastingly colorful characters.[5] Watson's streamlining of routine will be considered shortly, but first some consideration must be given to the characters who work with Purbright and to the citizens of Flaxborough who provide his cases. Among the former are his superior, Chief Constable Harcourt Chubb, and his immediate subordinate, Sergeant Sidney Montgomery Love. Also present are a number of lesser policemen, as well as a few equals from other jurisdictions with whom Purbright collaborates. Finally, there is his most unusual "aide," Miss Lucilla Edith Cavell Teatime.

Chief Constables have long been the butts of comedy in British detective fiction, and Harcourt Chubb is no exception. Though Purbright can say that Chubb is better informed than he pretends to be, the more typical comment is that Chubb has an "expression of mournful omniscience which betokened an inability to make sure of what he had been told" (Dog, 85). Whether he is truly stupid or merely pretends to be so as to avoid being troubled by the unpleasantness of policework, he becomes a comic foil for Purbright. When not compelled to fulfill his position's responsibilities, Chubb retreats to his greenhouse or his seven aggressive Yorkshire terriers. His only other activity is reading lurid books, which he obtains from the local library, telling the librarian they are for Mrs. Chubb. Improbably, at least once he visits Flaxborough's brothel; the act is improbable for he is otherwise an elegant model of rectitude. That rectitude is matched by his essential innocence towards crime, which is also surprising, his having been chief constable for over thirty years, but he is a "man who has never really worried about anything in his life" (Nuns, 82). He uses the word *nice* as a talisman to ward off trouble, as when a woman faints: "It was 'rather nice' he considered, for sensitivity to be so highly developed. Dogs were much the same: the better the pedigree, the greater the propensity to have fits" (Sinners, 25). Another method of preventing trouble to himself is always to stand—his wife says he even stands to watch television: "he had learned that his insistence on standing in the seated presence of callers disheartened petitioners, frustrated complainants and generally reduced interviews to a minimum" (Bump, 93).

Chubb's view of crime is one of well-bred distaste. He becomes very unhappy when respectable people, particularly the upper class, become involved in a case, for they have inexplicably let his side down. However, he is totally honest and will protect no one, but he will be dubious of their involvement until Purbright has proof, causing the latter to say, "He thinks that crimes in this town are committed only in his policemen's imagination" (Hopjoy, 14). Chubb's special dislike is the subtle murder, saying that murder is "such a beastly business in the first place. It becomes positively crawly when you have to strain a decent intelligence to sort it out" (Hopjoy, 114). He prefers to think of policework as being that of a gardener pruning and spraying to rid society of the canker and mildew of crime, the analogy providing detachment from the real thing. Likewise, from his point of view the world would be better if it were "a great dog show with policemen having nothing to do but guard the trophies and hold leads" (Coffin, 17).

Though Purbright says with a grin, "He thinks I'm a cad" (Sinners, 110), his relationship with Chubb is usually amicable because Purbright has learned the proper approaches to obtain his ends from his superior. He allows Chubb to pretend wisdom, finding it often helpful to his own thought; he knows when to stop overpowering Chubb with details; and he never criticizes Chubb's attempts to disguise his dependence upon himself. Purbright has to bear such Chubbisms as "All this questioning and poking into other people's business. I don't know how you bring yourself to do it, Purbright, I don't really" (Coffin, 129-21), and though Purbright's teeth may clench, he perseveres. For his part, Chubb is not so stupid as not to be somewhat uneasy in confronting Purbright. He does not fear impertinence, which he considers an acknowledgement of inferiority, but rather the acceptance of his own ideas, which may lead heaven knows where: "if there were one thing calculated to disturb the chief constable more than another, it was prompt and unqualified agreement with one of his opinions by Inspector Purbright" (Blue, 76). He much prefers "the reassurance of rebuttal" to easy acquiescence, for the latter destroys his carefully constructed defenses:

he had never been able to decide to his own satisfaction whether Purbright's observations were intended to flatter or to bewilder him. He therefore had evolved a specially pliable defensive shield which could take, as seemed apposite at the moment, the shape of wisdom absolute, of a democratic willingness to learn, of the remembrance of an important engagement elsewhere, or even of a good-humored and altogether spurious stupidity. (Dog, 115)

Thus, Chubb remains an enigma: either stupid or calculatingly lazy.

Unlike Chubb, Sergeant Sidney Love never poses problems for Purbright. This blushing, sixteen stone boy of forty-four—as of *Plaster Sinners*—who thinks all liquor except ginger wine tastes rather awful, whose favorite word is *dinky*, and whose fiancee of fourteen years is a thirty-three year-old who plays goal on a mixed hockey team, is a comically likeable aide for Purbright. Over and over, Love's unlikely youthful appearance is emphasized. His face is as innocent as that of a choirboy, a boy martyr, an eleven-year-old, or a Dresden pastoral. His boyish enthusiasm and eagerly offered omniscient store of Flaxborough gossip are combined with his equally boyish admiration for the rich, which is unsullied by envy: rather he is "a sort of amateur anthropologist, ready always to be happily surprised by discovery of such gewgaws of trivial chieftainship as a white telephone or a leopardskin lavatory seat cover" (Dog, 11). And in spite of his athletic Agnes, he still feels raffish staring at "mammary canyons" and "scrumptious totties" and can be "gee-whizzed" by those in revelatory costumes—another evidence of his unchanging boyishness.

Perhaps because Love is so literal-minded in his day-to-day life, he enjoys developing fantastic theories on cases, not thinking them through. Purbright likes Sid, as he calls him, but is well aware of his limitations as a detective: "In eighteen years' service, his natural guilelessness, like his rubicund complexion, had remained inviolate. Purbright was very fond of him and supposed that he would have been revered as a holy man had he been born into one of those societies which equate idiocy with sanctity" (Nuns, 45). Love's guilelessness is evident every time he undertakes a task for Purbright. An obvious instance occurs in *Coffin Scarcely Used:* "When he wished to see without being seen, he adopted an air of nonchalance so extravagant that people followed him in expectation of his throwing handsful of pound notes in the air" (127). Similarly, when he has to follow a smart lady-crook, she leads him on a merry chase through parts of Flaxborough even he has never seen. The lengthiest example of Love in action occurs in *Whatever's Been Going On at Mumblesby?* when he is sent to eavesdrop on the patrons of The Barleybird, Mumblesby's inn; for fifteen pages Love's inadequacy parades itself before the reader. He obviously will always remain a sergeant—though how he has achieved that rank remains a mystery—but he also remains a delightfully comic character.

Less developed than Chubb or Love are the other policemen who work for or with Purbright. The constables are essentially humors characters: aggressive Brevitt, phlegmatic Palethorpe and Fairclough, dumb Pook, irritable Braine, and luckless Burke. There is also policewoman Sadie Bellweather, most of whose cases seem "to be concerned with the more bizarre manifestations of male vanity" (Doctor, 25). Assisting in forensics is the satirically named Warlock, who possesses a breezy manner at odds with the frequently gruesome nature of his work and who makes Purbright feel like a straight man in a comedy act. William Malley, the coroner's officer, is fat, kind, and knows even more than Love about Flaxborovian private lives; as Purbright says, "He can tell you things about this town that even I don't want to know" (Nuns, 88). Malley has to serve Albert Amblesby, the town's deliberately cantankerous and senile coroner, in the first eight novels, but then Watson mercifully—for the police force—dispatches the old nuisance with a peaceful death. These recurrent officers handle much of the police routine in the novels, but that work is "ruthlessly streamlined" or played for laughs.

Purbright works with men of more or less equal status from other jurisdictions in three of the novels. *Hopjoy was Here* offers a parody of Ian Fleming's James Bond in "the man known as Ross" of Intelligence. While being very superior to Purbright, Ross is so obtuse that he becomes a bore—which is obviously Watson's intent. *Bump in the Night* finds Purbright on special assignment in nearby Chalmsbury at the request of County Chief Constable Hessledine, a much more serious senior officer than Chubb. A major reason for Purbright's being there is that Chief Inspector Hector Larch, who is technically in charge of investigating a series of bombings is himself a suspect—a situation which does not make for easy relations between him and Purbright, nor does Larch's prickly personality. Purbright, however, is not cowed by him; in fact, as already noted, he feels sympathy for him and is happy to clear him of guilt. Much friendlier relations occur between Purbright and Detective Inspector Edgar Bradley in *Plaster Sinners*. Bradley is sent from London as one of that city's criminals is the victim in the case. Bradley has a droll sense of humor, and he and Pulbright spend much of their time trading quips about their work and colleagues. In all of his dealings with other policemen—on whatever level—Purbright remains calm, good-humored, and always in control.

His most unconventional relationship is that with Miss Lucilla Edith Cavell Teatime, Watson's feminine version of the gentleman-crook who aids the police. She is such a masterful comic creation that she dominates three of the eight novels in which she appears: *Lonelyheart 4122, Just What the Doctor Ordered,* and *It Shouldn't Happen to a Dog.* Lucy, as she is known to friends, is a vaguely middle-aged, lady-like swindler, specializing in charity frauds, but with other scams as well, nearly all of which are successful. She is at various times director of Famtrees, a genealogical agency; owner of The House of Yesteryear, an antique shop; secretary-treasurer of the Edith Cavell Psychical Research Foundation; and director of Moldham Meres Laboratories, which produces an herbal remedy for impotence. Most important, she becomes secretary of the Flaxborough and Eastern Counties Charities Alliance— a sort of East Anglian United Way—a post which enables her to buy her "little sports car, the cost of which modest self-indulgence she managed to implant neatly amidst the managerial expenses of a charity devoted to the relief of greengrocers' horses" (Dog, 151). Charity is a business for Lucy—the business of bilking the credulous to insure a continued supply of modest self-indulgences.

In spite of her extralegal activities, Lucy works happily with and for Purbright. Though he is aware of what she is up to, he knows that to prove it would not only be difficult, but would deprive him of a principal source of information and a shrewd counselor. His recognition of her aid is stated most explicitly in *Whatever's Been Going on at Mumblesby?*: "A sidelong glance at her face told Purbright that Miss Teatime, looking pensive now, was nearing the moment when she would, with no sign either of concern or condescension, present him with some piece of relevant and perhaps even vital information" (53). In each novel she has at least one major scene with Purbright, in which he seeks her opinion on his current case and she gladly gives it. Of course, she usually finds a way for her help to increase her savings account, but Purbright does not seem to mind. There are a number of remarks by him to indicate his awareness of her true activities, as when he asks with "genuine affability" if her antique shop can supply him with "a nice second-hand treadmill" (Mumblesby, 48). When she says in *Just What the Doctor Ordered* that she has been astonished by the "yield of the milk of human kindness since the alliance honored me with the secretaryship," his response is "Ah, one skims where one can, Miss Teatime, does one not?" (125). Purbright knows and Lucy knows he knows: that is the basis of their relationship, the reason she aids him and the reason he does not interfere with her schemes. As she explains to a criminal friend in *Charity Ends at Home:*

> Mr. Purbright is not a policeman in our sense of the word. He is a most charming man and, as I hope and believe, a tactful and realistic one....
> And Mr. Purbright, I might add, is not insensible to the attraction of a *quid pro quo.* (163)

What are the qualities that enable Lucy to aid Purbright? There are at least eight. Being a swindler, she has to be able to judge people's character, to be an amateur psychologist, if she is to succeed. This close scrutiny of others, especially from her perspective of trusting no one, makes her analysis of them invaluable in a criminal investigation. Also from her own experience, she has knowledge of the criminal mind, particularly of the type that can appear respectable to other people. Conversely, she is able to call upon her criminal friends, whether an abortionist or a gangleader, for information unavailable to others, certainly not to the police. She is without fear—except possibly of arrest; she faces personal physical harm and threats from a huge conglomerate with equal aplomb. Being thorough and well-organized, as evidenced by her "soft touch list," a remarkably detailed file of possible contributors to her charities, she is, as Purbright notes, perceptive in noticing small discrepancies in evidence. This ability is most clearly seen in *Kissing Covens*. Furthermore, she can piece together clues in a systematic manner that would do justice to any of the great detectives; her identification of a partially defaced metal disk in *It Shouldn't Happen to a Dog* is a prime illustration. Finally, there is her intense curiosity, which is a necessity for her own safety. Anything that is unusual or puzzling must be solved to her satisfaction; otherwise, she may make an error in her operations that could be a disaster for her. Therefore, she is willing to help the police to perserve her own way of "earning" a living. Nor does she ask for any credit; she is pleased to help—so long as Purbright does not take the time to investigate her own activities, but continues their *quid pro quo.*

Whatever else she may be, Lucy is consistent; the same cannot be said for the other Flaxborovians. It is not surprising that at times Purbright can feel "a little like the visitor to a closed ward in a psychiatric hospital who notices for the first time that none of the doors has a handle on the inside" (Blue, 75), for Flaxborough and its inhabitants could produce such an impression on any thinking person. A town of 14,482 with the motto "In Boldness We Prosper," Flaxborough is based upon the Lincolnshire port of Boston, which is on the Witham River a few miles from The Wash of The North Sea. Flaxborough and its neighbors, Chalmsbury and Brockleston-on-Sea, constitute the closed world of the novels. Flaxborough's history goes back to the Romans and is throughout one long example of the bloody-mindedness—an often repeated word—which continues to provide entertainment to its citizens. In every respect, Flaxborough is the exact opposite of the cozy village of British detective fiction which Watson excoriates as Mayhem Parva in *Snobbery With Violence.*

Lucy Teatime observes that "a certain cachet attaches to knavery in these parts, even at the highest levels of society" (Mumblesby, 19). Other general comments on the moral tone of Flaxborough include "a town of earthy misdemeanours" (Coffin, 53) and a place of "endemic sexual impetuosity" (Doctor, 28). More specifically, a probation officer sells dirty postcards to his clients, a brothel hires efficiency experts, the chairwoman of a witches' coven is not "orgy oriented" but the members are, a Baptist lay preacher is drummed out of the church for "his too liberal interpretation of the word 'lay' " (Covens, 79), and an alderman drugs the Amateur Operatic Society's cast of *Rose Marie* on opening night. The list could go on and on. Such events take place on Abdication Avenue, Windsor Close, Jubilee Park Crescent, and

Coronation Street and amidst the "great" Church of St. Lawrence, the Ann Boleyn Tea Room, the Klub Kissinger, and Fen Street's Edwardian Gothic police station, made of "that peculiarly durable stone which looks like petrified diarrhea" (Charity, 24). Watson never gives a map of Flaxborough, saying in *Snobbery With Violence* that maps are a worn-out device, but it is a fully realized setting for comedy and murder.

Also in *Snobbery With Violence* Watson attacks what he calls "tennis-club literature, where no one ever is called Ramsbottom or Golightly or Snagg" (103). He makes sure that no one can say the same of his novels; in fact, the only avid tennis player in them is a murderess. The names of the Flaxborovians—like their activities—are rarely beautiful. Even Chubb is named after a fish. Among many are Walter Grope, a rhyming cinema doorman; Vernon Wellbeloved, irascible superintendent of Twilight Close, a home for the ungrateful elderly; Winston Gash, a farmer who flirts in public by wringing a chicken's neck; Henry Popplewell, a slang-ridden journalist; Bernadette Croll, the local nymphomaniac who becomes a victim in *Whatever's Been Going on at Mumblesby?*; Dr. Halcyon Cropper, the local medical officer; Gertrude Gloss and Flora Pentatuke, matronly coven members; bawdy old Mrs. Crunkinghorn; and two disreputable families capable of anything: the Trings and the O'Shaunessys.

A number of these appear in more than one novel, a technique which Watson uses with many secondary characters to make Flaxborough a knowable, if improbable, place. Often a minor figure in one novel becomes a major one in a later, or vice versa. For example, a lawyer for the murderer in *Plaster Sinners* is a victim in *Whatever's Been Going On at Mumblesby?* and the husband of the victim in *Charity Ends at Home* becomes a member of a murder conspiracy in a later novel. At other times, family relationships provide a connection: a victimized girl in *Kissing Covens* is the niece of one of the principal villains in *Coffin Scarcely Used* and the murderess in *It Shouldn't Happen to a Dog* is the grandniece of the victim in *Coffin Scarcely Used,* while her sister appears as one of those scrumptious witnesses for Love in *Kissing Covens* and her father is in several novels. Others are just recurrent figures of the town, such as shady garage owner Alf Blossom, pompous lawyer Justin Scorpe, and Leonard Leaper, whose life is based upon the conviction that some day he will become King of England. Leaper appears in the second novel as a journalist, the fourth as a Nonconformist minister, and the ninth as the less than successful manager of the local dog shelter; he is a perfect example of the

Flaxborovian eccentric who brings forth Purbright's psychiatric hospital-Flaxborough analogy.

During one of his few arguments Purbright says that 'this is not a frontier town in nineteenth-century America, Mr. Mayor, and you are not a sheriff. If Flaxborough can be said to have such a person, I suppose it's me" (Blue, 74). The last few pages should indicate that if Flaxborough is not a frontier town, it is, with its collection of zanies, at least a difficult one in which to have to practice detection. That Purbright recognizes the difficulty is evident in his remark that "if all the twos put together in this town had proved fertile we should be overrun with fours" (Hopjoy, 33). His cases are flooded with red herrings, often farcical, ranging from supposed espionage and grotesque public bombings to the dueling pistols of "a loony earl" and the variety of sexual shenanigans of the Flaxborovians. Though more comic than mysterious, these red herrings create complications for Purbright, confuse the reader, and keep the plots jauntily bubbling along. Also, nine of Purbright's cases are based totally on physical evidence, providing more opportunities, in context, for comic incongruity. The keys to the solutions may be a baptismal font, a nylon suture, a dog's identification tag, a "satanic" headmask, first issue stamps, a stethoscope, or "begging" letters from a charity. Usually this physical evidence is discovered early, but its meaning is unknown, for it is either so innocuous or seemingly so unrelated to the crime that its significance is missed until Purbright makes the necessary connection. Still another factor which complicates four of his cases—*Coffin Scarcely Used, Kissing Covens, It Shouldn't Happen to a Dog,* and *Whatever's Been Going On at Mumblesby?*—is that the crime is the result of some form of conspiracy, with multiple villains lying to protect each other. (Six novels use the least-likely-suspect device, and in three the murderer is either barely seen or only talked about.)

But no matter the complexity of his cases, Purbright perseveres and solves them—though Lucy Teatime actually discovers the motive for the crime in *It Shouldn't Happen to a Dog,* providing him the murderer without his ever knowing of her help. Watson gives Purbright a medley of qualities from various forms of detective fiction to enable his success. He is a keen observer without seeming so, like Sherlock Holmes noting the smallest details; keeps information to himself as well as does Hercule Poirot; sleuths in the most traditional sense; makes last-minute rescues a la the thriller; keeps his men in line like the precinct captain of a procedural; and feels pity at the wastefulness of murder in the manner of so many humane gentlemen-policemen. All of these qualities are enveloped by his common sense, evident in his pondering his first murder case: "Purbright supposed that a murder could be solved by the same procedure as was used to detect a bicycle thief or the perpetrator of a charabanc outing swindle, and he was probably right" (Coffin, 53). Allied to his common sense is his belief that his job "consists substantially of exercising patience" (Sinners, 45), his unfailing politeness to everyone concerned in a case, and his refusal to take "as a personal insult the unwillingness of a wrongdoer to be caught" (Bump, 180). Though he can be active when necessary, he is much more a thinker. The sifting of information by analytical thought is at the center of his method of investigation. The problem, of course, is to know the correct questions to ask, as indicated by his exasperated statements that he is "at the damn-fool question stage" and "the stage of not knowing what to throw away" (Coffin, 68 & 77). But he continues to ask questions, search for physical proof, accept help from anyone offering it, and send his men out for more information to examine.

In spite of his using his team of men, Purbright is not a procedural policeman. Watson sprinkles all of the novels with passages which have a procedural note, most notably in *Six Nuns and a Shotgun*, but they are more lip-service to the procedural school than the real thing. A paragraph in *Blue Murder* both illustrates such passages and, through its last sentence, indicates how Watson undercuts the true procedural tone and method:

> The inquiries into the death of Clive Grail were in the charge of Detective Inspector Purbright, acting on behalf of the chief constable, Mr. Harcourt Chubb. He was assisted by Detective Sergeant Sidney Love, Sergeant William Malley, coroner's officer; three officers in plain clothes named Harper, Pook and Hollis; and five uniformed constables. Subsidiary and specialized aid was provided by the East Midlands Forensic Science department; the Post Office; the acting police surgeon and the pathology department of Flaxborough General Hospital. Co-operation on less formal levels was forthcoming from Josiah Keeble, editor of the *Flaxborough Citizen;* from Chung Lee Ha, restaurant proprietor; and from an old gentleman in Brockleston-on-Sea who remembered the making of a cinematograph record of that resort's Armistice celebration in 1918. (126)

In that previously noted imaginary interview, Chubb says of his author, "There's a certain irreverence about him," that he is flippant, and that he has a "Very perverse sense of humour."[6] No one having read the Flaxborough novels can quarrel with these statements. In them Colin Watson creates a zany, bizarrely comic, and often bawdy world, which he views with detached amusement. At times the detectival element may take second place to the comedy and satire, but generally

Watson is able to weave the two into a seamless whole through the presence of Inspector Walter Purbright. Not comic himself, though as noted he can be witty, he is the quiet center of the whirligig that is Flaxborough. Always affable, unruffled, and commonsensical, he moves among his fellow Flaxborovians correcting, calming, and cleaning up the messy confusions, follies, and crimes in their lives. In spite of his middle-class status, he owes more to the gentlemen-policemen of such writers as Marsh and Innes than might be expected (or that Watson would probably have admitted). He has his team of officers and he uses them, but his cases are not examples of the police procedural; rather they are contemporary police versions of the British comic detective novel. To close on a typically Watsonian hypothesis, perhaps Purbright is an indiscretion of Roderick's Alleyn's youth!

Notes

[1]The editions of Watson's novels in which Inspector Purbright appears are listed below, preceded by the original date of publication. All quotations will be cited in the text using, where necessary for clarity, the abbreviation after the entry:

1958 *Coffin Scarcely Used* (New York: Dell, 1981). (Coffin)
1960 *Bump In the Night* (New York: Walker, 1961). (Bump)
1963 *Hopjoy Was Here* (New York: Walker, 1963). (Hopjoy)
1967 *Lonelyheart 4122* (Chicago: Academy Chicago, 1983). (4122)
1968 *Charity Ends at Home* (New York: Dell, 1983). (Charity)
1969 *Just What the Doctor Ordered* (New York: Putnam, 1969). (Doctor)
1972 *Kissing Covens* (New York: Putnam, 1972). (Covens)
1974 *Six Nuns and a Shotgun* (New York: Putnam, 1974). (Nuns)
1977 *It Shouldn't Happen to a Dog* (New York: Putnam, 1977). (Dog)
1979 *Blue Murder* (London: Eyre Methuen, 1979). (Blue)
1981 *Plaster Sinners* (Garden City: Doubleday, 1981). (Sinners)
1982 *Whatever's Been Going On at Mumblesby?* (Garden City: Doubleday, 1983). (Mumblesby)

The British titles of *Just What the Doctor Ordered, Kissing Covens* and *It Shouldn't Happen to a Dog* are *The Flaxborough Crab, Broomsticks Over Flaxborough* and *One Man's Meat* respectively.

[2]*Mortal Consequences* (New York: Harper & Row, 1972), p. 202.

[3]*Snobbery With Violence* (London: Eyre and Spottiswoode, 1971), p. 211. Further references will be cited in the text.

[4]"Interview With a Character," *Murder Ink,* ed. Dilys Winn (New York: Workman, 1977), p. 80.

[5]"The Classic Form," *Crime in Good Company,* ed. Michael Gilbert (London: Constable, 1959), p. 79.

[6]"Interview With a Character," pp. 79 & 80.

Bill Knox's Colin Thane and Phil Moss

Constance Hammett Poster

It is interesting that the British police procedural novel which best corresponds to the ideal type described by George Dove in *The Police Procedural* is not English but Scottish, and paradoxically the same characteristics which make Bill Knox's Thane/Moss series uniquely Scottish are the very ones which place it in the pure police procedural genre.[1] The description of the organizational structure and methods of the police follow the standard pattern of their type, but unlike their novelistic counterparts on both sides of the Atlantic who suffer from doubts about the conflict between their jobs and personal lives, seem overwhelmed by the prevalence of crime and corruption, and question the role of a police force in society, Thane, Moss and all their colleagues are shown to have a keenly felt sense of responsibility and duty and to believe that hard work is a virtue and one becomes a policeman in response to a calling.

That this set of attitudes and beliefs is part of Glasgow's Millside Division police force and rarely met with elsewhere, is attributable to the religious forces which have shaped Scotland's thinking for over four hundred years. It was John Knox, famous church reformer and politician, who single-handedly turned his country into a Calvinist stronghold, and that harsh creed with its emphasis on self-denial, discipline, thrift and hard work as a method of coping with the fears and uncertainties of predestination—known as the Protestant Ethic— is part of the ingrained habits of thought of the Scots. Religious adherance has declined but patterns of thinking based on Knox's Presbyterianism linger on.[2]

Not that Thane and Moss are shown as being excessively moralistic or consider themselves the hammer of God set on earth to punish the wrongdoer. Thane, the major character, and senior in rank to Moss, is portrayed as compassionate and understanding. He does not show prejudice toward minorities and, in fact, pays some lip service to gender equality. He dislikes unnecessary violence, and there are no scenes of policemen beating prisoners, although when he deals with a particularly heinous crime, Thane acknowledges the wish to give the malefactor "a good thumping." He has been division boxing champion in his youth, but although there may be punch-ups at the denouments of the stories, they have the innocence of old-time cowboy movie saloon fights.

Nor are Thane's attitudes toward sex particularly repressive; no criticism is made of people having affairs, although excess of any kind seems to lead to a bad end. The religious factor is to be discovered in Bill Knox's construction of motivations for criminal actions.

As a crime writer for a Glasgow newspaper, Knox, like any good city reporter, is familiar with a wide range of criminal behavior. The crimes about which he chooses to write are common to all technologically developed urban areas: fraud and robbery, with murder as a possible consequence. The emphasis on particular motivations, however, reflects Scotland's religious preoccupations. There is on the one hand, the stories that deal with the problem of order and discipline in the patriarchal family. A number of plots concern crimes committed as the result of a young person, usually male, rebelling against an authority figure (father, uncle, mentor), ending with the commission of a murder (*Draw, Grey, Antiques, Leave, Little, Live, Rally.*) In *Draw Batons*, Frank Walsh hates and envies his father, Jarrold, so strongly that at the conclusion of the novel when his part in murder and theft is revealed, Frank taunts him by saying that all his actions were just a way of getting out from under him. Parenthetically, it may be remarked that none of these plots lend themselves to any kind of simplistic Oedipal explanations; they are quite decidedly problems of authority and discipline.

Since Knox places the emphasis in his work on the use of police procedures in the solutions of crimes and the fast-paced action this entails, he does not spend much time discussing the psychological make-up of the criminal, but since motiveless crime is uninteresting to the reader, in all but one book (*Justice*) which deals solely with the professional criminal and possibly for that reason is the least successful in the series, motive is either directly attributed or implied. And while all transgressions against society can be subsumed under the Ten Commandments, the impression one has from reading the eighteen books in the series, is that it is as much the commission of one or more of the seven deadly sins as the fact that the actions are classed as illegal, that brand the man or woman as a criminal.

Knox would find himself agreeing with Karl Marx that the prime motive for human action is economic; for the most part crimes are committed for gain, but other quite important factors are involved. The following is a tentative outline: *Children*—pride, envy, covetousness; *Draw*—pride, envy, covetousness; *Deadline*—lust, pride (this is one of the three novels in which sex rather than love or possessiveness is used as a motive); *Death*—covetousness; *Deep*—envy, covetousness; *Grey*—gluttony (drink), covetousness; *Hanging*—covetousness, envy, anger; *Justice*—sloth?; *Kill*—lust, gluttony, envy, sloth; *Antiques*—pride, covetousness; *Leave*—pride, gluttony, envy, covetousness; *Little*—pride, envy, sloth, covetousness; *Live*—lust, pride, covetousness; *Man*—covetousness, envy, sloth; *Pilot*—covetousness, envy; *Rally*—pride, envy, anger, covetousness; *Taste*—covetousness, pride; *Tallyman*—gluttony, covetousness, sloth.

Tallyman is an interesting example. The plot deals with a loan shark operation run on the model with which Americans are familiar—twenty-five percent interest per week and physical violence if you can't pay up. The moral indignation of the judge who must sentence one of his victims who has been forced to embezzle to pay his debt, of Thane and even other crooks, is triggered by their detestation of the loan shark's gluttony, his need to have even greater amounts of money although he has a sufficiency. The total lack of restraint here is more important than the technical illegality.

The Series Team

Bill Knox is a prolific writer, author under his own name and others of three series and several non-series novels. Although his non-Thane/Moss series use neither policemen nor Glasgow settings, they show his continuing interest in the procedural. One series centers on a man who works for Her Majesty's Fishery Protection Service, giving us a fascinating picture of the workings of the bureau as well as affording Knox an opportunity for some superb description of sailing and northern Scotland. His love of, and ability to show us so vividly, Scotland is one of Knox's great strengths. At these moments he seems one of the true inheritors of the tradition of Stevenson and Buchan.

In the second series, the home base of the civil service bureau known as "Queen's and Lord Treasurer's Remembrancer" is Edinburgh, but in his pursuit of estates which may revert to the crown and the like, Jonathan Gaunt visits various spots on the continent. This bureau has its own set of procedures, some unorthodox. Taking the three series as a whole the reader can learn quite a bit about the manner in which government institutions operate in Scotland, and Knox organizes his presentation of information in a stimulating fashion.

Chief Detective Inspector Colin Thane, later Detective Superintendent of the Millside Division in Glasgow, and as of 1984, Joint Deputy Commander of the Scottish Crime Squad is remarkable not least in that he has managed to remain in his early forties for twenty-seven years. For most of his career he has been teamed with Detective Inspector Phil Moss, a most felicitious union since the characters complement each other so well. Thane is tall, muscular, rugged, putting on a bit of weight, although he still shows the fitness of a man who has been on the police boxing team. He has a wife, Mary, two children, and a mortgaged home. He's a thruster who likes to back a hunch:

He forcibly disciplined himself to tolerate the need for refinements, he would rely to the limit on every scientific aid he could find, but when circumstances dictated he would willingly act first and sweat out the result later. (*Taste*, 20)

Thane is impatient, dislikes procedure and paperwork at the same time that he admits, "they add up to the disciplined, grinding mills of police routine which so often held the key to successful police investigation" (*Sanctuary*, 20)

When his essential humanity gives way to hard, controlled anger is the time when Thane reaches peak efficiency. His partner, Phil Moss is unlike Thane in both physique and temperament. Less excitable and imaginative than Thane, Moss appears almost comic. Barely regulation height, of indeterminate age (most guess about ten years older than his partner), he is a victim of a legendary ulcer for which he takes an endless series of nostrums, each more loathsome than the other. Moss's ulcer provides one of the running gags of the series, since he refuses to have it surgically removed. However, uncomfortable as it may be, the ulcer never keeps him from his job. Nor does his slight build prevent him from "holding his own in the dirtiest back street battle."

Following the pattern of the pure procedural, the partners are very close and have a great fondness for each other. The bachelor Moss is regarded as an honorary uncle by Thane's children and in the one story in which Thane is seen as having a serious family problem— his son is getting into bad company and is in possession of burglar tools—it is Moss who straightens out the situation (*Antiques*).

With the publication of *Live Bait* in 1979, Knox presumably felt he had exhausted the possibilities of the team and the Millside locale, even though the district comprises areas as diverse as a Clydeside slum and an upper-middle class area called Monkswalk. Moss has his ulcer operation which keeps him from active duty for a while, and Thane is promoted to Detective Superintendent and assigned to the Scottish Crime Squad, which is not tied to any particular region. This gives Knox the opportunity to introduce two new possible partners: young, impetuous but intelligent Sergeant Francey Dunbar and Police Constable Sandra Craig, who is said to be a good, hard-working cop, whose weakness is constant hunger. In addition, there's Joe Felix, a scientific communications specialist, who affords Knox the opportunity to talk about new investigative procedures. None of these minor characters has crystalized into someone strong enough to take Moss's place as evidenced by his being reintroduced in a major role in the last series novel.

The same might be said of Chief Superintendent William "Buddha" Ilford, Thane's old boss. An instantly recognizable character who performed the function of representing the higher authority in the chain of command, pushing Thane, demanding impossible results and bestowing praise grudgingly, his quirks were a welcome part of the book. Hart, the new boss, is so far a supernumerary. The strain of keeping a series going over almost thirty years without losing the interest of either the reader or oneself is considerable. As consummate a technician as Knox is, he is undoubtedly aware of this, but it is as yet unclear how he will solve the problem.

Attitudes Toward Society

To his credit, Knox has avoided the more distasteful modes of thinking of some of the police procedurals. As previously mentioned, Thane is no bigot. Much of his work, even when interacting with factory owners, is among the street criminals, the "neds" of Glasgow. The early books and to some extent the recent ones make it clear that Knox holds to the school of criminology which places most of the blame on conditions of social disorganization—bad housing, unemployment. Occasionally, while not falling into the currently fashionable despair over the rise in crime rates, he admits that some people will always commit crimes. Thane observes in 1973:

Soon Columba Street would vanish, its families be rehoused—and even if the kids stayed grubby they'd then have a bath to be dumped into at night... It was taking time and money but very slowly the city was beginning to win on social terms, wiping out conditions that bred neds. (*Draw, 78*)

But earlier in 1967 he says that whereas at one time an outsider could have strolled through the middle of a Glasgow gang fight and emerged untouched, shielded by his neutral status, it is no longer true. The old gangs that had fought for the love of it and as a relief from the monotony of poverty were now "younger, vicious rat-packs with money in their pockets and contempt for the weak" (*Justice,* 46).

As for his attitudes toward women, the police department has always been a male enclave, with the traditional jokes about women. Knox makes an effort to be more up-to-date in this respect. If he does not show women in positions of authority, it is probably because they do not exist, for his knowledge of the police structure is awesome, but he does show us women in positions of authority in industry or interacting with men on a level of intellectual equality. However, his real admiration is for the Mary Thanes of the world, women who are loyal, uncomplaining homemakers and mothers, easing the policeman's job, and raising his children in a loving but disciplined fashion to internalize the values shared by herself and her husband. When Thane is offered a plush job as head of security for a regional bank, even though it means more money and a nine-to-five, free weekend existence, she tells him that he must make up his own mind and exerts no pressure on him to make the decision she prefers. (*Tallyman*)

Why does Thane choose to stay in the force? Knox details all the complaints we are familiar with from other police procedurals: overwork, a thankless profession, understaffed, seeing the underside of life every day, being caught between the conflicting demands of the public, those in charge, human feelings and the need to maintain professional standards. Here is one reason a policeman in this series offers to explain his choice of job: "Ach, who the hell would be a cop? I suppose somebody's always got to be around—maybe that's what it's all about" (*Tallyman*, 188). Thane's attitude is probably that found by Holdaway, in his study of the English police force. He says that the constables he worked with saw themselves as the last bastion between civilization and chaos. In their view, it was not the ties of kinship, friendship and comradeship, work and play that maintain society, but the police force.[3]

Another important fact about Thane that helps make him one of the most likeable of the procedural cops is that he has no desire for sweeping powers. In an investigation of whiskey adulteration, he works with a Surveyor in Customs and Excise who has extraordinary powers— the Scots take their whiskey seriously.

He could demand or force entry into any house or building in the course of his duties and search it without having to worry about the need for a warrant. He could arrest a suspect, have him lodged in prison for any one of a wide variety of offenses... All in all the Customs and Excise force had a sobering strength. It was a strength, however, used sparingly with a heavy and automatic disciplining of any enthusiast who went too far without adequate reason. (*Taste*, 67-8)

This is an authoritarian's dream, but Thane's sense of fair play and his awareness of the dangers of absolute power make him wary of it.

The police force, like other branches of the civil service is supposed to be a-political, but of course this is a myth. By its very nature it must uphold whatever group is in power. On a smaller scale, pressure is constantly being applied to go easy on Judge X's son or play down cases which might cause embarrassment to the rich or powerful. On the other hand, a poor record of solving cases will be a bar to further promotion. A stock figure in police procedurals is the policeman who ignores all this in order to maintain his integrity. Thane is no different from the rest. In one case involving whiskey fraud he finds himself going after a man in whose company Buddha Ilford owns stock. Needless to say, it does not stop him.

Knox has also written a story involving Scottish nationalists, an extremely touchy situation for him as well as his protagonists. He manages to take no position himself, except against violence in the pursuit of extremist goals, but states that although England and Scotland were merged in 1603, the Scots have remained independent and stubborn, cherishing their past, and angry at being ignored by successive London-based governments. Of the three political solutions—status quo, independence or federalism—Knox gives us no hint as to which he or Thane prefers.

Knox writes a fast-paced story, with ingenious settings in industry or related to hobbies such as racing or flying. In either case we see the use of one of the original functions of fiction: describing types of work and the social relations of the workplace. The novels are not diffuse; there is a major case which is followed through to a successful conclusion. While other pending cases are mentioned, they are relegated to the background unless they impinge in some fashion on the major theme. Subordinate stories about the criminal activities of neds may be brought in to illustrate a dead end, but never distract attention from the main theme. And just as there are few sub-plots, there are no pauses for deep introspection on the part of the characters. Knox's crime fiction does not make much of psychological insight, but this is not to say that the men and women are not clearly delineated. What brings them to life is the sharp eye and descriptive power Knox developed in his journalistic years. He would have made a good cultural anthropologist; his pictures of flat interiors place people in social class structures quickly and accurately. Nothing is extraneous; the detail is masterful:

Bare floorboards met peeling, faded wallpaper. Grimy cracked ceiling, stained brown with damp over much of its area boasted a single bare electric light bulb. There was a small fireplace in one corner, the grate overflowing with crumpled rubbish. Furniture was restricted to a sagging bed against one wall, a mattress with blankets on the floor near the window, a scarred table, chairs and an old wardrobe. A gas ring and chipped sink constituted the kitchen area, used dishes and empty bottles cluttered the tabletop. (*Justice*, 28)

This is writing with texture and, together with the swiftness of Knox's plotting, must be discussed within the framework of the police procedural. These are not whodunits; the identity of the criminal is known to us as soon as Thane finds out, and for the most part this is about halfway through the book. The interest is in the capture of the criminal and the securing of evidence for his conviction. Since, as was previously noted, these are cases of fraud and robbery, there is generally a hierarchy of criminals, the neds or small fry at the bottom being discovered fairly easily, the top men or women with greater difficulty. Generally Knox puts in a chase at the end which leads the police into the Scottish countryside. While this gives Knox a chance to use his descriptive talents on areas for which he has great fondness, it serves the more important function of providing great Buchan-like chase scenes in which man is pitted against nature as much as man. There is also the implication that retributive justice is meted out by Nature, in order to restore harmony and balance. In many of these scenes the criminal's defeat is effected as much by Nature as man; a higher justice prevails (*Live, Hanging, Antiques, et. al.*).

In order to show the use Knox makes of police procedures and how well they are integrated into story, I have selected a 1962 novel entitled *Little Drops of Blood* for detailed analysis. With one or two exceptions, such as his venture into spy story, in which Thane and Moss are involved (*Man*), every story contains a wealth of detail about procedures. Laboratory men, traffic officers, fingerprint experts, records keepers and the like are series regulars. We are told so much about the workings of the Scottish police organization that Knox has prefaced his books with a disclaimer:

The organization and methods of the Scottish Crime Squad are different in some minor details from those given in this story.
I know it and the Scottish Crime Squad know it. They want it that way.

Page one opens with an Occurrence Report:

Following radio message received from Control, time 23.48 hours, Thursday, April 22, proceeded to South Salisbury Road where beat constable was already in attendance. Deceased civilian was lying on the west side of the roadway at a point of 15 yards north of the engine factory entrance. Patrol radioman John Murray assisted beat constable in search for witnesses. None located. Roadway badly lit at locus. On preliminary examination, deceased appeared to be victim of traffic accident. Multiple injuries, and clear traces of car treads on raincoat. Second inspection of area, however, showed indications which decided me to request C.I.D. attendance. Detective Inspector Moss of Millside Division arrived at locus at 00.29 hours.

In one short paragraph Knox has managed a surprising number of plot developments and scene-setting devices.

1. We know what a Scottish Occurrence Report looks like and the type of information the officer must develop.

2. We have a preliminary description of the scene.

3. The penultimate sentence sets the stage for a murder investigation.

4. The report contains a partial outline of the police department chain of command.

5. We have a preliminary description of the victim's injuries and a probable cause of death.

6. The final sentence introduces second-in-command series character, Phil Moss.

The pace of the book and the police both move swiftly. Within minutes of joining Moss, Thane gets his crew going. Men are stationed fifty yards on either side of the accident. The body is examined for identification and to validate the preliminary explanation of the injuries. Knox starts a running joke by Thane at Moss's expense which will be unknowingly reprised by other experts. It both sets the tone of the relationship between Thane and Moss and puts a brake on the build-up of the intensity of a murder investigation to sustain reader interest. Moss is cold. Thane quotes an old Scottish proverb, "Never cast a cloot till May's oot." Although he has made a joke, it is clear that he is genuinely concerned about Moss's discomfort.

Moss's memory comes to Thane's aid as he semi-recognizes the corpse as being one of their villains, hastening the identification process since his prints can be run through the Criminal Records office. We are beginning to understand the workings of the organization. The doctor and Scientific Bureau men have come on the scene. In terms of the authority structure, Knox has started with beat cop and by the following morning we'll meet Ilford, thus encompassing the normal chain of command. The duties and responsibilities appropriate to each level will be clearly spelled out, and in the meantime we see how Thane exhibits leadership qualities. It is these qualities as well as his top-notch police work that will eventually gain him promotion.

Constable MacDonald, the man in the patrol car, draws his attention to the fact that the jagged edges of the blood drops point both north and south, making it probable the victim has been run over more than once. Thane congratulates him on his attentiveness and later commends him to Ilford.

The doctor's preliminary medical report indicates the victim was rendered unconscious before being placed on the road to be run over. Were he to have been standing, his legs would have been hit first by the bumper, but there are no signs of leg injuries and no broken glass from where the headlights would have struck him had he been standing.

In less than six pages we've seen a police machine galvanized into activity as the result of what seems to be a simple case of murder, but of course is later shown to be extremely complex. The facts are brought out through the dialogue; plot exposition does not consist of a series of leaden, declarative sentences. The reader has been whirled up into the investigation as it proceeds and is eager to follow it. The beginning is always the busiest time; dead ends, the disappointment of false leads may come later but by then the reader has so empathized with Thane and Moss that he or she will put up with the checks in the action knowing it will recommence shortly.

Thane gets only three hours sleep that night on a cot in his office; police work is grueling. He sees Ilford the following morning, and we know about Thane's discomfort at entering Buddha's office. Too often a summons to that place spells trouble. He is able to tell Ilford that the dead man, Sammy Bell, an ex-convict is a mechanic. Ilford in return explains the burgeoning stolen car racket. Since there may be a connection between Bell's death and the racket, they decide to let his death appear as the result of an accident to lull the gang's suspicions. Thane's supposed ignorance of the workings of the racket is a device to describe it to the reader. Knox is at his best with these accounts, showing very solid research. Ilford puts Thane in charge of the investigation which doesn't please him. He comments to Moss that Millside Division is being asked to pull Headquarters' chestnuts out of the fire. This intra-service rivalry is standard in the pure police procedural. Knox allows Thane to become introspective at this point. He criticizes himself for not paying more attention to the stolen car reports, but how can he be both at his desk reading reports and out in the field catching crooks? Once more the theme of the overworked and unappreciated cop.

At this juncture his wife calls to remind him that it is his son's tenth birthday and he should be home. He thinks he can be, but they are both aware that duty overrides personal concerns. Knox continues to run through the litany of police procedural formulae. Police start tracing the known associates of the deceased. Thane can use the formal networks for this or tap into the informal ones such as asking a fellow officer who specializes in the area for help. If he gets the information he wants, he may obligate himself to return the favor in kind or some other fashion.

Thane and Moss call at the garage where Bell worked and meet Erick Millan, the well-known racing driver, who manages it. In order to find out about him, since he is not a known criminal, they call on Jock Mills, a newspaperman. The cooperation between the newsmen and police is edgy and potentially dangerous. The reporter may promise to keep quiet in order to curry favor with the police or get a scoop later, but cops know that while their own loyalty is to the department, Mills is an outsider and outsiders can never be trusted totally. While the full extent of Millan's villainy is not yet apparent, the information developed about him calls his character into question. He is a womanizer, an egotist, letting his uncle's business decay while he concentrates on his driving; unlike the police group, he cannot subordinate his personal desires for the good of the organization.

When Knox finally lets his readers meet Erick's uncle, Ludd Millan, he turns out to be a member of a class Knox uses frequently, the self-made man. The idleness of the nephew is juxtaposed against the hard-working Ludd, whose blunt fingertips still show faint scars of knuckle-barking, skin-tearing spanner work. His kindness toward his nephew is not reciprocated. He goes so far as to warn Erick when the police come to arrest him even though he knows him to be a killer.

The final chase scene takes place in the Cairngorms, rough, mountainous country, where the Glaswegian police are at a disadvantage compared to their country colleagues. Moss's leg is broken (not a serious injury for a series hero), and Millan is taken back to the city to be charged and eventually receive a life sentence. By removing Millan from society and themselves from the Cairngorms, Thane and Moss assure the reader that the balance of nature and society will be restored.

Knox and the Future of the Scottish Police Procedural

It would not be overstating the case to say that until recently, Bill Knox *was* the Scottish police procedural. There are a goodly number of Scottish detective story writers and even more born outside Scotland who have used it as a setting for their novels, but only Knox has made use of the procedural formula to gain international fame. Asked to characterize his books, one would say first and foremost that he is a "good read." Vice, sexual assaults and the rest of the sleazy criminal activities that pervade the American police stories cannot be found in Knox's work. There are no four-letter words, no sexual encounters, and Thane, while he may admire a pretty leg, does not appear to be tempted into adultery. One can only speculate as to the reasons for this reticence, but one suspects that it was a deliberate choice to attract a specific audience, which has signified its approval by continuing to buy his books.

The desire to appeal to a wide audience on both sides of the Atlantic may also explain why little broad Scots dialect is to be found in Knox's work. The essence of a good read is that the book should not cause discomfort as would happen if there were too much violence or one were not assured from the start that the good guys would win and the wicked ones be punished. Nor should the reader have to sit with glossary in hand. For the sake of versimilitude, and possibly for the same reason that shops in Scotland deck everything in sight with tartans for the tourist season, when Thane visits rural areas, a few words are sprinkled in the conversation. Otherwise Knox uses a literate, straightforward prose style which suits the characters he creates.

The shape of the Scottish police procedural may be changing with the entry of two new writers in the field. Peter Turnbull, who works in Glasgow, but is a native Englishman, writes tough, ultra-violent police stories that put in all the cynicism and negativity Knox leaves out. There is much less science and more informers and the police personnel are certainly less idealistic and more self-involved. There is very little about them that is particularly Scottish including the language.

The most interesting of the new Scots writers is William McIlvanney, who is regarded as much more a novelist than a writer of police novels. Two of his books have been published in this country: *The Papers of Tony Veitch* and *Laidlaw*. His policemen are also unlike Knox's. Laidlaw works in a tough Glaswegian slum where violence is the norm, but he is an intellectual who reads Camus and tries to rid himself of the guilt instilled in him by Calvinist parents. As with Turnbull, the individual policeman seems to overshadow the group. While these authors may be writing a new kind of police formula novel, Knox remains the pre-eminent practitioner of the classic form.

Notes

[1]The editions of Knox's novels in which Colin Thane and Phil Moss appear are listed below, preceded by the original date of publication. All quotations will be cited in the text using, where necessary for clarity, the abbreviation given after an entry:

1957 *Deadline for a Dream* (London: Long, 1957); as *In at the Kill* (New York: Doubleday, 1961). (Deadline)

1959 *Death Department* (London: Long, 1959). (Death)

1960 *Leave it to the Hangman* (New York: Doubleday, 1960). (Leave)

1962 *The Grey Sentinels* (London: Long, 1962); as *Sanctuary Isle* (New York: Doubleday, 1962). (Grey)

1962 *Little Drops of Blood* (New York: Doubleday, 1962). (Little)

1963 *The Man in the Bottle* (London: Long, 1963); as *The Killing Game* (New York: Doubleday, 1963). (Man)

1965 *The Taste of Proof* (New York: Doubleday, 1965). (Taste)

1966 *The Deep Fall* (London: Long, 1966); as *The Ghost Car* (New York: Doubleday, 1966) (Deep)

1967 *Justice on the Rocks* (New York: Doubleday, 1969). (Justice)

1969 *The Tallyman* (New York: Doubleday, 1969). (Tallyman)

1970 *Children of the Mist* (London: Long, 1970); as *Who Shot the Bull?* (New York: Doubleday, 1970). (Children)

1971 *To Kill a Witch* (New York: Doubleday, 1971). (Witch)

1973 *Draw Batons!* (New York: Doubleday, 1973). (Draw)

1976 *Rally to Kill* (New York: Doubleday, 1976). (Rally)

1977 *Pilot Error* (New York: Doubleday, 1977). (Pilot)

[2]See Roland H. Banton, *The Reformation of the 16th Century* (Boston: Beacon Press, 1952).

[3]See Simon Holdaway, *Inside the British Police: A Force at Work* (Oxford: Blackwell, 1983).

Peter Lovesey's
Sergeant Cribb and Constable Thackeray

Jeanne F. Bedell

"Do, sir? Do nothing. Talk to us. That's all." (*Wobble to Death*)

In writing his first Victorian detective story, *Wobble to Death,* Peter Lovesey emphasized the creation of atmosphere: "For me, the main thing in that book was establishing the atmosphere of the race and getting my characters and getting the crime underway. Cribb was brought in simply to be a working Victorian policeman of the time, quite different from a Sherlock Holmes character."[1] His now famous detectives, Sergeant Cribb and Constable Thackeray, do not appear until almost halfway through the novel, which opens as a train carrying reporters and athletes arrives at Islington Green station. Through dense fog the men grope their way to the Agricultural Hall, where a six-day pedestrian race is being staged by sports promoter Sol Herriott. The reader first gains a general impression of Victorian sporting activities and then meets a varied group of competitors and trainers: Captain Erskine Caldwell, formerly of the Third Dragoon Guards, a gentleman-pedestrian; ex-bricklayer Charles Darrell, who had "prepared for the race to a punitive schedule of massage, steambaths, and abstinence" (14); young Billy Reid, whose ability does not match his determination; and Francis Mostyn-Smith, an anomalous entrant whose reasons for participation form a minor mystery in a novel where suspense is continuous on two levels. Neither the winner of the race nor the identity of the criminal is known until the last pages. The first five chapters set the scene, identify characters, establish possible motives, and conclude with the murder by poison of Darrell. Only then do the two Scotland Yard detectives enter the scene.

This technique, also used in *Mad Hatter's Holiday*, enables Lovesey to develop his Victorian background before concentrating upon the process of detection. The careful, even loving, attention to period detail and its unobtrusive interweaving with the narrative is characteristic of all his suspense fiction,[2] and although most of the novels open conventionally with the early discovery and investigation of crime, all

170

possess noteworthy variety in setting and character. Each introduces a specific and sometimes little known aspect of Victorian life: seaside holidays at Brighton in *Mad Hatter's Holiday;* the music-hall stage in *Abracadaver;* spiritualism in *A Case of Spirits;* bare-knuckle prize fighting in *The Detective Wore Silk Drawers;* and Irish terrorism in *Invitation to a Dynamite Party.* Limitation of subject and setting allows the historical background to emerge naturally through incident and conversation and makes Cribb's knowledgeable approach to investigation credible. Lovesey's grasp of Victorian life is also crucial to his characterization of Cribb and Thackeray and their methods of detection. Hampered by rudimentary forensics, the absence of a fingerprint system for identification of criminals, inept superiors, and a social system which makes questioning of upper-class suspects difficult, the two men, especially Sergeant Cribb, display competence and undoubted expertise.

Cribb's reputation is established early when, in *Wobble to Death,* a bookmaker greets him as "Wally Cribb! Sharpest crusher in London!" (80). He does not, at first appearance, possess either a compelling personality or an obvious flair for detection, but his patient and methodical investigation is successful. Shrewd, practical, and experienced, he bears a strong likeness to Wilkie Collins's Sergeant Cuff, whom he resembles physically in his height and leanness. Cribb is tall, "spare in frame," long-nosed, and adorned with notably bushy sideburns; he dresses conservatively but fastidiously. Thackeray finds his superior "exasperatingly well-turned out." This keen eye for sartorial excellence extends beyond the personal, however, and is turned to good use when Cribb is undercover. Whether wearing formal evening clothes or a striped blazer and white flannels, he can, when necessary, blend comfortably and unobtrusively into his surroundings.

In his late forties and at sergeant's rank, Cribb has divisional responsibilities ordinarily assigned to inspectors. His desire for promotion, continually thwarted because of his sardonic, outspoken attitude toward his superiors, seems unlikely to be realized, as does Thackeray's. Cribb tells the constable that "there's a streak of malice in you I never knew was there. We'll make a sergeant of you yet" (*Abracadaver,* 94), but Thackeray's laborious handwriting, inaccurate spelling, and failure to pass examinations set by the Education Inspector indicate his continuing in that rank. And Thackeray himself, despite discontent with his meagre salary (seventy-eighty pounds a year for a constable first class) and irregular hours, recognizes his limitations: "Explanations were a sergeant's job" (*Abracadaver,* 103).

The two men work well together although Thackeray occasionally resents Cribb's high-handedness and brusqueness, and Cribb has no illusions about the constable's capabilities; nor has the reader. In *Abracadaver,* narrated largely from Thackeray's point of view, Cribb's superior intelligence and *savoir faire* become clearly and ironically evident. Called to Scotland Yard to assist Cribb in investigation of a series of supposed accidents in music halls, Thackeray from the start is uncomfortable with the case, the suspects, the atmosphere, and, until murder is committed, with what he feels to be a waste of time: "I just can't take all this music hall stuff seriously. It don't seem like your class of investigation. It's not really worthy of you, Sarge. A blooming bogus bulldog in a basket and a strong man with a twisted ankle—that don't seem worth losing a night's sleep over. We've taken on some odd cases, I know, but there's always been a corpse to make the whole thing worthwhile" (64-5).

Cribb is, however, delighted with the case and fascinated with the statistical implications that bring him into it. Dressed in "opera hat and Inverness cap," Cribb "whistled a music hall tune to the rhythm of the cab-horse's canter along Southward Street" as he and Thackeray proceed to the Grampion Theatre. But his subordinate is unhappy; ordered to wear his "swallowtail suit," he feels that "Scotland Yard might own your body and soul, but it was a confounded liberty to assume they owned our best suit as well" (31). His reluctance is compounded by embarrassment, in direct contrast to Cribb's light-hearted ability to enter into the festive music-hall atmosphere. Upset by the noxious fumes from the "unwashed of South London," Thackeray is further distressed when Cribb only "lifts a wicked eyebrow" at the ticket seller's suggestion that they might "like a pair of dainty companions to share their box" (32). He looks, says Cribb, "solemn as a blasted tombstone," an appearance reinforced when another "accident" sends them backstage and he is confronted with ballet girls in tights. The gentle irony which pervades Thackeray's characterization in this novel is reflected in the description of his reaction to this incident: "A veritable outrage on decency! He dipped his head instantly, like a barge just seeing a low bridge. Then by degrees, and strictly in the case of duty, he mastered his modesty and raised his eyes" (47).

Smiling at Thackeray's discomfiture provides innocent pleasure for the reader, but his embarrassment—and his fear of appearing ridiculous—are important to the theme of *Abracadaver,* and to the solution of the case. "The common element" in the music-hall accidents, as Cribb says, "is ridicule. Absurdity" (66). Turning performers into laughingstocks makes it impossible for them to continue their careers; Thackeray has difficulty understanding this, but the reader, sharing the constable's fear of provoking laughter as he walks the back streets of Lambeth in borrowed knickerbockers or appears on stage as a footman in white silk stockings, realizes the insidious nature of the weapon used to spirit away "artistes" from their usual jobs. The theme is reinforced by the antic behavior of a private detective whose attempts at disguise offer both policemen occasions for merriment. An obvious parody of Sherlock Holmes, Major Crick, as postman or plumber, putting his "resources" at the disposal of the Yard, is a figure of fun. Thackeray is not. His outlandish garb is donned under orders, and his discomfort at appearing as someone he is not emphasizes the distinction between honest man and criminal: illusion is not only the mainstay of the theatre; it is crucial to the success of the criminal. Cribb's comfortableness, even familiarity, with this world indicates his superior intelligence; his ability to use and simultaneously see through illusion leads to his discovery first of the purpose of the staged accidents and then of the identity of the murderer.

But Thackeray too has his moment of perception. Incredibly naive about the entertainment choices of the upper classes (he cannot believe that "Peers and Parliamentarians" actually enjoy witnessing female nudity or listening to off-color jokes), he can yet see immediately through the pretensions of Inspector Jowett. More politician than policeman, Jowett is less distressed by an "indecent show" than by the presence of "two common members of the Police Force" at a function which attracts influential members of society. He berates his officers for wishing to uphold the law and emphasizes the importance of "discretion" in its enforcement. Jowett's belief that a man-of-the-world attitude somehow links him to peers and Members of Parliament is an illusion, a stage trick without substance, as Thackeray intuitively knows:

Even so, the inspector rose to take up a stance on the tiger-skin rug in front of the mantlepiece. A sepia photograph of himself in hunting-kit was displayed behind him. Thackeray reflected without much clarity that the chair in the picture was identical to one he had seen in a studio in Bayswater (158).

Described in *The Detective Wore Silk Drawers* as "a sandwich man without boards" (5), Inspector Jowett is a pretentious bore who toadies to his superiors and exploits his subordinates. He is more impressed by an "impeccable accent" and family background than by sound police work, and at the conclusion of *Silk Drawers* when Cribb confidently expects promotion, Jowett instead promotes the young constable who has assisted Cribb and Thackeray. Jago, the inspector explains to Cribb, has conducted a "first-class investigation," comes from a "damned good family," and is engaged to the daughter of an old friend. Lovesey's novels are, as he has described them, "light-hearted,"[3] and while he does not dwell on the injustices of the Victorian class system, it is clear that that system imposes barriers which impede not only Cribb's promotion but occasionally his investigations.

In *Abracadaver* Jowett, intent on discretion and the protection of the influential, orders him to stay away from the Paragon Theatre, the scene of a murder. In *A Case of Spirits* Jowett's friend Dr. Probert addresses him as "Policeman" and refuses to supply a list of guests who had been at his home shortly before it was burgled: "Respectable people, every one. I'm not having them subjected to an inquisition simply because they visited my house..."(24). Cribb obtains the list by effectively exploiting Probert's class bias and threatening to bribe the servants. And when Mrs. Probert tells him that he is not a gentleman, Cribb responds simply, "I wasn't brought up to be one, ma'am" (157). The stern moral sense which enables Cribb to link indecent entertainment for the upper classes to "penny gaffs in the backstreets of Cairo" (*Abracadaver,* 145) allows him to dismiss Probert's collection of erotic art with characteristic irony. When Probert offers to show him "a magnificent *Rape of the Sabine Women,*" Cribb replies, "Thank you sir, but not just now. We policemen come across quite enough of that sort of thing in our work" (21). Inurred to insult by years of association with Jowett, he is confident enough to accept comments on his social status dispassionately. He is also presentable and well-mannered, assets which allow him to move with relative ease in the world of his "betters." In *Swing, Swing Together,* a comic romance within the detective-story format, he mingles easily with the fellows of Merton College, Oxford, and is impressive enough to convince the principal of a training college for female teachers to place one of her charges under his supervision. In some cases he conducts initial interviews without revealing his identity, posing as a swimmer who has mislaid his towel in order to meet a suspect in *Mad Hatter's Holiday* and as an ordinary traveller in *Swing, Swing Together.* While investigating the illegal sport of bare-knuckle prize-fighting, he entertains habituees of a country pub with an impersonation of "a street tragedian in the Strand contesting his pitch with a German band" (*Silk Drawers,* 40) and convinces the local police he is a journalist. With careful attention to detail he sends constable Henry Jago undercover to infiltrate a group of fight promoters and tells Thackeray, as they prepare to attend a second illegal fight, "We'll need to look a trifle different from the last time, though. Can't be known as regulars. Tweeds and deerstalker for me. You're easy. You just shave off your beard" (73). This is no doubt hard on the constable, whose full beard is a source of pride, and it demonstrates what Thackeray sees as a "callous streak" in his sergeant, but it also emphasizes Cribb's talents in the art of disguise.

This talent, plus a genuine flair for impersonation, is the key factor in *Invitation to a Dynamite Party* in which Cribb, after a course in explosives at Woolwich Arsenal, poses as a freelance dynamite expert and infiltrates a group of Irish terrorists. Lovesey has referred to this book as a Victorian James Bond and admitted to having modelled it on *Goldfinger*,[4] an approach that allows both Cribb and Thackeray to reveal new facets of character. When Cribb is sent to spy on "decent, dutiful, dependable Thackeray," who is suspected of consorting with terrorists, he embarks on a series of adventures that test both his ingenuity and his morality. He learns that the constable, with whom he had worked five years but never met off duty, has interests and goals of his own. Bored with his current posting where "fallen women and ferocious dogs" make up his caseload, Thackeray is drinking at an Irish pub for "professional reasons." He tells Cribb that "I've never forgotten something you told me the first time we worked together. There's more useful information to be learned in a public taproom than in the *Police Gazette* (24). This desire to do some "detective work on my own" ends in disaster and near death for both men when Thackeray disappears and Cribb joins the terrorists as a "professional adventurer." As "Mr. Sergeant" he impresses the terrorist leader, a beautiful young woman named Rossanna McGee, with his skill as a dynamite thief and attracts her with the force of his personality. Rossanna's obvious desire for him complicates an already tense situation as he tries to discover the plotters' next point of attack, free Thackeray from imprisonment (*his* attempt at infiltration failed immediately, and he was locked up in a storeroom at terrorist headquarters), and avoid discovery. To succeed Cribb is even willing to put aside his moral principles:

Could she actually have been expecting him: Was she lying there in anticipation of a development she regarded as the logical consequence of having a mature professional adventurer in the house?... He took two measured steps in the direction of the bed. The room was so dark that every movement was a small adventure. Her scent, the fragrance of stephanotis, lay on the air...A Scotland Yard career was no preparation for boudoir atmosphere. Still, he was determined not to forget that he represented Law and Order; without that, his present situation was unthinkable. He was doing this for protection of the realm (108).

Cribb's devotion to duty does not, fortunately, require unfaithfulness to Mrs. Cribb, but this incident, with its mock serious tone, shows that he is not insensible to feminine charms. And after a rousing conclusion which involves a hairbreadth escape from a miniature submarine and the thwarting of a plot to assassinate the Prince of Wales, Cribb seems pleased to learn that Rossanna will not be prosecuted and responds "wistfully" when he hears that the Special Branch, not he, will keep an eye on her.

Sergeant Cribb in *Wobble to Death* is an effective, if not especially interesting, policeman. With each successive appearance, however, he has gained in complexity. His relationship with Inspector Jowett reveals a man disillusioned and sometimes bitter, while that with Thackeray demonstrates loyalty and a concern for his subordinates entirely foreign to Jowett. In *Abracadaver* he tells Thackeray:

"I don't ask for much...I'm not particular about the hours I work or the cases I'm put on, or the company I have to rub shoulders with... There's malcontents enough in the Force, but I've never counted myself one of 'em, though I've more cause for complaint than most. But an officer's entitled to look to his superiors for support, ain't he?" (177).

This support Cribb offers to Thackeray when Jowett accuses the constable of "blundering"; he did, says Cribb, "immaculate detective work, as discreet as you could wish and deserving of the highest commendation" (162). He is first angry and then confused when Thackeray is accused of terrorist activities and even suspected of murder: "secretly he envied the easy irresistible logic of six-penny novel detectives, and would have liked to employ it in his own investigations. But now that Thackeray had disappeared, he was hard put to summon two consecutive thoughts" (38). Essentially fair-minded, Cribb, unlike Jowett, cannot condemn a man without evidence or ignore that of established character. This quality is noticed by Albert Moscrup, the mild-mannered voyeur of *Mad Hatter's Holiday,* whose vacation hobby of watching women through a variety of optical instruments brings him to police attention. Moscrup, after a two-hour interview with Cribb, finds the sergeant "a sensitive listener, tolerant of others' little whimsies, not in the least disparaging about the optical experiments" (110). Cribb is intelligent and psychologically acute enough to recognize that Moscrup, who observes instead of participating in life, did not murder and dismember a servant girl but that his observation may be of great importance in finding out who did.

Cribb's patient approach to detection and his skill at interrogation, which *requires* careful listening, are of course part of his personality. As is his awareness that the facade of even so pleasant a place as Brighton during the season conceals crime and is indeed particularly suited to it: "Place is full of strangers right through the summer. Irregular behavior isn't noticed" (95). Cribb's clear-sightedness is crucial to the thematic structure of *Mad Hatter's Holiday,* where, as James Hurt has noted, Moscrup's optical instruments give him a distorted view of reality while Cribb sees clearly with the naked eye.[5] And in fact this novel shows him at his best as a detective.

Summoned to Brighton to handle a case too difficult for the local force, Cribb and Thackeray investigate the discovery of a severed human hand in the aquarium's crocodile cavern. Cribb inspects the hand through a magnifying glass, an approach that effectively separates him from Moscrup, whose use of binoculars and telescopes symbolizes his distance from reality, and deduces from the presence of fish scales and sand under his fingernails that the body had been dismembered on the beach. Aided by the inaccurate but useful testimony of Moscrup, he is led to the Prothero family and by diligent researches of his own to the identity of the murderer. School records and up-to-date medical information figure in the solution, but here as in his other cases, interrogation is his principal method. "I can pick wheat from chaff," he tells Thackeray in reference to the reliability of pub conversation (*Silk Drawers,* 38), and in *Wobble to Death* he advises a suspect, "Do, sir? Do nothing. Talk to us. That's all" (98). His cases are built up by a combination of physical evidence, background information, and interviews. He is capable of Holmsesian deduction, but his conclusions, soundly based on experience and practical knowledge, are valid deductions rather than flights of inspired fancy. And in this process even the slow-thinking Thackeray can occasionally follow: in *Silk Drawers* the two men are confronted with a headless corpse. By examining the body, Cribb determines that the man had been a worker, possibly a tanner, puddler, or bricklayer because of muscular development between the "deltoids and biceps." He first settles on bricklaying, noting the scarred palms, an opinion confirmed by Thackeray; but then the constable notices evidence which leads Cribb to whistle in surprise:

These hands. Not the palms. The knuckle side. There's a pattern of old scars, and it ain't from brickmaking, I'm sure. No brickie's that careless with the backs of his hands. He's a well-built man, and his work's thickened his wrists, but that don't account for the size of his fist nor its coarseness. If it made any sense, Sarge, I'd say that hand's been pickled—soaked in vinegar, though you can't smell it any more. And scarred from knuckle-fighting" (15).

Examining physical evidence is, however, only part of the process of detection. In *A Case of Spirits*, the only novel in which Cribb stages a reenactment of the crime, he must discover how the victim, a fraudulent medium, was electrocuted during a supposedly foolproof experiment. This he does by ingenious use of his knowledge of spiritualist practices and the properties of electrical current, but the re-enactment occurs only after Cribb has built up the case by his usual methods and become thoroughly familiar with the personalities involved. "There was more to detective work than clues and statements," he tells himself in *Waxwork*. "It involved people, their ambitions and fears, innocence and guilt. You needed solid evidence to determine the truth, but you could divine a lot by meeting them face to face" (69). Lacking evidence, however, he will resort to trickery, suitably used in the theatrical setting of *Abracadaver*, and his approach in the holiday atmosphere of *Swing, Swing Together*, is equally unorthodox.

Drawing inspiration from Jerome K. Jerome's *Three Men in a Boat (to Say Nothing of the Dog)*, an extremely popular novel first published in 1889, the year of the novel's action, *Swing, Swing Together*, despite its reflections on the Ripper murders, is the lightest of Lovesey's books. In pursuit of three murderers who have supposedly escaped in a boat, Cribb, Thackeray, young Constable Hardy, and Harriet Shaw, on leave from her studies at the Elfrida College for the Training of Female Elementary Teachers, follow Jerome's itinerary down the Thames. Harriet, a delightful, spirited young woman who saw the murderer during a forbidden midnight swim, is treated gallantly by all the men, especially Hardy, her rescuer when she emerged unclothed from the river. Harriet is at first suspicious of Cribb but realizes almost immediately, as Thackeray has long known, that "he was obviously the sort who gave nothing away unless it suited him, and enjoyed the sensation of power his reticence gave him" (29). This technique, essential to the detective story, becomes an integral part of Cribb's personality, doubly effective here since Hardy lacks the experience and Thackeray the intelligence to follow the convoluted chain of events. Cribb, elegantly dressed in striped blazer, white flannels, and red boating cap, questions lockkeepers, publicans, and Oxford dons, prescient and at ease with all. He is relaxed and even mildly facetious in his role as amateur sportsman; when Constable Hardy is bitten by a dog belonging to the three men they are following, Cribb's enthusiasm for this bit of "evidence" is understandable, and he promptly sends Hardy to London for comparison tests. Solving a murder by a comparison of toothmarks would surely have been a detective first, but Cribb is doomed to disappointment here, although his solution is eventually based on material as unique. Fittingly, in a novel whose source is literary, Cribb finds in the murderer's habit of quotation the key to his identity.

The good-natured, insouciant Cribb of *Swing, Swing Together* becomes an altogether darker, more realistic figure in *Waxwork.* Lovesey has said that "if there's any common theme in my books about the Victorian period, it's exploitation,"[6] and the dominant mood of *Waxwork* is one of loss and wastefulness. Opening with a carefully factual description of the quite ordinary life of hangman James Berry and his desire to achieve both profit and fame by selling the clothing of convicted murderess Miriam Cromer to Madame Tussaud's, the novel simultaneously reveals the circumstances which led Cromer to murder and the process by which Jowett uses Cribb's skills to avoid a major legal scandal and appropriates credit for his work. Because doubts have been raised about the validity of Cromer's confession, Jowett assigns Cribb to re-investigate the crime, thereby playing, Cribb thinks, "his meanest trick." Proving the confession false would embarrass the judiciary and the Home Office; proving it valid would simply confirm the accuracy of the initial investigation. And as Jowett makes clear, "Justice has had its opportunity... There are other interests to be considered now...."(154). Knowing that his work is only a formality, Cribb is bitter.

This bitterness does not, however, prevent his carrying out his usual thorough investigation during which he uncovers substantially more— and more damning—evidence that the original officer, Inspector Waterlow who owes promotion to having suggested that truncheon pockets be sewn into uniforms. Cribb's competence and his regard for truth stand out in *Waxwork*, where instead of forming a comic duo with Thackeray, he works alone or in conflict with other policemen of low level intelligence and performance. He is succesful, even brilliant, in his discovery of Cromer's plot; she is a worthy antagonist, but the case brings him neither satisfaction nor pleasure.

The source of his despair—and his feelings can come close to this—begins when Jowett fulfills that part of the Police Code that stipulates the visiting by inspectors of the quarters of all sergeants and constables who do not live in Section Houses "*to ascertain that the places are fit to reside in.*" Still rankling over the carefulness of Jowett's inspection ten years before, Cribb understands that his lack of respectful demeanor toward the man has been responsible for not being promoted. Jowett's visit this time is only a cover for his request that Cribb work on the Cromer case, but the sergeant's resentment persists. Jowett earns three hundred pounds a year, Cribb a hundred and forty, an amount that does not even stretch to giving his wife her greatest pleasure: "On an inspector's wage they could visit the theatre sometimes. Millie's idea of Heaven was the dress circle at Drury Lane" (34). Cribb's domestic life assumes importance for the first time in the series, and while it does not intrude into the investigation, his affection for Millie forms a contrast to the married life of Miriam Cromer. Millie still believes that he "would make it up to inspector if he treated Jowett right," and her sage advice that Cribb treat Jowett *"civilly for my sake, love. If he was one of the criminal class you wouldn't think twice about buttering him up to smooth the way, now would you?"* (35) reveals an understanding of her husband and an intelligent appreciation of his foibles.

Howard Cromer, as Cribb's interviews establish, saw his wife as a photographic model, not a human being, and in fact preferred her photographic likeness to her living presence. Cromer is guilty, but as Cribb learns about this young woman whose life deprived her of any outlet for her emotions or abilities, he comes to feel a measure of sympathy for her. "She agreed," explained her husband, "to arrange the flowers in the studio and fill the decanters—things a lady might legitimately undertake—but there were still hours when she was unoccupied" (97). Prevented by social background and social mores from expressing herself in any meaningful fashion, Miriam Cromer turned to murder when her way of life was theatened. In a moment of rare insight,

Cribb saw in her an implacable force: the strength of her will. It was a force that in other circumstances might have made Miriam Cromer a social crusader of her time, for it refused to accept defeat. But events had turned it inwards. It had become an impulse toward self-gratification. She had coveted marriage. She would not be thwarted. She had murdered her own friend. Marriage had brought frustration, not fulfillment. She had discovered what it was to be the object of someone else's obsession. Isolated and unloved, yet treated with devoted kindness, she had concentrated her will into playing the part of a wife. When blackmail had intervened, she had expunged it ruthlessly. The trial and sentence had provided a fresh challenge for her strength of purpose. She had come within an ace of cheating the hangman (227).

Toward Jowett, Cribb's manner is "not respectful"; yet he feels for Cromer "a measure of respect." When he leaves his final interview with Jowett, knowing that neither his work nor his name will be mentioned in the inspector's report to the Commissioner, and makes his way "unimportantly home," the reader shares his disillusionment and sense of loss—for his own potential and that of the woman whose death by hanging he has ensured.

Waxwork, published in 1978, is the last of the Sergeant Cribb novels, although Lovesey and his wife Jackie have written six additional adventures for television, all of which retain the comic, ironic approach of the first novels. But the striking differences between *Waxwork* and its predecessors perhaps explain Lovesey's departures in new directions, the Crippen case in *The False Inspector Dew* and the wacky world of Mack Sennett comedies in *Keystone*. Omission of Thackeray from *Waxwork* is also indicative of a change in approach; although Lovesey has said that in his "more depressed" moods he sees himself as Thackeray, "a rather put upon character...blundering about in the world and not getting any breaks and generally being taken advantage of..."[7] It is probable that he had developed the Watson-like constable as far as he could while retaining his comic characteristics. Inspector Jowett, also a comic creation of the first rank, has become more ominous in *Waxwork*, partly because Cribb is thrown back on his own resources and cannot vent his frustrations on Thackeray, partly because we see effects of Jowett's manipulative and inconsiderate actions upon Cribb as a private individual. Although the narrator in *Waxwork* tells us that Cribb's "sense of irony kept him tolerant of others in most situations" (34-5), he gets "near the limit of his tolerance" in an interview with Waterlow, and his disturbed dreams reveal unconscious pressures not seen in previous cases. He seems here, for the first time, tired. At fifty he has accepted his place in the hierarchy and ceased to hope for anything better: "Cribb was a realist. After seventeen years at sergeant's rank, it would take fireworks on the Crystal Palace scale to get him lifted" (58). Cribb's last and technically most successful case, one in which he is forced to work without confrontation with the major suspect until the very end and in secret without overt official support, ends on a note of sadness.

But the development of Sergeant Cribb from mere "working policeman" to complex human being is a major achievement in detective fiction, as is Lovesey's integration of his Victorian background with Cribb's cases. Without conspicuous moralizing, he presents the underside of Victorian life; with deft comic touches he re-creates a lost world in its innocent and not so innocent diversions. And with pervasive irony he offers a detached perspective that enables readers to see the world if not as it was, then surely in some ways as it might have been.

Notes

Editions used for this study are listed below preceeded by original dates of publications. All references will be found in the text.

1970 *Wobble to Death.* New York: Penguin, 1980.

1971 *The Detective Wore Silk Drawers.* New York: Penguin, 1980.

1972 *Abracadaver.* New York: Penguin, 1980.

1973 *Mad Hatter's Holiday.* New York: Penguin, 1981.

1974 *The Tick of Death;* published in the United States under this title and as *Invitation to a Dynamite Party.* New York: Penguin, 1980.

1975 *A Case of Spirits.* New York: Penguin, 1971.

1976 *Swing, Swing Together.* New York: Dodd, Mead, 1976.

1978 *Waxwork.* New York: Penguin, 1980.

[1]Lovesey to John C. Carr, *The Craft of Crime: Conversations with Crime Writers* (Boston: Houghton Mifflin, 1983), p. 282.

[2]For Lovesey's own comment on the historical mystery see "The Historian: Once upon a Crime," in *Murder Ink,* ed. Dilys Winn (New York: Workman Publishing, 1977), pp. 475-76. Lovesey follows the precept given here: "All we ask of the historical mystery is that it tell a story consistent with known facts and that those facts arise naturally from the plot. If we want a history lecture, we can go to college."

[3]Lovesey to Diana Cooper-Clark, "An Interview with Peter Lovesey," *Armchair Detective,* 14 (Summer, 1981), 214.

[4]Cooper-Clark, pp. 211.

[5]James Hurt, "How Unlike the Home Life of Our Own Dear Queen: The Detective Fiction of Peter Lovesey," in *Art in Crime Writing,* ed. Bernard Benstock (New York: St. Martin's, 1983), p. 150.

[6]Lovesey to Carr, p. 265.

[7]Lovesey to Cooper-Clark, p. 216.

Contemporary British
Fictional Policemen

Donald C. Wall

Earlier essays in this volume have dealt with famous fictional policemen who have achieved and retained popularity over the years. To judge from the number of contemporary authors writing about policemen and police work in the United Kingdom, interest in novels featuring policemen has remained strong. And with the spate of recent police fiction has come considerable variety, both of type and of diversity within a type.

Novels about policemen are far too numerous to be discussed with anything approaching thoroughness in a short essay. To provide a brief overview, however, they may be conveniently divided into different categories and sub-categories, with a discussion of the contributions of a few authors working in each category to illustrate something of the variety to be found within a type.

One main category is that of the "Great Policeman" (to use George Dove's label), the most traditional kind of police novel. A newer type is the police procedural, which may be further divided into those using a single protagonist, those relying primarily upon a pair of (usually opposed) policemen, and, far less common, those using multiple protagonists. Finally, there is the newest type, the police novel. Each of these will be dealt with in turn.

The first category, the best established type, is that which focuses on the "Great Policeman." According to Dove, the Great Policeman is usually a dominant, solitary figure who solves cases on his own, although he may work closely with a subordinate. The Great Policeman often gets involved in a case accidentally rather than by assignment, often finds himself in a different, perhaps exotic setting, is imaginative, insightful, and intuitive, and is generally far more cultured than an ordinary detective.[1]

The Great Policeman type might appear on the surface to hew to the actual practices of police work and thus be procedural. The main character might wear a uniform, have a superior to whom he is supposed to report, have underlings to order about, question witnesses, and use police records and laboratories to gather evidence.

All this, however, is only ornamentation. In actual practice, authors bestow upon their fictional Great Policemen a freedom from regulated behavior which no real cop has. This freedom also allows authors to invent for their protagonists the kinds of quirks, peculiarities, and particular genius that gives any one series its distinctiveness. While none of these Great Policemen would last long on a real police force, this type of police novel has achieved a popularity which makes its longevity seem assured.

Colin Dexter provides us with a good current example of this type with his Chief Inspector Morse of the Thames Valley Police.[2] Morse, whose first name no one ever learns, is a loner, a bachelor who has little that could be called a personal life. His main pastimes are solving crossword puzzles and word games, listening to music, especially Wagner, going to an occasional strip joint or pornographic film, and drinking copious amounts of beer.

Dexter makes some attempt to integrate these traits into his plots; some of Morse's pastimes become useful in his work. In *Last Bus to Woodstock*, a case centering around a young girl found murdered and apparently raped in a pub car park, Morse's ability at word games enables him to discover that the mistakes and illiteracies in a letter actually convey a secret message (53). In *Service of All the Dead,* an investigation of a series of murders in an Oxford church, Morse picks up an important clue by recognizing that one name is an anagram of another (128). And in *The Silent World of Nicholas Quinn,* a murder case that leads to the uncovering of an Oxford examination scandal, when several of the suspects try to use their supposed attendance at a porno film for an alibi, Morse's experience here enables him to sift through the stories and find the truth. Finally, Morse's passion for beer is also no mere device for personalizing his character. It seems to be the essential fuel that fires his thinking apparatus: "He had long since recognized the undoubted fact that his imagination was almost invariably fired by beer, especially by beer in considerable quantities" (Silent, 51).

Like most Great Policemen, Morse is a loner at work as well as play. He does have a sidekick, Sergeant Lewis, whom Morse keeps assuring "we are a team," but in practice, Morse keeps most of his knowledge and hunches to himself, often withholding information and insights from his partner, to the latter's chagrin. Nor is it only his subordinate Morse keeps in the dark. He has a superior, Superintendent

Strange, who rarely appears, seemingly content to let Morse pursue any investigation without oversight.

Morse's method of solving a case is not through the painstaking accumulation and analysis of information but, in typical Great Policeman fashion, by means of intuitive flashes. Early in one case, we are told, "He felt in his bones that there was an urgency about this stage of the investigation" (Bus, 34). In another, when Morse goes to Oxford to investigate Professor Nicholas Quinn's death, he decides almost at once that the murder is connected to Quinn's work at the university. As Morse knows hardly anything of Quinn's personal life at this point, this notion must be an intuitive one. In *Service of All the Dead*, when Lewis objects to the lack of evidence implicating a witness, Morse says, "Evidence? No, we haven't. But you've got to use a bit of imagination in this job, Lewis..." (110). Not just everyone could duplicate Morse's imaginative efforts, however, to judge from this description: Morse "for half an hour let his thoughts run wild and free, like randy rabbits in orgiastic intercourse" (Silent, 92).

Morse's "imagination," while it eventually leads him to solving each case, is by no means infallible. In *The Dead of Jericho*, stimulated by the knowledge that a murder victim has been reading Sophocles, Morse gives a virtuoso performance in which he explains all the ramifications of the intricate case by drawing painstaking parallels between the facts as he knows them and *Oedipus Rex*. It is an astonishing and convincing feat, with only one drawback; it turns out to be dead wrong.

It is perhaps fortunate that Morse's hunches do eventually lead him to successful conclusions in each case, for his ignorance and disregard of established police procedure and restrictions are enough, otherwise, to bounce him off even a fictional police force. When questioning a suspect in *The Dead of Jericho*, he fails to get a statement and must send Lewis back to cover the same ground (140). In the same book, he questions Lewis minutely about how traffic tickets are given and doesn't know there are duplicates made or what happens to them. When Morse says, "How do you come to know all this," Lewis replies, anticipating the reader, "I'm surprised *you* don't, sir" (Jericho, 125). In another case, by handling a letter, he ruins any chance for fingerprints, as he belatedly and sadly realizes. More often than not, in fact, his procedure seems sloppy and spontaneous, so much so that he occasionally becomes his own severest critic: at one point he reflects, "even a superficial scrutiny of his conduct of the case thus far would reveal a haphazardness in his approach almost bordering upon negligence" (Bus, 62). He is negligent, too, in questioning suspects;

he rarely seems to conduct a thorough interview, but characteristically gets one tantalizing bit of information and then rushes out to follow that inadequate lead. Nor is Morse scrupulous about observing the law. When Lewis asks him if he won't need a search warrant to go through desks in an office, Morse complains, "I never did understand the legal situation over search warrants" (Bus, 33). Again, he has Lewis illegally obtain a sample from a suspect's typewriter by posing as a repairman, though he is aware of the illegality. Whatever vicissitudes Morse's fanciful theorizing and haphazard procedures lead him into, however, his brilliance wins out in the end. And Dexter's plots are so complicated and tortuous that perhaps only a random genius could cope with them.

Another popular example of the still-current Great Policeman type is Chief Superintendent Henry Tibbett of Scotland Yard, the creation of Patricia Moyes.[3] Like Morse and others of this type, Tibbett is very much a loner, although he doesn't seem so because he is married. His wife, Emmy, serves as the partner with whom he works, and as is the case with Morse and Sergeant Lewis, Tibbett tells his partner only what he wants her to know. She is perfectly willing to do whatever he asks, with no questions asked, and apparently no resentment.

Tibbett fits the pattern, too, in the ways he gets involved in cases and in where those cases are located. Typically, he is sent to an exotic setting when the Yard is called upon for help. Thus in *The Black Widower* he is requested by the government of Tampica (a recently independent Caribbean island) to investigate a murder at their embassy in Washington, D.C., a case which takes him also to Tampica. In *The Coconut Killings,* he goes to another Caribbean island to investigate a murder when the ruling British authorities call London for assistance. In *Death and the Dutch Uncle,* a young interpreter for the Commission for Permanent International Frontier Litigation becomes suspicious when two of its elderly members die, apparently by natural causes, and he interests Tibbett, who ends up chasing around Holland trying to apprehend a former Dutch resistance fighter who is now head of an international gang of crooks. Occasionally Tibbett gets drawn into cases accidentally, as in *Season of Snows and Sins,* when he and Emmy visit a friend in Switzerland who has been a witness in a local murder. The investigation involves an exotic (and erotic) group of jet-setters. In *A Six-Letter Word for Death*, Tibbetts has accepted an invitation to lecture on police procedure to a small group of mystery novelists, who have sent him a crossword puzzle to test his intelligence. Solving the puzzle leads him, acting in an entirely unofficial capacity, to solve murders past and present.

There is little attempt to describe actual police work in these books. In Tibbett's running about in Holland, for example, he seems to get whatever official help he needs without unravelling a bit of bureaucratic red tape, even though he is in a foreign country. When a realistic-sounding case is mentioned, it is only there for background color: "And then came a call from the dock area of East London, where a seaman off a Liberian-registered ship, long suspected of drug-running, had been found stabbed to death in a sleazy rooming house, and the unpleasant facts of real life closed in on Henry...." (Six, 13). The case is hastily disposed of: all we are told is that it was "the work of greedy amateurs...and Henry was able to make an arrest within the week" (13). Obviously, both Tibbett and his creator prefer more exotic cases.

Tibbett's methods of solving cases rarely involve realistic police procedures such as gathering evidence by forensic techniques. In typical Great Policeman fashion, it is his perceptions, insights, and guesses that lead him to successful solutions. Midway through *The Black Widower,* when the murder seems to have been solved, Emmy senses that he isn't satisfied. He admits, "You're absolutely right, of course. My nose...I mean, I find it difficult to believe that things happened so conveniently and neatly. Or, let's say, I don't want to believe it" (127). When summing up the case in *Death and the Dutch Uncle* for his audience (the way these novels typically end), he again refers to his olfactory guidance when he admits he figured things out by means of "a bit of 'nose,' a few facts, a coincidence or two" (237). In his summary of *The Coconut Killings,* Tibbett says, "Look, I can't lay this thing out for you precisely, because it's too complicated, and in any case...well, I was playing hunches" (210).

Tibbett is blessed with a singularly unprepossessing appearance and manner. This appearance disguises the fact that Tibbett is an astute observer and incisive questioner who is extraordinarily good at seeing through the lies that people throw up, to the truth of the matter. In *A Six-Letter Word for Death*, two mystery fiction writers, who jointly write a series starring their "Miss Twinkley," assert that "her great strength lay in the fact that she was an amateur, unhampered by police procedure. This...was the reason that most great fictional detectives were not policemen" (29). Tibbett, amateurish as his procedures are, is nevertheless a great fictional detective who at least appears to be a policeman.

Tibbett is as different as could be from Morse in the kinds of cases they investigate, in the settings of those cases, and in their personal manners. Both, however, fit the pattern of the Great Policeman. The amplitude of that pattern and the diversity it allows doubtless accounts in large measure for this type of police fiction's enduring and continuing popularity.

While this type thus seems destined to live on, the emerging vitality of a new type, the true procedural, has been noteworthy. Here, too, we find enormous variety. But the distinction between the Great Policeman type and the procedural is not always clear-cut. There is sometimes a blending, as in the two very popular novels by William McIlvanney featuring Detective Inspector Jack Laidlaw of Glasgow.[4]

For the most part, Laidlaw solves his cases by standard means: questioning, use of informants, forensic science, and police teamwork. He does have a touch of the Great Policeman about him, however, in the freedom he enjoys. Laidlaw's superior, the Commander of the Glasgow Crime Squad, refers to Laidlaw as "one of our less conventional men" (45), and decides to let him go his own way in trying to apprehend a sex murderer. This departure from actual police procedure is made a bit more plausible by the Commander's decision to pair Laidlaw with young Detective Constable Harkness, who must report on Laidlaw's movements and progress to DI Milligan of the Central District, the man in charge of the investigation.

This first novel, *Laidlaw*, develops the tensions that emerge among the three policemen, Laidlaw, Harkness, and Milligan. Harkness has previously worked under Milligan, a brutal, insensitive cop who draws a sharp distinction between criminals and others. As he tells Harkness, "I've got nothing in common with thieves and con-men and pimps and murderers. Nothing! They're another species" (52). He has nothing but contempt for Laidlaw, who in turn despises Milligan. Harkness is caught between the two: having been trained by Milligan, he must now try to comprehend Laidlaw, a sensitive, thoughtful man who seeks to analyze and understand everything.

In discussing the case—a particularly brutal rape/murder/anal necrophiliac rape—Harkness wonders how they can possibly think their way into the mind of the murderer. Laidlaw says it can be done "Because he relates to us," an idea Harkness rejects with horror. Laidlaw asks, "You resign from the species?" and goes on to explain that the murderer is not some monster: "monstrosity's made by false gentility. [There are] no monsters. Just people. You know the horror of this kind of thing? It's the tax we pay for the unreality we choose to live in. It's a fear of ourselves" (71-2).

Later, Laidlaw explains to Harkness that he despises Milligan because "Milligan has no doubt," and adds: "I mean if everybody could waken up tomorrow morning and have the courage of their doubts, not their convictions, the millenium would be here. I think false certainties are what destroy us." As a result of people's inability or unwillingess to admit their own potential for any kind of action, "where they should see a man, they make a monster" (134). By the novel's end, the reader sees the young man who has committed this terrible crime as Laidlaw has: not as a monster but as an agonized, tortured human who is undergoing tremendous suffering. He has created his own punishment to a degree that a Milligan could never understand—but Laidlaw does.

McIlvanney's second novel, *The Papers of Tony Veitch,* puts Laidlaw onto a case that would never have developed except for Laidlaw's compassion. Receiving word that an old wino informant of his on the verge of death is asking for him, Laidlaw leaves his wife and some guests and gets some puzzling information from the old man, which leads to another very complicated case in which Laidlaw, again working with Harkness, sifts through the lies and lives of Glaswegians to uncover the unsavory truths he seems condemned to seek. An incidental truth here is his final acknowledgement that his shaky marriage is at an end. His wife is unable to accept the human realities that Laidlaw has come to know and accept as a result of his police work.

A major strength of both novels is the exploration of human psychology. In the police world, McIlvanney portrays the stresses with which policemen must deal and focuses upon the conflicts between personal ethics and duty that can result. The motivations of ordinary citizens and Glaswegian hard men are equally well presented. Thus we have a thoughtful portrait of a reflective, hard, compassionate cop trying to do his job without becoming a mindless cog in a bureaucratic machine or losing sight of his common bond with all humanity.

A far more prosaic and less thoughtful figure is Jack S. Scott's Detective Inspector Alfred Stanley Rosher, known among his colleagues (and not with affection) as "Old Blubbergut."[5] Near retirement age, he is still a powerful monolithic man who is built like a gorilla, has an intimidating face (with "teeth like brown tombstones"), and a surly manner. He is a solid, persevering cop whose career ranges from the sad to the comic to the triumphant. Without the kind of flair that characterizes Laidlaw, Rosher plods and stumbles his way to truth—usually.

The setting and circumstances of Rosher's cases are quite varied: the strangling of a young female teacher in a small village (*The Shallow Grave*), an armored car robbery outside an industrial city (*A Clutch of Vipers*), the search for a fanatical religious killer at a huge rock concert in a rural setting (*The Gospel Lamb*), the attempted robbery of a multimillionaire (*The View from Deacon Hill*) and the successful robbery of same (*An Uprush of Mayhem*), and a complicated jewel robbery masterminded by London thugs in another city (*The Local Lads*).

As varied as the cases is Rosher's career. In *The Shallow Grave*, Rosher arrests the wrong person—the real murderer confesses afterward. Rosher, who has made a local pub the headquarters for the investigation, becomes enamored of the publican's wife, a voluptuous and flirtatious contrast to Rosher's fat wife. When Rosher literally stumbles into making what appears to be an ardent assault on the woman, her jealous husband knocks him down the stairs. The case ends with Rosher in the hospital with a broken arm; Rosher's superintendent, who dislikes him, must scramble to get the couple to drop charges. This mess leads to Rosher's demotion, his wife's leaving him, and his having to work under his former subordinate, Sgt. Cruse, who has been promoted to Detective Inspector in Rosher's place. When Rosher advertises for a housekeeper, a crook who hates him gets him to take on the wife of a man he has convicted, and her supposed two children—a couple of depraved delinquents. The crook also plants stolen goods in Rosher's house, then informs the police, which leads to his suspension. He is ready to resign in disgust. When Rosher—purely by accident—manages to catch the fanatical killer in *The Gospel Lamb*, however, his career is saved, even though he has also arrested an undercover cop and ruined a drug investigation. And when he foils the attempted robbery of the multi-millionaire, he is promoted back to D.I. His success continues when he solves a jewel robbery first from a hospital bed and then on crutches.

Rosher is at times unlikeable, at times a buffoon, and sometimes a pitiable figure because of his grim loneliness. As a policeman, he seems believable and realistic enough. He follows traditional investigative technique, writes reports, has run-ins with superiors and bullies subordinates, intimidates and rewards his stable of informants, and worries about holding his temper to secure his pension. The series presents a rather ordinary (though individualistic) cop dealing with believable cases, and Scott has taken some trouble to pay attention to established police procedures.

Another procedural series which concentrates on the career of one man is that by James Barnett, who is a retired Commander, C.I.D., Scotland Yard. As one might expect, the attention to procedure, evidence gathering, and methodical investigation is carefully worked out and fully developed. Not so predictable, however, is the convoluted and intricate nature of the cases described, or the sensitive and thorough exploration of the protagonist, Detective Chief Superintendent Owen Smith.[6]

Owen Smith is a single, intelligent, hard-working policeman with hardly any private life. His lack of "private life" tends to carry over into his work, where his integrity and dedication make him something of a thorn in the side of police (and governmental) bureaucracy: he is not a good team player, but an individualist whose actions sometimes impede an investigation. In demand because of his ability, he is nevertheless regarded with caution, suspicion, or hostility by his superiors.

Smith makes his debut in *Head of the Force,* which begins with the discovery of the body of the Police Commissioner, Sir Charles Steype, in his office at Scotland Yard, sitting in full uniform behind his desk. "All except his head. That was impaled by the neck upon the spike of a ceremonial dress helmet" (7).

The policeman put in charge of this investigation, Deputy Assistant Commisioner Angus Craddock, asks to use Smith, which bothers Hicks, Assistant Commissioner-Crime, an oleaginous political type. As Hicks recalls, "We sent him out [to the Caribbean] at the request of the Foreign and Commonwealth office to make discreet inquiries, with the accent on discreet, into a series of political murders. He winds up arresting the island's Attorney General and about to arrest the Financial Secretary, when they throw him into an aeroplane and deport him" (13). Craddock is well aware of Smith's reputation, and when he first calls him in, it is to warn him: "You've got the gift. But you are colour-blind to red light. You don't know when to back off. You're good but you're a fucking chancer, Owen. Don't take any chances with this one" (18).

With this warning, Smith finds himself in over his head on a case that involves the Britain First Movement, an ultra-conservative political group whose burgeoning popularity has the government worried, a terrorist group calling itself The Soldiers of the People, agents of an unnamed communist country, and governmental deals and corruption with links to all of the above. Despite the efforts of various high-ranking police, intelligence, and governmental officials to control the investigation, Smith manages to discover most of the truth, but is thwarted in his attempt to bring the case to the conclusion he believes is right.

At the end, he is cynical and embittered by what he has discovered, wondering whether his version of the truth can lead him anywhere.

Smith's next investigation, *Backfire is Hostile*, does little to restore his confidence in the system. At the outset, he has just completed a three-month inquiry into a complaint against the police initiated by one Dickerton, an M.P. whose constituency includes a good many people who have had run-ins with the law. Smith assures a colleague, "Take it from me, old son, it doesn't do for a politician to ignore the criminal vote" (10). He is then sent to inquire into the murder of a young female Flight Lieutenant at Cladenham Air Base. Here again, Smith encounters interference, this time from the various military services and British Intelligence. The murder is connected to a Russian General's desire to defect, delivering his country's new Backfire bomber to the British, and a British traitor's deal with the Russians to expose and prevent the defection, all complicated by the British government's desire to have no untoward incidents occur that might upset a forthcoming peace conference. At the end, Smith has become even more cynical about the possibility of his ever doing his job the way he knows it should be done.

In *Palmprint*, Smith finds himself enmeshed in the spiderweb of international intrigue when he is sent to a Caribbean island to investigate the murder of an American, Eli Voden, who has been strangled and thrown into the sea. He discovers that Voden was a professional hit man and, in pursuing his inquiry in Toronto and back, stumbles up against an international arms dealer's plan to foment revolutions in the area, local politicians' plans to seize the island when the British give it independence, and a rivalry between the CIA and FBI to apprehend the munitions dealer.

Smith solves several of the novel's mysteries by the use of technology. Having the American's body exhumed, he discovers Voden's fingers have been cut off. Smith then has the skin from the palms cut off, put between glass, and sent to Scotland Yard, which reveals Voden's identity and background. Taking the head of another exhumed murder victim, wrapped in aluminum foil and packed in dry ice, to Toronto, Smith is able to prove the innocence of the harmless islander charged with the crime.

While on the island, Smith falls in love with Louise Debriel, the sister of the black local police chief, and asks her to marry him and return to England. She is reluctant, primarily because she is protecting her brother from Smith's inquiry. Debriel, when Smith tells him that he has proposed to Louise, notices that Smith does not mention love, and asks, "Is it because you are incapable of love? As an emotion, I mean...a psychological condition gradually induced over years of police service?" (150). At the end, when Smith has arrested Debriel for murder and has become Acting Chief of Police, he goes to inform Louise. Seeing the red-tinged bath water from the overflow pipe of her house, he sends a sergeant in, telling him what he'll find. "It was not a matter with which he, as Chief of Police, need become personally involved" (186).

In the first two cases, Smith is able to find little satisfaction in his work because of the powerful, corrupt forces which thwart his efforts. In this one, police work makes impossible the personal relationship he very much needs, and ironically it is his identity as a policeman which provides the anesthesia for his feelings to survive.

Smith's cynicism is furthered by his next investigation, the execution of a man in England by a firing squad. . The case leads him into a tale of revenge that began during World War II, and the plan of some ex-soldiers to punish the officers who turned traitor. This is the most methodical of Smith's cases; every phase of it—the taking of statements, the establishment of a complex system of cross-reference files, the identification of firearms use—is painstakingly described. The case seems to be concluded, in that the executioners have been apprehended and put on trial. Public sympathy is such, though, that the jury, in defiance of all the evidence, finds them "Not guilty." Punishment is meted out, however, in a most unexpected manner.

In *Marked for Destruction*, the case begins with an infanticide, which seems to be only a very ordinary domestic case. As the investigation proceeds, however, the deaths mount rapidly. Smith, who has been exiled to an outlying district, finds himself taken off the case but, burdened by guilt for some of the deaths, he suppresses evidence and strikes out on his own. The cumulative effect of his disillusionment from previous cases leads him to take a holiday in America where he pursues leads which prompt him to illegal acts, including a number of killings. Early on, Smith thinks of himself as "the detective, the hybrid human in whom the oil and water of means and ends, of logic and absurdity, were emulsifying into an unstable plasma" (78).

Smith's instability and disorientation grow as he gets caught up in the fanatical religious cult he is pursuing. He realizes he has rejected the orderly, logical system and disciplined thinking that had given order and meaning to his life, "granting his mind and body the freedom to wander in pursuit of a self-indulgent crusade" (213). The book ends chaotically with both the U.S. and British governments suppressing information and with Smith, broken in mind, in a British mental institution.

Overall, the series delineates with careful detail the struggle of an intelligent idealist to find meaning and purpose by working within established systems and discovering, increasingly, that he must circumvent those organizations in order to follow his quest for truth and meaning. Ultimately, the quest breaks him. Perhaps. This is the most thought-provoking of series, and the serious and significant nature of the issues Smith must face shows how broad a spectrum the police procedural offers.

The struggle of the "loner" with a sense of integrity which brings him into conflict with the establishment appears also in two novels by Peter Hill: *The Fanatics* and *The Washermen*. Hill spent thirteen years in the C.I.D. and his novels, like Barnett's, are procedurally accurate. Hill's protagonist, Commander Allan Dice, C.I.D., Scotland Yard, is a loner because of his deep religious beliefs.[7] He insists upon bringing his convictions to the job, and the application of morality to police work leads to complications.

Dice's cases, like Owen Smith's, tend to bring different government agencies into conflict, and the cynical maneuverings which result frustrate Dice. In *The Fanatics*, a breakway group of communist terrorists from a foreign country seeks to destroy the fledging Christian Democratic Party, a group that brings militant Christianity to politics. The terrorists seize and hold the minister, Paul Carpenter, head of the CDP: they wish to destroy the CDP because they see its militant religious ideology as a potential threat to communism. The British Government wants Carpenter alive, lest his death make him a martyr and allow his party to reap enough public sympathy for it to carry the next election. The KGB shares this reason and also wishes to destroy the terrorists as a deterrent to other would-be-independent groups.

Dice has both personal and professional problems during all this. The personal stem from his failing marriage to a nymphomaniac and his refusal to consider divorce because of loyalty and religious conviction. The professional involve a colleague who wishes Dice to fail, to further his own advancement, and Dice's repugnance at any concern for saving Carpenter's life simply for Carpenter's sake. Dice's idealism constantly runs up against governmental cynicism, and only his personal faith keeps him going.

In novels about policemen such as Laidlaw, Rosher, Owen Smith, and Dice, the concentration on one character makes it possible for authors to explore in some depth the many different ways in which police work can affect the lives of these loner protagonists. Procedurals involving multiple protagonists are also becoming quite popular, and the most common type uses a pair of policemen whose marked differences combine to make them an effective team.

One such pair, DCS Bob Staunton and DI Leo Wynsor, also the creation of Peter Hill, exemplifies this type.[8] Staunton is happily married, fifty-ish, an earthy Cockney who solves cases by plodding, painstaking attention to detail. Wynsor is single, in his late twenties, well-educated, and given to imaginative, intuitive solutions to crimes. Staunton has taken on Wynsor as his protege, recognizing his talent, and tries to educate him in the ways of police politics, which the outspoken Leo must master if his career is ever to advance. They function together well; the earthy Staunton gets people to talk who would be put off by Wynsor, and Leo's upper-class accent and breeding allow him an entree into situations where Staunton would not be welcomed.

As members of a Murder Squad which travels wherever their expertise is needed, they appear in four novels which place them in East Anglia, Cornwall, Wales, and Oxfordshire. This allows Hill to describe a variety of local customs and to show his detectives' flexibility. The plots, too, are varied: a search for a rapist-strangler, involving a local coven (*The Hunters*); the search for the killer of a Cornish Don Juan (*The Liars*); the hunt for an army-trained sniper roaming the wilds of Wales and using people for target practice (*The Enthusiast*), and the investigation of a prominent man's disappearance which includes a marvelous psychological portrait of the making of a murderer (*The Savages*). Staunton and Wynsor are an engaging and effective pair who prove versatile enough to solve their varied cases with the help of established police procedure which is always carefully detailed.

Similar in many respects is another pair by a different Hill, Reginald, whose team of Detective Superintendent Andy Dalziel and DI Peter Pascoe, plus a few other supporting policemen, are headquartered in Yorkshire.[9] Dalziel (pronounced "deel") is divorced, shrewd, and crude— rather like a dyspeptic Staunton, boasting a tongue that could be used as a flensing knife. Pascoe is married (to an intelligent, liberated woman, Ellie), well-educated, and as astute in his way as Dalziel. Like Staunton and Wynsor, the differences in temperament make them well suited to engage a broad spectrum of people in their investigations.

Those investigations are quite as varied as those to be found in any series: a man who goes about strangling young engaged girls, to save them from the disappointment of marriage (*A Killing Kindness*), an inquiry into a supposed snuff film (*A Pinch of Snuff*), the search for the killer of a rugby player's wife (*A Clubbable Woman*), and a chilling portrait of an engaging psychopath, who gets off (*Deadheads*). During the progress of these investigations, Dalziel's crudity protects him from any personal effect, but the thoughtful Pascoe becomes increasingly disillusioned with people in general and with the efficacy of police work. His wife's often hostile comments about Pascoe's profession do not help, but their otherwise good relationship provides a sanctuary from the sordid realities he must face.

Reginald Hill also takes takes some pains to depict correct police procedures, and so the novels are both true-to-life accounts of police work and incisive, reflective excursions into society's problems from the different viewpoints of the major characters.

Expanding the number of major characters through whose eyes a story is told allows an author to present a fuller description of police procedure during an investigation. By switching back and forth from one viewpoint to another, the author can present a broadly realistic coverage. However, no one character can be as fully developed as those in novels using a single protagonist or a pair.

The procedure using multiple protagonists seems to be rather less common, but one author who manages this very successfully is Peter Turnbull, who has aptly been called "the Scottish Ed McBain." Turnbull's three novels present a realistic group of characters whose enforced interaction during the course of an investigation rings true, and he balances his account of the police work by economically slipping in details of their personal lives.[10] While there are brief appearances by Chief Superintendent Findlater and assorted constables, the novels are developed mainly through viewpoints of four cops of Glasgow's "P" Division, DI Fabian Donoghue and DC's Malcolm Montgomerie, Richard King, and Ray Sussock. The four are different enough to illustrate a nice variety of types of policemen and their attitudes toward their profession.

Donoghue, something of a dandy, is competent at both orchestrating an investigation and in helping to perform much of the donkey work that goes with it. A cautious man, concerned about advancing his career, he is terrified of press conferences but holds them anyway, lest Superintendent Findlater step in and take credit.

The three constables working under him are all quite different. Richard King is happily married to a Quakeress and has two young children; the contrast between his tranquil home life and the squalor and suffering he sees on the job occasionally makes him feel guilty about his happiness. Montgomerie's police experience affects his personal life too, but in another way. A young, swinging bachelor, he tells an even younger constable, "Let yourself get involved in this work and you're finished.... Detachment, that's the word. Stay detached or you'll take it home with you" (Fair, 28). But Montgomerie takes his detachment home with him, causing him to struggle against a full emotional commitment to the young physician he loves. Far stormier is the life of Ray Sussock, in the process of divorce and carrying on an affair with a young WPC, Elka Willems. His shrewish wife blames the marital failure on police work, citing it as the cause of inattention he has given his family: her and their homosexual son. Sussock is in his mid-fifties, has not advanced in police service, and lives a hand-to-mouth existence. He has nevertheless applied for extended service, as there is nothing else he knows how to do.

The cases they work offer quite a range. *Deep and Crisp and Even* concerns the quest for a psychopathic killer who murders at random. *Dead Knock* is about the cracking of a heroin smuggling ring and brings in an impetuous Dutch policeman whose action oriented methods bring him into heated conflict with the cautious Donoghue. *Fair Friday* begins with the death of a harmless journalist who, threatened with redundancy, desperately scrapes up a story which gets him killed. In the search for his killer, the men of "P" Division uncover municipal corruption linked to a Glaswegian syndicate. All three novels, like McBain's, pay close attention to the accurate depiction of police procedure.

Whether novels about police are variations of the procedural or the Great Policeman Type, they all explore the cop world to some extent. No discussion of police fiction would be complete, however, without mention of one more kind: the police novel. Policemen are the protagonists, and police work is its focus. Here, though, the depiction of police work is not a means to an end—solving a crime, unraveling a mystery, apprehending a criminal. Often, there is little or no mystery to be found. Instead, this type of fiction has as its end the evocation of the world of the policeman. The subject is how that world shapes and is shaped by those who inhabit it, and the aim is to show outsiders "reality" as viewed through a cop's eyes. In the United States, the work of such writers as Joseph Wambaugh, Robert Daley, and Bob Leuci provides good examples of the type, but England has its own contributors. One is John Wainwright (another ex-policeman).

In *The Bastard*, a violent, suspenseful tale of revenge, Wainwright gives us "reality" as seen through the eyes of DC Ray Cameron of the Yorkshire County Police, as tough and embittered a cop as has ever appeared in literature.[11] He is not one of those who has been soured by his job; Cameron was a hard man before he joined the force, and the power that comes with the position simply provided the means for him to better express his toughness. His violent, unyielding nature has worked in opposite ways: it has enabled him to subdue and intimidate the villains on his "patch," but it has prevented his advancement.

In this novel, it is Cameron's job to guide a young CID Inspector from Scotland Yard up into the snowy northern wilds to apprehend Cameron's arch-enemy, a man as tough as he is. The young Inspector serves as a contrast to the other two. His insistence upon following police procedure is his downfall, for he makes the mistake of thinking that others will observe the same rules that he does. In a life or death struggle with someone who will do anything and everything, as Cameron knows, one had better be prepared to resort to any means himself.

If Wainwright's portrayal of a policeman's view of the world is a grim one, G.F. Newman's is sordid. In a series delineating the career of his cop, Terry Sneed, Newman plumbs the depths of police corruption.[12]

In *Sir, You Bastard*, which covers the first seven years of his career, young Sneed is early introduced to the ways and means of corruption by the cops who are training him. Realizing that those who balk at dishonest actions are never going to advance, the amoral Sneed learns fast. In a short time he has dozens of scams going, but, while the money piles up in his hidden bank accounts, it is not wealth but power he seeks.

Ironically, in many respects Sneed is a good—or at least effective— policeman. He solves a great many cases, often because he lies, cheats, plants evidence and does whatever he must to get a conviction. His career advances rapidly as a result of his conviction rate, but he speeds up that advance by blackmailing superiors, by blowing the whistle on fellow cops to create vacancies—in short, by doing anything he needs to, without regard to ethics or morals. Sneed's world is one where nearly all the police are "bent," but his cynicism (or realism?) is such that, to him, the corruption is simply another example of the nearly universal corruption of society in general. The lawyers, judges, and businessmen Sneed knows are as venial and amoral as he is, and the man who flourishes in society is the one who acquires power over others.

In another novel, *The Guvnor*, Newman presents a somewhat different view of an equally corrupt world.[13] The protagonist is DCS John Fordham, at thirty-nine the youngest man at his rank. In the course of a murder investigation, Fordham discovers that societal corruption extends up to cabinet rank. Like Sneed, Fordham uses the techniques and powers of the police to get what he wants, but where both use corrupt means, Fordham's ends are idealistic. His aim is to bring to justice the influential and socially prominent men who are associated with a crime syndicate, and his struggle to accomplish this illustrates the plight of the modern policeman faced with police bureaucracy on the one hand and the "old boy" network on the other.

While it is chancy (and perhaps foolhardy) to try to identify trends in contemporary police fiction, certain changes do seem to be taking place, though their significance is debatable and speculative.

One change shows up in a marked contrast between the Great Policeman type and the procedurals. The former emphasizes the use of human cleverness and imagination to solve and control crime, while the latter adds a heavy reliance on science and technology. It is logical enough that technology should be given an important role, for as it becomes ever more useful, its use increases. This emphasis might only be a more accurate and up-to-date representation of police work as it is actually carried on. But it may also reveal a cause of change in the way policemen function, in that the use of technology can replace other ways of acting. The bobby with his personal radio no longer has to use psychology to defuse a situation; he can call in massive reinforcements, and he does. Thus technology can use the men who rely on it, as well as the reverse, and the narrowing of options for human interaction may have a dehumanizing effect.

Certainly police work has always carried with it the possibility of its own kind of dehumanization taking place—the tendency to think of oneself as a policeman, not a civilian, which creates an "us" and "them" outlook. But at least there was an "us" to whom one could turn for a sense of belonging. In the current police procedural especially, however, that comforting camaraderie seems to be missing. A strong theme running through this fiction is the struggle of the cop to retain his individual integrity. The tortured loners like Laidlaw and Dice, the thoughtful and well-educated like Wynsor and Pascoe, and the rebels like Owen Smith all fight this battle, and the police force, far from providing a psychic sanctuary, is often their chief antagonist.

Nowadays, the cop must not only combat corruption in society; he faces it in his own department. Where a Henry Tibbett or Inspector Morse never worries about departmental politics or crooked colleagues, the Smiths, Wynsors, and Dices cannot escape them. Such concerns inevitably interfere with the way policemen perform and add to the frustrations of a job that has enough of them built into it.

Whatever the reasons, the cop's world portrayed in current fiction is an increasingly grim, dark, and less idealistic one. More and more, this world is being described as becoming uninhabitable for those of sensitivity, intelligence, and ethics. Society is degenerating, and law enforcement agencies which should regulate it are overwhelmed by the magnitude of the task or partake of the corruption they are supposed to combat. Is all this a true picture of the deterioration of the social order and the species, or is it only a new realism which reflects conditions as they have always existed?

Time and historical perspective will settle the question. But in the meantime, novels about British police continue to proliferate and diversify. The devotee of this fiction has a rich choice at hand, running from novels that are steeped in gloom, frustration and despair to ones wherein good triumphs unfailingly over evil, from those rendering dark visions of humanity to ones which treat human inhumanity as an aberration to be tracked down and stamped out. Given the almost infinite complexity of human behavior, perhaps this is the way it should and must be.

Notes

[1]George N. Dove, *The Police Procedural* (Bowling Green, Ohio: Bowling Green University Popular Press, 1982), 36-7.

[2]The editions of Colin Dexter's Inspector Morse novels consulted are as follows, in order of original publication date. Quotations are cited in the text using, where necessary for clarity, the abbreviation given after an entry. (This same format is used throughout).

1975 *Last Bus to Woodstock* (London: Pan, 1977). (Bus)
1977 *Last Seen Wearing* (London: Pan, 1977) (Wearing)
1977 *The Silent World of Nicholas Quinn* (London: Pan, 1978). (Silent)
1979 *Service of All the Dead* (London: Pan, 1980). (Service)
1981 *The Dead of Jericho* (London: Pan, 1983). (Jericho)

[3](1968) *Death and the Dutch Uncle* (N.Y.: Holt, Rinehart and Winston, 1968). (Dutch)
1971 *Season of Snows and Sins* (N.Y.: Holt, Rinehart and Winston, 1971). (Season)
1975 *The Black Widower* (N.Y.: Holt, Rinehart and Winston, 1977). (Black)
1977 *The Coconut Killings* (N.Y.: Holt, Rinehart and Winston, 1977). (Coconut)
1983 *A Six-Letter Word for Death* (N.Y.: Holt, Rinehart and Winston, 1983). (Six)

[4](1977) *Laidlaw* (N.Y.: Pantheon, 1982).
1983 *The Papers of Tony Veitch* (N.Y.: Pantheon, 1983).

[5](1977) *The Shallow Grave* (N.Y.: Harper and Row, 1977). (Grave)
(1979) *A Clutch of Vipers* (N.Y.: Harper and Row, 1979). (Clutch)
(1980)*The Gospel Lamb* (N.Y.: Harper and Row, 1980). (Gospel).
(1981) *The View from Deacon Hill* (New Haven: Ticknor and Fields, 1981). (View)
1982 *An Uprush of Mayhem* (New Haven: Ticknor and Fields, 1982). (Uprush)
(1983) *The Local Lads* (N.Y.: E.P. Dutton, 1983). (Local)

[6](1978) *Head of the Force* (London: Secker and Warburg, 1978). (Head)
(1980) *Backfire is Hostile!* (London: Magnum, 1980). (Backfire)
(1980) *Palmprint* (London: Magnum, 1980). (Palm)

(1980) *The Firing Squad* (N.Y.: William Morrow, 1981). (Squad)
(1982) *Marked for Destruction* (London: Secker and Warburg, 1982). (Marked)

[7](1977) *The Fanatics* (N.Y.: Charles Scribner's Sons, 1978).
(1979) *The Washermen* (London: Peter Davies, 1979).

[8](1976) *The Hunters* (N.Y.: Charles Scribner's Sons, 1976).
(1978) *The Liars* (Boston: Houghton Mifflin, 1978).
(1978) *The Enthusiast* (Boston: Houghton Mifflin, 1979).
(1980) *The Savages* (London: Heineman, 1980).

[9](1970) *A Clubbable Woman* (London: Collins, 1970).
(1978) *A Pinch of Snuff* (London: Collins, 1982).
(1980) *A Killing Kindness* (N.Y.: Pantheon, 1980).
(1983) *Deadheads* (N.Y.: Macmillan, 1983).

[10](1982) *Deep and Crisp and Even* (N.Y.: St. Martin's 1982), (Deep)
(1982) *Dead Knock* (N.Y.: St. Martin's, 1982). (Knock)
(1983) *Fair Friday* (London: Collins, 1983). (Fair)

[11](1976) *The Bastard* (London: Macmillan, 1976).

[12](1973) *Sir, You Bastard* (London: Sphere, 1978).
(1974) *The Price* (London: New English Library, 1975).
[13](1977) *The Guvnor* (London: Panther, 1978).

Contributors

Earl F. Bargainnier is Fuller E. Callaway Professor of English at Wesleyan College. Currently President of the Popular Culture Association, he is the author of more than fifty articles and *The Gentle Art of Murder: The Detective Fiction of Agatha Christie*. He has previously edited *Ten Women of Mystery* and *Twelve Englishmen of Mystery* and is editor of the forthcoming *Comic Crime*.

George N. Dove, Dean Emeritus of Arts and Sciences, East Tennessee State University, is the author of two books, *The Police Procedural* (1982) and *The Boys From Grover Avenue* (1985). He wrote the essay on Dorothy Uhnak for *And Then There Were Nine* and the one on Michael Gilbert for *Twelve Englishmen of Mystery*. He is a contributor and member of the Advisory Board to *Twentieth Century Crime and Mystery Writers*.

Martha Alderson is an editor with the Webster Division of McGraw-Hill Book Company. With Neysa Chouteau, she has written essays on Anne Morice and Lillian O'Donnell for *And Then There Were Nine* and entries for *Twentieth Century Crime and Mystery Writers*. She was a contributor to *Adolescent Female Portraits in the American Novel, 1961-1981* and has also written articles and reviews for *The Mystery Fancier, Clues,* and the educational publication *Reading in Virginia.*

Liahna Babener is Head of the English Department at Montana State University in Bozeman, MT. She is President of the Popular Culture Association and has published articles on nineteenth century American fiction, regional literature, and film, as well as detective fiction. Her present project is a book-length study of autobiographies of Midwesterners, to be entitled *Growing Up in the Heartland.*

Jane S. Bakerman, Professor of English at Indiana State University, teaches detective fiction, American Literature, and women's studies courses. She publishes articles, interviews, and reviews about crime fiction in such journals as *Clues, The Armchair Detective,* and *The Mystery Fancier,* and served as adviser and contributor to *Twentieth Century Crime and Mystery Writers.* Her essay on Ruth Rendell appeared in *Ten Women of Mystery*, and she is the editor of *And Then There Were Nine.*

Jeanne F. Bedell is on the faculty of the University of Prague. She was Program Chairperson for the 1985 meeting of the Popular Culture Association in the South. She has published articles on Conrad, Alcott, and composition, as well as on detective and espionage fiction. Her special interests are nineteenth century sensation fiction and mysteries before and during the early twentieth century.

Neysa Chouteau is a Senior Editor with the Webster Division of McGraw-Hill Book Company. With Martha Alderson, she has written essays on Lillian O'Donnell and Anne Morice for *And Then There Were Nine* and entries for *Twentieth Century Crime and Mystery Writers*. She was a contributor to *Adolescent Female Portraits in the American Novel, 1961-1981.* She is co-author of the *Learning Basic Arithmetic Series* and has contributed to *The Mystery Fancier, Clues, Grass Roots Editor,* and *Ellery Queen's Mystery Magazine.*

Mary Jean DeMarr is Professor of English at Indiana State University, where she teaches courses in American literature and women's studies. Her articles on detective fiction have appeared in *The Mystery Fancier* and *Clues*, for the latter of which she also serves as a member of the advisory board. She has recently published, with Jane S. Bakerman, *Adolescent Female Portraits in the American Novel 1961-1981: An Annotated Bibliography.* She is American Editor of the Modern Humanities Research Association's *Annual Bibliography of English Language and Literature.*

Barrie Hayne is Associate Professor of English and Associate Chairman of the Department of English at the University of Toronto. He contributed the essay on Anna Katharine Green for *Ten Women of Mystery* and the one on A.E.W. Mason for *Twelve Englishmen of Mystery.* He contributed several entries for *Twentieth Century Crime and Mystery Writers* and is currently Vice-President of the Popular Culture Association.

Frederick Isaac is Circulation Librarian at the University of Santa Clara, California. His articles have appeared in library journals and mystery-oriented magazines. He also contributes reviews regularly to the San Francisco *Chronicle.*

Constance Hammett Poster is a free-lance editor and writer in New York City. She has previously taught sociology at Brooklyn College and West Georgia College, and has been an advertising copy chief. She is past editor of *The New York Element: a Journal of the Arts and Politics*, author of *Social Problems and Social Policy*, and has published articles in such journals as *The Gerontologist, The New Leader, Ballet Review, Clues, Sociology, Social Forces*, and *West Georgia Review*, as well as in *Dictionary of Literary Biography*.

Leah A. Strong is Professor of American Studies and Chairman of the Division of Humanities at Wesleyan College. She has held numerous positions in a variety of academic organizations, such as the Southern Humanities Conference and the Southeastern American Studies Association. Her research has been primarily in the American novel, American folklore and Mark Twain. She is the author of *Joseph Hopkins Twichell: Mark Twain's Friend and Pastor* and many articles. She was a founding member of the Popular Culture Association.

Donald C. Wall is Professor of English and Humanities at Eastern Washington University. He has published criticism on John D. MacDonald and James McClure and has presented a number of papers at meetings of the Popular Culture Association. His published fiction includes short stories in *Mike Shayne's Mystery Magazine* and a young adult novel about soccer, *Best Foot Forward*.

Joan Y. Worley is Visiting Lecturer, Department of English, University of California at Santa Barbara. Her publications include short pieces on film, detective fiction, and composition.